STRATEGICS

STRATEGICS

The Art and Science of Holistic Strategy

WILLIAM J. COOK, JR.

QUORUM BOOKS

Westport, Connecticut • London

Library of Congress Cataloging-in-Publication Data

Cook, William J., 1938–
    Strategics : the art and science of holistic strategy / William J.
    Cook, Jr.
        p.   cm.
    Includes bibliographical references and indexes.
    ISBN 1–56720–278–0 (alk. paper)
    1. Strategic planning.   2. Management.   I. Title.
    HD30.28.C6625   2000
    658.4'012—dc21   99–33205

British Library Cataloguing in Publication Data is available.

Library of Congress Catalog Card Number: 99–33205
ISBN: 1–56720–278–0

First published in 2000

Quorum Books, 88 Post Road West, Westport, CT 06881
An imprint of Greenwood Publishing Group, Inc.
www.quorumbooks.com

Printed in the United States of America

The paper used in this book complies with the
Permanent Paper Standard issued by the National
Information Standards Organization (Z39.48–1984).

10 9 8 7 6 5 4 3 2 1

Copyright Acknowledgments

The author and publisher are grateful for permission to reproduce portions of the
following copyright material:

John A. Byrne, "Strategic Planning: The Rise and Fall and Rise of Strategy," *Business
Week,* August 26, 1996, 48–49. Reprinted with permission.

Samuel Taylor Coleridge, "Biographia Literaria, From Chapter XIII," in *The Norton
Anthology of English Literature,* ed. Robert M. Adams (New York: W.W. Norton and
Company, 1968), 272–273. Reprinted with permission from David Campbell Publishers,
Everyman's Library Ltd.

Unnumbered exhibit on page 93, from Images®, copyright 1999 PhotoDisc, Inc. Reprinted
with permission.

Exhibit 6, "The DNA Double Helix," from James Watson and Francis Crick, "A Structure
for Deoxyribose Nucleic Acid," *Nature,* April 2, 1953. Reprinted with permission.

Exhibit 12, "Traditional vs. Emerging Organization," from Dr. Gerrita Postlewaite.
Reprinted with permission.

FOR JACK HARBER

Friend, Confidant, Mentor

Contents

Preface

It seems that I have been involved in strategic planning my entire life, either as the person responsible for developing the plan, as the planning facilitator, or as the trainer of other facilitators. My first involvement in strategy was in the military, where I learned the art and science of *strategos*—"to lead an army." When I was asked to serve on the team that was to build a new university, I discovered an entirely new application of strategy. Because of that success, I have been given the opportunity to facilitate the strategic plans for numerous corporations (some *Fortune* 500 companies) in a variety of industry types. In addition, since 1980, my firm and I have facilitated over 700 plans for educational systems, both throughout the United States and abroad.

From all this experience I have realized two things. First, most attempts at strategic planning fail to realize the power implicit within the concept of strategy. Thus, all too often the results of planning are disappointment and frustration, and in some instances the organization suffers irreparable damage. Second, and more personal, I have discovered that the concept of strategy is far more than a methodology or a technique. It is actually a philosophical view of oneself, the world, and the way things work. Furthermore, we only know its full power by discovering our own.

Looking back, it is abundantly clear that I have been truly privileged to work with the very best organizations of their kind. And each project, each relationship, has been an opportunity for research and learning. Taken together, those experiences have provided me with a unique education, unavailable anywhere else or in any other way. It is as though 25 years ago I was planted on a huge, uncharted island, and since that time I have been making my way, little by little, into the interior and discovering all kinds of wonderful people and things along the meandering journey.

I am still not sure what it all means, but this book is an attempt to report my findings thus far. I hope it will serve as a useful guide to other explorers. Although I have attempted to make this book as friendly and as useful as possible, one should not be surprised to find unfamiliar, even foreign, vistas now and then with an occasional patch of dense forest. But for all that, it is an honest recollection of one who has been there.

In addition to expressing my gratitude to all of my faithful clients and students, I am deeply indebted to my associates for their many insights and assistance. Also, I am especially grateful to Howard Feddema, my senior associate, who drafted the original version of the Action Team Leader's Guide, The Facilitator's Guide, and the protocol for unit planning; also, to David Title for his refinement of the Action Team Leader's Guide. I particularly want to acknowledge the splendid support provided to me during the research and preparation of this manuscript by Mrs. Jill Cook Bryan.

And I extend special thanks to Judy Wallace, my life's partner, for her unfailing love and encouragement.

STRATEGICS

Chapter 1

Introduction

When a word enters the popular culture, quite often its original meaning is eroded, its definition obscured, and its whole concept lost. This is what has happened to the word "strategy." Most often used in the context of planning, "strategy" always carries a certain mystique, perhaps even a sense of panache, but any attempt at definitive, practical specifications typically ends either in confused generalities or in a suffocating restriction in the narrowest of contexts. For example, "strategic planning" is now defined, at least in practice, as long-range planning by most corporations and as comprehensive planning by non-profit institutions. Furthermore, in both instances, it is not uncommon for "strategic planning" to be reduced to program or project planning. While it semantically may be perfectly logical to ascribe any definition to words according to the specific context, to do so with "strategy" robs the original idea of its power to create systems of new dimensions, new realities. Unfortunately, the dilution of meaning has occurred at the precise time that contemporary systems need strategy most.

This is not an academic matter. At any time, under any circumstance, the loss of meaning regrettably would diminish both the system and the persons involved. But present time and circumstance—that is, the end of one epoch and the beginning of another—seem particularly evocative of the creative energies and new possibilities found only in the full implications of "strategy." There is an abundance of dramatic evidence that, at the beginning of this millennium, all of Western civilization, if not the entire world, is suspended in a cusp of historical proportions. All around, the orders that have been built up for the past three centuries are disintegrating and collapsing. Every day, new orders are being created, orders that radically change every aspect of human life and human society. No existing system is exempt. And, as in all previous epochal shifts, the only way any system can guarantee its future is to create for itself completely new realities. That means, simply, a return to the original concept of strategy—from methodology and technique to a fundamental assumption about the world, human beings, and the way things work.

The conceptualization that best recognizes and appropriates all the possibilities of strategy may be termed *strategics*. Each of the three aspects is essential in the others: *Strategic Thinking, Strategic Planning,* and *Strategic Action.* While all of these subjects have been variously acknowledged and explained by both practitioners and theorists, strategic planning has of course commanded most of the attention and is in fact typically undertaken without the benefit of either thinking or action.

Although much has been written about strategic *Thinking,* little has actually dealt with current strategic issues. Specifically, in the late 1940's, 1950's, and 1960's, strategic planning usually was utilized in *de novo* situations—start-up enterprises, without precedent, based on assumptions about the potential market or actual demand. But by the 1970's, owing to the sterility of financial analysts, this kind of planning had degenerated into the development of formulaic "business plans."

During that same decade, strategic planning was properly applied to change issues—specifically Level I change issues, which means changing within a system only through "improvement," "restructuring," or "reforming"; however, it still remained the same system. It is regrettable to note that most of today's so-called strategic planning still uses the vocabulary and concepts of Level I change.

Since 1986, strategic issues have been redefined in terms of Level II change, and that demands planning that creates something other than the original system. The questions of "who," "why," and "what" are still valid, but the results are in a new language and constitute a complete metamorphosis.

It is probably an indication of the seriousness with which strategic planning is taken that virtually nothing has been written or said about strategic *Action.* Perhaps that is the reason most so-called "strategic plans" are never realized. The offices of chief executives are commonly filled with strategic plans whose only effect is occupying otherwise useable shelf space. In fact, most planning methodologies seem to assume that the strategic plan itself is the result, so typically there is nothing in the plan that can be taken to action. For example, the Minister of Health for a British Commonwealth country recently lamented that his agency had invested an inordinate amount of money in a voluminous planning document prepared by a consulting firm, yet he could not find anything that actually could be "implemented." But it is not enough that a plan be translatable into action; it must provoke the action. Strategic plans cannot be ignored or denied. Furthermore, the process of planning must be such that it continually tests the action against the plan and the plan against the action.

For all of the great exuberance for strategic *Planning*, most do not realize the full power of strategy. Because the plans are not infused with strategic thinking or carried to strategic action, the vast majority of strategic planning is worse than futile—it is destructive. Not only is the future of the planning enterprise placed at great risk, but both credibility and competence are seriously compromised.

The most superficial approaches are the ones based on the assumption that strategic planning is merely a methodology; that is, a process and a discipline with certain prescribed components which, no matter how defined or developed, constitute a plan. Even the most precise terminology within the most technically accurate methodology will not produce a strategic plan unless the issues dealt with are, in fact, strategic.

Strictly in an attempt to clarify the subject and to prevent disappointment and cynicism, strategic planning requires: (1) a strategic organization; (2) dealing with strategic issues; and (3) making strategic decisions.

First, strategic organizations are only those that are, in fact, autonomous; that is, they are self-identifying and self-governed. Strategic planning is not some kind of optional luxury that can be utilized by sub-systems such as departments or divisions of strategic organizations. It is impossible for non-strategic organizations to make or to realize strategic decisions.

Second, with regard to addressing strategic issues, no other kind of planning is sufficient. In fact, no other kind even pretends to result in strategies. For example, "long-range planning," while probably never reduced to a specific discipline, is based on pre-adaption to future conditions. Its basically behavioristic (and many times naturalistic) philosophy is "prepare yourself for the future." So it always begins with an "environmental scan," thereby acknowledging that the locus of control is external to the planning organization. Adaption is the height of ambition. Strategic planning, on the other hand, confidently asserts that the locus of control is internal, that the organization can look into the future and see what it aspires to be, can write specifications, and can then actualize that future by dint of its own efforts—usually sooner than it expects. It actually can prepare the future for itself. Thus, it is requisite that the first concern in strategic planning is the character of the organization—its values and principles.

Nor is strategic planning "comprehensive planning." That is the kind of planning typically done by institutions just before some accreditation agency or some other regulatory authority sweeps down on the organization to prove its adherence to orthodoxy. Rigid, pre-tacked, preconfigured, and cast in institutionalized "standards" and the like, this kind of planning, at best, "improves" the organization according to self-serving internal criteria or, at worst, perpetuates organizations that are already obsolete. In fact, comprehensive planning has the ultimate effect of making institutions out of all organizations. An institution is an organization that exists solely for self-perpetuation.

Strategic decisions are those commitments that challenge the existing orders, create disequilibrium, and encourage risk toward new realities. They are decisions that, at the time, are often completely unrealistic and generally considered unachievable. But they are all predicated in the fact that the only reality anyone will ever know is that which he or she sees. And what one sees is always and only a matter of choice. Strategic decisions create those new realities. The ultimate test of a strategic decision is this: If the organization that develops a strategic plan can implement the plan, then truly strategic decisions were not made in the planning process. High risk? Yes. But not as risky as the alternative.

"Strategics," then, is a single concept with three critical facets:

1. *Strategic Thinking.* This is the idea. It establishes the context that gives meaning to human activity. It defines reality.

2. *Strategic Planning.* This is the technique by which all variables are synthesized and the means by which all energies are dedicated to one ideal intent. Understanding and commitment are set forth in a plan that is, in effect, both stimulus and expedient.

3. *Strategic Action.* This is the realization of the plan and the discovery of new possibilities within the action. This is the idea.

Part I

Strategic Thinking

Chapter 2

The Five Arenas

He thinks too much: such men are dangerous.
—Shakespeare, *Julius Caesar*, I, ii, 191

Any attempt at strategy that does not begin and end with strategic think-ing is worse than futile; it is destructive. The results are always the same: disappointment, frustration, and cynicism for all those involved; loss of credibility by those who instigated the activity; and eventual obsoles-cence or irrelevance of the enterprise under consideration. Worse still, there is the forfeiture of the power inherent in strategics to leverage existing systems into new dimensions, new realities.

Even though "strategic thinking" is implicit in strategy, it is a rather presumptuous phrase. It gives the impression that the thinker knows something, or knows *about* something, that ordinary non-thinkers do not. It is that aura of mystery—part excitement, part intimidation—that seems lately to have captured the popular fancy. A quick visit to the Internet will discover a plethora of experts professing to know the secrets of strategic thinking, from specific products and markets to the origin, nature, and meaning of the cosmos. At least one expert claims to have invented the whole idea. Unfortunately, these contemporary versions of strategic thinking are not strategic. The problem is twofold. First, the modern mind, ironically, has been lured by rationalistic science into a world of abstractions. But strategic thinking is not abstract. It is practical, everyday common sense in action. It requires no theory, no fabrication, no proof. Only the results are extraordinary—simply so.

Second, Cartesian "critical" thinking has been the predominant intellectual cast of the twentieth century, so creativity is sacrificed to rational analysis. In fact, "thinking" has been so narrowly defined that intuition and other non-rational powers are all but excluded.

There are five arenas of strategic thinking that are especially critical in the present circumstances:

I.   Definition of Strategy

II. Leaders vs. Leadership

III. Condition vs. Cause

IV. The Nature of Systems

V.   The Dynamics of Human Organization

These arenas were not selected arbitrarily, nor are they the result of scientific analysis, for the simple reason that the answer is always in the question. And, to be sure, there may be many more irregularities and outright misconceptions about strategy, as popularly applied, that deserve consideration. But these five issues represent not mere technical aberrations; they contain fundamental, insurmountable perversions of the original idea of strategy. The loss is not one of argument but of the inherent capability of human beings to create their world. Furthermore, logically, each arena has become a contradiction within itself.

Definitions are tricky business, especially in a relativistic age that seems to have a passive aversion to certain meaning. But the issue must be addressed if for no other reason than the prevention of uncontrollable confusion, to say nothing of lost opportunity. Strategic planning has become a matter of unmitigated confusion for one simple reason: while it is true that context always determines meaning, modern attempts to move the idea of strategy out of its original context into one both foreign and incompatible are doomed from the start because, in this case, the idea is the context.

The scientizing of human relationships has the pronounced tendency to destroy not only the particular relationship in question but also the very possibility of that or any other relationship. The dual fallacy of so-called modern science is that it originates in paradox and results in perversity. That is the woeful story of *"leadership."* If contemporary society is bereft of leaders, as many observers allege, it may be a simple case of mistaken identity. There is no connection whatsoever between modern "leadership" and leaders.

It is a happy world which realizes that circumstances are not *causes.* It is an even happier world which realizes that none of these external factors necessitates, or deserves, a direct response. Responding merely turns these factors into advantages and disadvantages, requiring or inviting more response. The secret to happiness is understanding the implications within and beyond the conditions and circumstances. Why is the ultimate cause.

It is not surprising that *systems* would become the fascination of a generation living in a cusp, that shifting never-never land between the nostalgia and trepidation of the deteriorating old orders and the exhilaration and tentativeness of the new ones that are not quite yet discernible. Cybernetics, quanta, holism, and spiritualism captivate the minds of those not especially earthbound, while frenzied electronic networking and the accumulation of information distract the attention of those given to the mundane. Most people consider it a victory just to connect with someone (or something) else in the vast complexity of randomness to which they vainly try to impute order. If they are successful, further consideration of systemic order is academic. The only real verification of any system is what happens when it does not work. The assumption about systems is the major premise for planning.

The basic question about *organization* is whether it is a noun or a verb. That is, grammar aside, is it a thing or an action? Is it static or dynamic? A construct or a formation? The answer offered by contemporary society is that it is a static thing, namely, the corporation, a construct originally fabricated for commercial enterprises but ultimately the design of every aspect of modern society. It is pervasive, dominant. Curiously, organization ended in the United States in the late seventeenth century, almost exactly a century before the nation was established. Even more curious is the fact that, since that time, there has been no recognition of any other kind of organization—until now. Now is always the critical time. From now on, it will be organization that separates the future from the past—and the verbs from the nouns.

Chapter 3

Arena I: Definitions

There are three popular interpretations of strategy: the corporation-management, the institutional-administrative, and the futuristic. Of course, there is crossover, cross-pollination, and cross-breeding, but the types are distinct enough for identification. While this initial discussion will not be the final word on the subject, the matter of definition is the only place to start.

CORPORATION-MANAGEMENT VERSION

The best takeoff for this discussion is the feature article in *Business Week* (August 1996) in which both the history and the philosophy of corporation strategy is summarized and, in fact, greeted as an idea that had unexpectedly returned after a long, unexplained absence.

The Rise and Fall and Rise of Strategy[1]

Early 1960s. Harvard professors Ken Andrews and C. Roland Christensen articulate the concept of strategy as a tool to link together the functions of a business and assess a company's strengths and weaknesses against competitors.

Early 1960s. General Electric (GE) emerges as the pioneer in strategic planning, creating a large, centralized staff of planners to ponder the future. Consultant McKinsey & Co. helps GE view its products in terms of strategic business units, identify competitors for each, and evaluates position against them.

1963. Under founder Bruce D. Henderson, Boston Consulting Group (BCG) becomes the first of many strategy boutiques. BCG pioneers a series of concepts that take Corporate America by storm, including the "experience curve" and the "growth and market-share matrix."

1980. Harvard professor Michael Porter's book *Competitive Strategy* provides a generation of MBA-trained executives with new models to plot strategy based on economic theories.

1983. New GE Chairman Jack Welch slashes the corporate planning group and purges scores of planners from GE's operating units. Numerous companies follow his lead.

Early 1980s. Battered by global competition, companies turn away from strategic planning and begin to focus on operational improvement. Executives embrace the Total Quality movement and the teachings of guru W. Edwards Deming.

Late 1980s. Corporate America begins massive downsizing and reengineering of operations to increase efficiency and productivity. Guru Michael Hammer leads the reengineering revolution.

1994. After ten years of downsizing, companies begin to focus on how to grow. Academics C. K. Prahalad and Gary Hamel become the most influential of a new group of strategists with the publication of *Competing for the Future*.

Now. A bevy of new books are out from a new group of strategy gurus who are capturing the attention of corporate executives and redefining the process of strategy creation.

Inexplicably, the account completely overlooks the real origin of strategy in the world of corporation. In 1954, Peter Drucker, in his book *The Practice of Management*, devoted a single paragraph to what he called "strategic management." As it turns out, that was, and is, an oxymoron. Management by its very nature is not and cannot be strategic. Nothing pertaining to management can ever partake of strategy. What he was trying to do was to somehow take advantage of this ancient concept of warfare as applied to the battlefields of business. After all, business means competition and, as Clausewitz had said, competition is war. Strategy thus interpreted, especially in the dynamic post-war economy of the 1950's, made perfect sense. Of course, planning had always been considered a principle of management. Typically, after 1926, it was listed as the first activity of management, but the application was limited to tasks, jobs, or, perhaps, projects. Drucker's idea went far beyond that, potentially affecting the totality of organization.

Questions of originality and ultimate intent aside, this interpretation of strategy very quickly became not only the definitive but also the permanent standard, especially when applied to planning. "Strategic organization" would not be thought of until 50 years later. Whether this immediate and enduring acceptance was because of actual validity of the concept, the absence of any other reasonable alternative, or simply because it was a matter of convenience is a debatable issue. But the fact remains that "strategic management," with all of its implications, has persisted as the dominant philosophy and methodology of strategy, not just in the corporate world but in every aspect of organized society. In all fairness, the original idea was probably bent in popularization, but that does not ameliorate its legacy. It is precisely this kind of thinking that diminishes action, taming the most radical initiatives. Creation is out of the question. Discovery is out of mind.

There are two fatal flaws in the corporation-management version of strategy: (1) the subordination of strategy to the existing organization, and (2) the diminution of strategy to only corresponding response to external factors.

Regarding the first flaw, just as the science of management exists only within the context of the corporation general, so is the context of strategy restricted to and by the context of the corporation specific. That should not be particularly surprising; the only purpose of management is to serve the corporation by "getting work done through people," that being the first and only definition of management. Therefore, anything related to management—past, present, and future—will be first and foremost a loyal and faithful thrall. What that means is that strategies, as used by the corporation, are devices, employed or deployed, to achieve whatever goal has already been decided. ("Whatsoever ye shall bind on earth shall have already been bound in heaven"—or words to that effect.) The function of strategy, thus, is nothing more than "implementation." Strategies, therefore, become management exercises and the methods those of management practices. There is no leverage here, no possibility of transformation. It is possible for the blind to lead the blind. Misunderstandably, it is not even necessary for the strategies to be strategic. The final absurdity was the development of strategy by non-strategic organizations, that is, those without autonomy.

This way of non-thinking about strategy reached its climax in the 1990's with a paroxysm proudly heralded as "Total Quality Management" (TQM). Other than the lingering confusion over which adjective amplified what (or was one a noun), the apostles of this creed were very clear as to the secondary role of strategy. The way to the future lay in continuous improvement of existing systems through quantitative operational research. According to this doctrine, once the desired improvements in the existing system had been settled on, based on the analysis of data, then "strategies" would be developed to accomplish them.

But the question of which should come first was not really the problem. Quite often, popular opinion held that it did not matter which preceded the other; and, with that degree of understanding, the assessment was probably accurate. It made no difference because, quite frankly, neither made any difference. Some managers-administrators even suggested that TQM and strategic planning were two approaches ultimately leading to the same place. That is the real problem. Nothing could be further from the truth. They are polar opposites: strategy is intent on creating new systems; TQM is dedicated to perfecting those systems already obsolete.

Thereby, the organization, whatever it is, is condemned to remaining what it is. The loss is compounded by the fact that not only is stasis impossible to maintain, but the very idea of strategy causes serious allergic reaction throughout the corporation-model organization. On the one hand, hopes are raised in promise, and straightway dashed; on the other hand, threats are insinuated into intimidation. In the first case, the prospect of strategy causes those in its path to slink into reclusiveness; in the second case, to retreat and pull up the drawbridge. The bottom line is this: if this is the interpretation of strategy, any organization would be better off never to mention the word; or, if it must have strategy, to keep it secret.

Just as the definition of strategy was confined to management activities, so were the methodologies and processes conformed to the rigid corporation structure. Basically and thoroughly, the order was "top-down, bottom-up." The language varied, but the process was always the same. Major initiatives conceived at the "strategic level" were delegated downward for the development of "operational" plans. Usually such activities were carried out under the rubric of expected gains, both in substance and support. However, in all cases, the strategic authority maintained veto power over the operational recommendations—even the most high prerogative of benign disregard.

The likely precursor of this kind of planning process, certainly for Professor Drucker, was "Management by Objectives (MBO) and Self-Control." Reflection on why MBO failed seems especially relevant to this discussion. The failure was probably more in practice than in philosophy, but seven practical errors of MBO were carried forward into strategic planning as a management exercise: (1) accountability and authority were separated and made disproportional; (2) objectives were established for only selected components of a person's job; (3) the establishment of "priorities" destroyed any concept of system essentiality; (4) objectives were often conflicting, competing; (5) commensurate support was not provided for individuals pursuing the objectives; (6) there was inconsistent, often unrelated, follow-up; and (7) evaluation was punitive and connected to remuneration. Obviously, the effect of such an approach to organization could only be debilitating, even self-destructive. It would be impossible for any organization to rise above its top.

The second flaw, corresponding response to external factors, was somewhat more subtle and consequently more pervasive as a contaminant of strategic thinking. To fully appreciate the significance of this fallacy, one must recall the intellectual milieu in which the idea of "strategic management" was conceived. By the 1940's, the prevailing view of humanity was a very unhappy combination, or collision, of rationalism and naturalism. The corporation found itself stranded on an isthmus between the contemporary manifestations of those philosophies: behaviorism—pertaining to the individual, and Darwinism—pertaining to society at large. Betwixt and between, the corporation characteristically partook of both strands, reducing the person to effect and organization to survival.

There was no fancy terminology for corporate thinking, no theoretical expositions; the corporation mentality revealed itself in one simple resignation: "I go where I am pushed." From committees to consolidation, from being union-whipped to market-driven, from the urgency of profitability to customer focus, the corporation mentality was thoroughly and only reactive. Opportunism was the epitome of intervention. Most recently, it has become painfully obvious that all of the late corporate machinations—reinventing, restructuring, downsizing, merging—were not the result of strategic thinking but of episodic reaction. The legacy of the corporation is that radical innovation always comes from the outside.

There are many examples of attempts both to warn of the pitfalls of corporate planning as well as to actively displace it. The most notable example of the first is that of Professor Henry Mintzberg who, in his book aptly titled *The Rise and Fall of Strategic Planning*, chronicled the disappointments and frustrations of eternal analysis and number crunching without synthesis, without creation. Unquestionably the most dramatic example of the second is the decision by Jack Welch, president of General Electric, to completely eliminate the corporate planning office and place the responsibility for creating new futures within the operating units of the company. Unfortunately, these examples are still the exception.

THE INSTITUTIONAL-ADMINISTRATIVE VERSION

There are several metaphors that could be used in the discussion of the institutional-administrative version of strategy, and probably the only similarity among them would be that they each represent an attempt to symbolically express comparison or contrast with the corporation-management version. The medium and the message are the same.

For example, one instructive way of looking at these two interpretations of planning is through the imagery of twin pillars. Interestingly, that could be made to work in two ways: first, to signify that there were two dominant influences in each version (behaviorism and Darwinism in one, behaviorism and materialism in the other); and second, to symbolize the two versions themselves. And it is also true that, either way, "pillars" are human constructs designed as the foundation (or portal) of all human activity—immovable, changeless, mindless. The only difficulty with this symbolism is that it is too simple, and that is an open invitation to misunderstanding. The modern scientific mind could not rest until it had explained all of the possibilities of matrices, force-field analyses, *et cetera* inherent in the symbolism, thus complicating the whole thing beyond any practical meaning. But, amazingly, such fruitless activity would make the imagery come true.

Or, another perhaps more practical analogy may be that of "mirror image"—a peculiar reflection in which all of the features are there, only reversed. Distortion poses constant uncertainty. This imagery works exceedingly well to accurately portray both the philosophical concepts as well as the operational practicalities of the two versions. For example, institutional-administrative theory claims that it is not a science, but nevertheless it creates a complete organum of scientific principles by another name, a name implying wisdom—"proverbs." More has been written on the subject of administration than about any other human endeavor; and much of that unprecedented and unparalleled volume of commentary has been by or about Luther Halsey Gulick, who pursued the subject relentlessly in "notes" published over several years in the 1930's and 1940's. The term *proverb* gave the impression of being less scientific than "principle," as in management, and it enjoyed the luxury of accommodating mutually contradictory postulates. Administrative theory never overcame the fundamental error of this ambiguity.

So it should not be surprising to find that, operationally, institutional-administrative practice simply adapts the principles of management, often using the same language. The best critical admission of this duplicity is by Herbert A. Simon, who very early reduced the "proverbs" to four principles, directly out of the corporation-model organization's field manual:

1. Administrative efficiency is increased by a specialization of the task among the group.

2. Administrative efficiency is increased by arranging the members of the group in a determinate hierarchy of authority.

3. Administrative efficiency is increased by limiting the span of control at any point in the hierarchy to a small number.

4. Administrative efficiency is increased by grouping the workers, for purposes of control, according to (a) purpose, (b) process, (c) clientele, or (d) place.[2]

The only difficulty with the "mirror-image" analogy is that it could be construed as suggesting, and rather pointedly so, that institutional-administrative strategy must be or should be an imitation of the corporation-management version. That is still the popular view. The result is that *wealth-appropriating* organizations are taught and expected to emulate the attitudes, practices, and methodologies of *wealth-producing* enterprises. Public agencies, for example, are admonished in no uncertain terms to operate "more like a business." Astonishingly, this notion has never been questioned.

But perhaps the only imagery that fully captures the relationship between these two versions is the extended metaphor of twins—evil twins. Of course, it would be easy to push this already offbeat comparison too far (or to tease about whether two evils make one good, or one really big, evil). But the fact remains that both of these ostensible human perspectives have a common ancestry. It almost requires a genealogical chart to trace the common origins and differing branches of philosophy. Yet, the matter is really quite simple: both the corporation-management and the institutional-administrative versions originated in the context of rationalism-naturalism, but the institutional-administrative twin suffers a genetic deficiency even more debilitating than the behaviorism-Darwinism that characterized the corporation-management version. Somehow it inherited (instead of Darwinism) the latent defect of materialism, along with the dominant strain of behaviorism. So while the corporation model organization is best described as behavioristic-Darwinistic, the institutional-administrative organization is accurately characterized as behavioristic-materialistic. The difference is the question of survival.

The difficulty with this imagery is that, genetics aside, the philosophical issues are not exactly topics of everyday conversation. The first confusion would be over the many questions associated with materialism. That could take a considerable amount of explaining, perhaps to no avail. For instance, it probably would be extremely difficult to explain that materialism is the other side of Darwinism; and it would be almost impossible to get across the very important point that materialism, as a worldview, is not about survival of the fittest through the insatiable accumulation and consumption of things and money but is about the pursuit of human salvation in this present world, devoid of any spiritual dimension. Actually, materialism is a very old philosophy, dating back at least to the fifth century B.C. Oversimplified, its major tenets were that there is a sharp demarcation between the spiritual and the material, that all matter is evil, and that the only hope for human beings is to make the best of the material world of which they are a part. In its later stages, there was a lessening of emphasis on the natural evil state and eventually an almost exclusive emphasis on the prospect of creating a perfect world. This view, whether from optimism or resignation, was certainly the legacy of rationalistic science. Furthermore, what really matters is not the actual achievement of perfection but the everlasting "progress" toward it. Final judgment is impossible. The ultimate false premise of incremental, continuous improvement, certainly by implication, is that human perfection is possible; otherwise, why improvement? The very unhappy prospect of impending doom gave the corporation-management version of strategy an anxious vitality that the institutional-administrative version could never have, or, for that matter, never needed. But permanence is an unworthy substitute for performance.

Whatever the metaphor, these are the unadulterated facts of the case, at last report. Any one of the following institutional-administrative misconceptions will seriously compromise the concept of strategy. Together, they will destroy it completely.

(1) *Any application of strategy, as in the corporation approach, is undertaken only in the context of the existing organization and is therefore subservient to the existing system.* But institutional thinking goes much further—backwards. It actually attempts to perpetuate the organization long after it has become irredeemably ineffective, even after it is obsolete. Typically used by entities that are not subject to the harsh realities of the marketplace, this kind of strategy exempts *carte blanche* the organization from any kind of objective judgment. Planning becomes the means for holding everything in place. And everyone can find ample cover in the luxuriant growth of bureaucratic foliage. There are indecipherable layers, stifling density, and plenty of threatening loose ends dangling about. Any attempt at real strategic change is immediately overgrown and stifled.

(2) *Institutional planning begins with the assumption that the institution is a uniform, intractable structure directed in minutiae by centralized control.* Although very much authoritarian, the personal nature of real authority gives way to impersonal "policies" and "procedures"—greatly enhancing the *ex cathedra* aura of all directives. Planning thus becomes not a set of specific plans to be realized but a continuing desperate attempt to write enough regulations to control every aspect of the organization, to be enforced by the guardians of the establishment. And the control is strictly top-down, issuing in mandates without commensurate resources or authority; there is no bottom up, except the accountability for carrying out dictates. The problem is that results cannot be mandated. Planning not only takes on the characteristics of the institution, it reinforces them. Rather than changing the system, planning is adapted to the defense of the system. These features, taken together, amount to an inescapable lock on the status quo.

(3) *The institution is process.* There is no understanding of results. In fact, the institution has an inherent aversion to measurable or observable outcomes. Results threaten the status quo and force individual accountability. Therefore, any and all "objectives," or "goals," true to the institution's dual nature, are stated in terms of process, or as a demonstration of certain kinds of behavior. Colleges and universities have so impressed "process objectives" into the minds of aspiring young bureaucrat hopefuls and slightly worn but retreadable master bureaucrats that it is now impossible even to hold an intelligent conversation with them about the

authentic meaning of "objectives." Just as sure as the old axiom about the tiger and his stripes, it is impossible for the institutional-administrative mentality to comprehend objectives.

(4) *The institution exists in an isolated eternal "now."* Therefore, hyper-analysis of every aspect of the organization becomes both rationale and justification of its existence. Research replaces thinking. Something called "institutional research" continuously disgorges polluted streams of data, but, typically, no information. Synthesis, therefore, is impossible. But that is not a problem here. It is also unnecessary. Planning is misappropriated into "paralysis by analysis." The plethora of studies, reviews, and re-ports—all based on makeshift statistical exercise—eliminates any possi-bility of results-based planning. The institution exists only in its own data.

(5) *Paradoxically, the total organization control endemic in the basic dispo-sition of the institution is not carried out in actual systemic development of the whole organization.* Fixes are the institution's daily bread; all are piece-meal, usually imported, and always succeed into programs, projects, and packages that are "installed" or "adopted." Nothing comes from within the institution, and nothing is holistic. In many instances, "planning" is little more than the accumulation of junk from seasonal intellectual flea markets. So, after a while, the thing becomes a crazy patchwork of used materials where nothing matches or fits. In organizational terms, sys-temic necessities such as integration, synchronization, coordination of effort, and unity are rendered impossible. Planning takes on exactly the same "un-characteristic." Concentration of effort in any purpose is im-possible; energies are dissipated. Random "plans" become ploys for sandbagging, stonewalling, and the old game of "cover your ass."

(6) *The institution has a blatant disregard for its lower levels.* That is tan-tamount to saying that it has a contempt for actual work, for the business at hand, and for the clientele it is purported to serve. Neglect and distance breed a litter of trouble—sloth, disaffection, resentment. In that environ-ment, planning is always after the fact, and it never quite catches up. Lag time is not between plan and action but between activity and plan.

THE FUTURISTIC VERSION

There are all kinds of debris in the intellectual galaxy. From time to time it rains down on the heads of unsuspecting people and knocks them senseless, but in the process it leaves them either with a warm glow and an overwhelming feeling of personal well-being or adled beyond words. While there are many other hypotheses, that is the only logical expla-nation for the unearthly phenomenon known in the land of oxymoron as "futuristic planning." Fortune seeks its own.

Actually it is not accurate to refer to the futuristic type as "strategy," and there is serious reason to question whether this version, in any of its forms, really has anything to do with planning. Furthermore, there are so many variations of the futuristic approach that it is impossible to categorize them either discreetly or fairly. The problem is not one of quantity, or that there is occasionally very unlikely blending and mixing; rather, it is that, in almost every case, shadings obscure the lines, evidence perhaps of imprecise thinking. But at the risk of being judged both inaccurate and unfair, this discussion will suggest that there are three kinds of futuristic thinking: the *spectacular*, the *speculative*, and the *spectral*. Sufficient critical attributes exist for each to identify them as actual kinds, yet they have a common character.

All are based on the assumption that prospective future realities serve as the stimulus of some kind of immediate response. From anticipation to adaptation to preparation, the reaction of human beings and human systems is always precipitated by that which is predicted or has been predetermined—by forces and factors outside. The reaction is the plan.

The *spectacular* ranges from *tours de force* in Newton's laws of predictability to the confidence game of the snake-oil hawker. While based on slivers of credible evidence, the future portrayed is little more than a skillful concoction calculated to serve a predetermined agenda. Bill Gates writes a book about the only future being in cyberspace in order to prepare the hearts and minds of nervous ninnies to convert all of their earthly goods, all of their net worth, into technological apparati—Microsoft, of course. The Sierra Club blares out alert after alert, warning of horrifying natural disasters being brought about by marauding lumberjacks and campers, to provide everyone else absolution from guilt by association through easy penance—preferably cash. Environmentalistic politicians funeralize over global warming in an attempt either to fuel their own campaigns and local defense funds or to provide general admission to the public treasury for constituent green groups. Chicken Little quickly grows up to become cock of the walk. And the National School Board Association issues apocalyptic predictions about the imminent collapse of America's public schools and the general heathenizing of children obviously aimed at creating panic "yes" voting in local referenda, no matter how inconsequential the thing to be approved. The spectacular approach transforms planning into little more than inciting herd instinct, but always with individual motive. In a perverse irony, this kind of "futuring" actually becomes strategy, a gambit designed to achieve a specific outcome. Strangely, of all the futuristic versions and kinds of strategy, this may be closer to the original idea than any other.

The second kind, the *speculative*, is also based on responding to assumptions about the future, and that should be taken as an indication of the persistent passive-reactive attitude inherent in the futuristic approach. Yet it is true that this kind of thinking holds considerable promise as a reasonable exercise. Sometimes the results are quite impressive, worked out in compelling scientific detail and providing an intriguing, perhaps accurate, description of the future. But here again the starting point for action is external and, perhaps, fixed. Any action is response.

There are three shadings of speculation. The first is the purely philosophical. While perhaps not as evident as the others, this approach nevertheless is still prevalent in Western culture, especially in the upper strata of political, academic and business planning, and direction and control (i.e., the Federal Reserve). Economic cycles, political cycles, historical cycles—that is the basic idea. The idea of cycles as the pattern of human existence originated, at least in Western culture, with the Cynics in ancient Greece. They believed that human systems would be born, rise to maturity, then fall into complete and uttter disintegration, and from the ruins another system(s) would arise. In modern times, the idea of cycles took on a more logical, if not rationalistic, cast. Deeply rooted in a misunderstanding of the dialectic, and far more Marxist that Hegalian, speculation about the future more or less presupposes in human events a continuous repetition of thesis, antithesis, and synthesis. Even if this were a valid interpretation of human history, that is no reason to accept it as the interpretation of future. The most possible influence, probably the only influence, that the idea of cycles can have on future events is its effect as a self-fulfilling prophecy. Cycles and futures are two different subjects. Stripped to fundamentals, the difference can be stated as a simple formula:

Past $\times$ Present $=$ Future

Interpreted, this means that the past as it conflicts witht the present produces the future. Of particular significance is the notion of "conflict" between past and present rather than between future and past. The result is that the future casts no shadow backward. Thus, the future, in any of its manifestations, becomes coincidence at best, accident at worst. And, as usual, the extent of human influence is the understanding of certain natural principles and learning how best to use them to advantage— never to cause, but to adjust behavior for the most desirable results under the circumstances. "Influencing" the external factors is the highest ambition. This way of thinking, while not generally admitted, is the fundamental predisposition of virtually all contemporary strategy. Even the most new-age thinking is suddenly rendered very old: "The purpose of strategic thinking in the new planning paradigm is to help an organization identify, respond to, and influence changes in its environment."[3]

This reductive philosophy is in stark contrast to legitimate strategic thinking, which holds that life does not consist of cycles, and the true formula is, "the future as it contrasts with the past yields the present."

That is to say, the starting point in creating futures is the future—imagined imperatively. Only then does the past have any meaning; only then does the present have any context.

The second version of the speculative is purely practical. Based on the Newtonian assurance of unerring predictability, current circumstances are thoroughly analyzed and scientifically extrapolated into the future, yielding surprisingly accurate pictures or scenarios. Only the current situation is in doubt. It is called "environmental scan." That tells the story. Obviously Darwinistic in its origin, this way of thinking yields several very unhappy conclusions: the world is characterized by scarcity; competition is the way of life; survival is the highest aspiration; "adaptation" is the only mode for survival; finding and keeping to a "niche" is about the only chance available. In actual sessions, planning groups, using this approach, have become so discouraged that they have abandoned the field altogether, given up any idea of action, and given themselves up to luck, fate, chance, and magic—not to mention the lottery. That being the case, once again it is eminently better to not plan at all. Anxiety is greatly reduced; and every day brings another exciting surprise. In fact, the only constant is surprise.

The third version is reflexive. This kind of "strategy" ranges from simple stand-by knee-jerk reaction—unreasoned, even non-rational—to fairly sophisticated contingency planning. Contingency planning usually consists of preliminary analysis of possible "futures," either as events or circumstances, and prescriptive response to each situation. The knee-jerk attitude obviously involves little in the way of strategy, unless in some sort of metaphysical way there is strategy in waiting to act until the impact is felt. In the meantime, conceivably any sort of activity could be pursued. The conditional is manifested along a broad continuum: from standard operating procedures (S.O.P.'s) contemporary theory of organization. S.O.P.'s are common; they are simply planned prudent measures activated by threat or opportunity. But the "contingency" theory of organization proved to be a rather unfavorable critique of all other such theories. It is important here because of what it says about contemporary thinking. There were four such theories during the twentieth century, progressively: scientific, social, humanistic, and contingency. Reduced to its basic doctrine, this philosophy acknowledged the inadequacy of each of the previous approaches, but it recommended selectively combining them with one another as well as with other principles freely drawn from any science into a pastiche appropriate to the immediate challenge. Contingency planning may be the better part of discretion, and contingency organization may cover a multitude of sins, but none of that changes its basic disposition. It is still reactive—pure and simple.

The most sophisticated reflexive approach was something known specifically, and probably generically, as "future search." The original future search methodology was a rather soft version of the participatory/quality craze that swept North America in the 1960's, blended with the mind-mapping (association of ideas) of the 1970's, and based loosely on the historical dialectic (the first two steps in the process: "review the past; explore the present"). And while there was much of real value incorporated here and there into the process, there was little integrity in the total system. Although it actually developed "action plans," typically there was little emphasis on achieving results. While it did indeed focus on the future, the idea was not to *create* a future but rather to *choose* among various fantasized options—hence, "future search." "Our purpose is always joint action toward a desired future."[4]

That was ostensibly accomplished by "creating ideal future scenarios" and then "identifying common ground." Action plans become a tentative assertion of will over circumstance, but in the end circumstance prevailed. But that is the nature of reflexive planning. It is quite similar to the old carnival game (lately upgraded and refitted for interstate truck-stop arcades) in which the young aspirant attempts to manipulate the arm and claws of a mini-steam shovel to grab the most desirable prize from all of those scattered about in the glass box. Sometimes one gets lucky, but usually not.

The third kind of futuristic perspective, the *spectral* (with apologies to Mark Twain), "sees through a glass eye darkly." The disorientations and sense of detachment that accompany focused obscurity call forth demonstrations from mysticism to outright silliness. Complicating the matter further was the general outbreak of "envisioning" that swept the newly scientized world beginning in the mid-1980's. Just as soon as it became apparent that most of the current generation might actually see the twenty-first century, and even more dramatic, a new millennium, visions became more or less commonplace, *de rigueur* for people on the move, or those seeking to give the impression of motion. Unfortunately, no one cautioned that illusions, delusions, and hallucinations are also visions. So visions flashed or floated about erratically. For example:

- Every public bureaucracy in the nation developed (or photocopied) a document boldly emblazoned with the promise of "Vision 2000."
- Cities and towns rushed to create mass effusions about "(Podunk) 2000: A Vision for the Next Century." One such publication declared the city's vision as:

    To provide quality service for our community through professionalism, communication, and teamwork.[5]

- Every industry group searched the horizon for a vision of what lay ahead:

    Visions of the Future.
    What will the food distribution business look like in the next cen-

tury? A blue-ribbon panel of consultants sat down with a progressive grocer to chart the future. What they say may encourage you,
or frighten you, or both.[6]

- "Vision" became an obligatory component of strategic plans, even though the
  actual declaration seemed most like a description of current events, a justification of the existing system. The verb tense is the first clue.

  ASCD (Association for Supervision and Curriculum Development)
  makes a difference for children by serving those who shape their
  learning. ASCD helps educators prepare children for their future
  roles as citizens in an interdependent, ever changing world. We are
  a powerful advocate and invaluable resource for excellence and equity in education. We build partnerships that advance teaching and
  learning worldwide. We live our beliefs through our actions, products, and services.[7]

- All chief executive officers were hired (and fired) based on the "vision" they
  brought to their companies. This was the typical expectation:

  Leaders (top managers/administrators) are responsible for the creation of vision, and the vision provides the basic energy for moving
  the organization toward the future.[8]

- From out of nowhere people begin having visions with the frequency and reg-
  ularity of hot flashes:

  One scientist's vision revolutionizes the hearing industry, benefit-
  ting millions of people. . . . [9]

Some of the many puns were downright cute, such as the ophthal-
mologist who advertised "visionary eye care." Suffice it to say that very
soon visions lost sight. It was a good idea gone bad. Whether arising
from conjuring, dreaming, or revelation, visions entice with fantasy and
escape, so they are either entertaining diversions or a tacit abnegation of
responsibility—none can be realized. As a general rule, people have visions when they have no purpose. Primarily sought by government
agencies and institutions of higher education, visions require no real
commitment, only "sharing," or maybe "buy-in." But visions are popular also in the world of business, especially among companies attempting to blunt the edge of autocratic management by getting otherwise
dismal and disinterested employees to get psyched up about the vision
of the "leader," a.k.a. the CEO, who has just floated in on a magic carpet
borrowed from Kubla Khan, Ph.D. The problem is that such visions are
never, ever transferred into action, simply because they cannot be.

The basic problem with visions is that they are always fleeting and
elusive. Palpability is of no significance to the bright or shadowy images
that haunt the landscape of tomorrow. Proverbially the realm of prophets

and soothsayers and closely associated with dreams, visions waive both certainty and substance. Legendarily, visions were the means by which gods and other supernatural beings revealed to mortals, via some chosen seer, pictures of either a heaven or a hell, figuratively—literally. For some perverse reason, there were always more visions of hell, usually accompanied by a clamorous divine warning and a last chance to mend one's ways. Beatific visions are so rare that they are enshrined, the visionaries canonized. Even so, there was considerable tolerance in the visions' specifications and veracity. The overall effect was the thing. After all, details lead only to trifling misunderstanding, argument and squabbling.

Yet beyond the unresolved questions raised by visions as such, there is today a rather placid and general confusion about the word(s) itself. Visionists have the disturbing habit of quoting an ancient Hebrew adage, "Where there is no vision, the people perish" (Proverbs 29:18) as the authentication for beginning and ending every discussion about the future with some invocation of vision. It is disturbing because even an amateur exegesis will quickly discover that original wisdom speaks of something far more meaningful than the fascinations of a blue-ribbon panel. The subject here is vision—singular—not visions. There is no hint of artificial stimulation by drugs, hypnosis, dream-sleep, or professional vision-meisters. The prophets evidently knew the difference, because in another context another prophet declared, "Your old men shall dream dreams and your young men shall see visions." But here the prophet speaks of vision, that is, simply and only the ability to see. He is merely pointing out the absolute necessity for individuals to see meaning and purpose in their lives day to day. Otherwise, they become lost, despondent, and lethargic, even to the point of death. That kind of sight requires no magic-lantern show, and it is certainly not a mandate for those who think themselves possessed of a vision (or visions) to share it or impose it. There is nothing mysterious here; nothing concocted; nothing derived from neo-scientific incantations. It is simply a matter of faith in oneself and in purpose beyond oneself. Unfortunately, the *fin de siècle* bouillabaisse of visions was something else completely.

The end of the matter is this: practically speaking, any planning process that begins with vision is immediately suspect. There is little chance that anything of substance will come of it. No one can be exactly sure about what goes on in the spectral realm. Every day brings a new revelation. But discernible words, now and then echoing from the outer mists, suggest many strange things—all apparently aimed at creating an air of mystery, heavy with the fragrance of the supernatural. Some, especially those drawn from Native American traditions, probably cross the line in the profanation of sacred traditions. Ultimately, the spectral raises this improbable question: how is it possible that strategic thinking can be anti-thought? Admittedly, much is to be said for the attempt to escape the shackles of purely rationalistic processes—certainly a blow for emotional freedom, popularily known as "thinking out of the box." However, one would expect that strategic thinking would be at least intellective, if not intellectual, but that is not the case. Instead there is a distinct tendency toward rationalistic ambiguity, indicative no doubt of a psychology of ambivalence about oneself, others, and the way the world works.

While each of the following techniques may be stimulating in any kind of planning, and although they certainly push against traditional linear rationalistic schemes, none by itself, nor all together, constitutes a plausible strategic planning process.

- *Metaphors* became the currency of planning, especially those drawn from quasi-scientific jargon. In fact, it seemed that there was considerable competition among new-age gurus to discover the next faddish naturalistic or biological symbolism as an antidote to thinking.

- *Visualization* purported to depict in one flowing collage, the past, present, and future of the universe. Recalling the prehistoric pictographs, drawings served as the technique of placing a human perspective on the events and conditions of the day. Words ceased to be effective symbols of communication and became, rather, putative action. At least one dreamy-eyed prognosticator had the audacity to declare visualization as the next "revolution" in strategic planning. Ironically, high-tech morphing returned civilization to the walls of the cave.

- Imitations of the *spiritual rituals*, often sacred, of aboriginal cultures held a special fascination. The First Nations of North America were pillaged for traditions pertaining to dreams, quests, journeys, and communication with spirits.

- Intimations of *Eastern mysticism* began to appear somewhat incongruously in Western constructs. Isolated aspects of completely other realities lost all meaning when they were taken out of context. The results were ridiculous combinations, for example, the Tao of leadership and Hoshin planning.

- The promise of the so-called *"new age"* was irresistible, a world free at last from all of the constraints, boundaries, and limitations of the past 2,000 years. It was a world in which the only realities were "chaos, complexity, and change." Truth was irrelevant, and abstraction was easily rationalized away.

There is little doubt that the proponents of such devices were earnestly seeking ways to achieve breakthroughs or breakouts from the rationalistic constructs that have dominated Western civilization for over 300 years, and they are to be congratulated for the attempt. Yet, with all due respect to them, they themselves, as a generation, are trapped in a world that has so minimized the power of the human mind, through rationalistic constructs, that the realization of another world is virtually impossible. Math and science and logic are only very small parts of the universe.

Perhaps it would be both explicative and instructive to recall the precise distinction made by Samuel Taylor Coleridge between the intellectual facilities of "imagination" and "fancy." In context, he was expounding on literary processes, but the principles are universally applicable to human thinking. He proposed that the imagination "struggles to idealized and to unify"; "fancy," quite in opposition, is merely a "mode of memory emancipated from the order of time and space." The latter is the most succinct description of current planning theories and practices imaginable. According to Coleridge, and a whole school of thought, fancy was "mechanic," "logical," "the aggregate and associative power." Imagination is "organic" and "creative," held in check by reason. As the highest level of human thought, the imagination is the "shaping" and ordering power; and the assumption was that the "new creation" emanating from the imagination is a completely new reality— not a fantasy or a "fanciful projection." Contemporary visions, even when raised to the highest power, are exactly that—"fanciful projections." There is a world of difference between projecting and creating.

It is worthwhile to contemplate the implications of Coleridge's own words:

The imagination, then, I consider either as primary, or secondary. The primary imagination I hold to be the living power and prime agent of all human perception, and as a repetition in the finite mind of the eternal act of creation in the infinite I Am. The secondary I consider as an echo of the former, coexisting with the conscious will, yet still as identical with the primary in the kind of its agency, and differing only in degree, and in the mode of its operation. It dissolves, diffuses, dissipates, in order to recreate; or where this process is rendered impossible, yet still, at all events it struggles to idealize and to unify. It is essentially vital, even as all objects (as objects) are essentially fixed and dead.

Fancy, on the contrary, has no other counters to play with, but fixities and divinities. The fancy is indeed no other than a mode of memory emancipated from the order of time and space; and blended with, and modified by that empirical phenomenon of the will, which we express by the word choice. But equally with the ordinary memory it must receive all its materials ready made from the law of association.[10]

In conclusion, it is not academic fastidiousness that compels this distinction between legitimate strategy and the modern imitations. Rather, it is the matter of practicality: anything other than the original is bound to result in frustration, disappointment, and loss of will.

Chapter 4

Arena II: Leaders vs. Leadership

Those who know and care about definitions tell us that there are two kinds—real and nominal. The real are meanings ascribed to words at a given time and place—in other words, the vernacular. So the meaning of the same word may change radically from one generation to the next or from one locale to another synchronistically. The designation "real" is potentially misleading because it may easily be mistaken as a mark of authority. But that is so only in terms of contemporary understanding. Real definitions are an accommodation of current usage. And, in any actuality, it probably makes no difference whether "marshal" means "horse-servant" or a special law enforcement official. But it does make a difference whether "strategy" is reduced to any number of devices, techniques, and methodologies for any and all ordinary activity, or elevated to extraordinary creative action.

Nominal definitions, on the other hand, have to do with the original intent of the word. Here the word is not so much any utilitarian instrument of communication—as say, linking verbs*—but the linguistic expression of a simple idea or a profound concept. It is meaningful, for example, that the word "barbarian," currently interpreted as "an uncivilized person," originally meant "one whose speech sounds like 'bar-bar'." There is a fullness in the distinction between the accentual language of the Germanic tribes and the qualitative classical tones. It is, in fact, no less than cultural distinction. But when the context is lost, so

---

*Experts say that one-fourth of the task of expression in English is accomplished by nine words (*and, be, have, it, of, the, to, will, you*). See *The Development of Modern English* (Englewood Cliffs, N.J.: Prentice Hall, 1954), p. 174.

is the meaning. That is what happened to the word "strategy." Lesser real definitions supplanted the original meaning, but it was the original definition that held the concept.

The nominal definition of strategy (*stratos* + *agein*) is "to lead an army." The word *strategos* was much in vogue among the Greeks as early as 3500 B.C. The date is significant because it dispels any recent claim that strategy is a child of the corporation or the sibling of management. Strategy predates the corporation by 5,200 years and management by over 5,400 years. The etymology of the word is significant because it makes strategy forever a matter of *leading*. If strategy is to be true to its name, it will partake of the qualities of leaders. The more, the truer. Therein lies the rub. Unfortunatley, "strategy" has lately entered the popular culture with about as many "real" definitions as users, very likely because there is no longer any understanding of the nature of leaders or leading. The situation is rapidly becoming hopeless. Leaders have been replaced by management scientists; leading has been supplanted by technique. The twentieth-century idea of "leadership" has negated both.

LEADERSHIP

King Solomon graciously offered this discouraging word: "That which is crooked cannot be made straight." So it is with "leadership." Actually, the confusion over this subject may rival that of the famous Schleswig-Holstein controversy, a boundary dispute so indecipherable that Lord Pemberton rose in Parliament to declare the situation so confused that only three men ever understood it: one died, another went insane, and the third forgot. So it is with leadership.

The best and worst place to start this discussion is with the simple question of the relationship between leadership and management. Historically, they seem to have developed at about the same time—"leadership" appearing first in about 1918, "management" emerging as a science between 1908 and 1926. But from the beginning there was serious confusion over the meaning of "leadership," specifically as it related to management. And the confusion, over the years, rather than being resolved, has been exacerbated by both intellectual neglect (it is all a matter of semantics) and popular myth (leadership is also a rationalistic science). Either way they have been reduced to strictly non-intellectual propositions. The ultimate consequence was the extinction of leaders from contemporary organizations. One school of thought assumes that rationalistic management and leadership are pretty much the same. No muss; no fuss; no bother. The words are commonly used interchangeably, even within the same discourse. This is the basic disposition of the corporation model's belief and practice: leadership is expected to exist in direct proportion to management authority. As one goes up the ladder in management rank, his or her leadership is supposed to increase commensurately. The CEO is, ex officio, the leader of the organization, the first tier of managers, the "leadership."

Accordingly, the catalogs of all the major graduate schools of business in North America carry many courses variously labeled with the word "leadership." Most of the course descriptions promise some kind of "leadership development." But close reading of the text quickly reveals that every one of these offerings is pure and simple management training. There is only one exception: one university lists two courses in something called "cultural leadership." Even the author of the textbook admits that he does not know what that is. If any differentiation between management and leadership is evident, it is only as a marketing gimmick. For example, some of the business school brochures announcing summer programs seem to make a distinction in gibberish such as, "You have been given the responsibility of management, now learn the principles of leadership," or vice versa. It seems to work either way. And either way, the connection is mentally forged. In the hinterland of academia, leadership degenerates into little more than first-line supervision. For example:

Tactics for Effective Leadership: Interaction Management[11]

This three-day workshop is designed to give you fundamental skills to address and improve performance-based issues with your staff. The workshop covers:

- *Core Skills for Managers*: introducing you to the key principles to build commitment with your staff.
- *Facilitating Improved Performance*: helping you focus on what your staff does and how they do it.
- *Following Up*: completing the circle by giving your staff effective feedback to support improvement.

Recently, six experts were asked to answer the question "What is leadership?" Their answers clearly demonstrate the rife confusion of management and leadership.

What Is Leadership?[12]

- The art of mastering change . . . ability to mobilize others' efforts in new directions. Leaders define future needs and opportunities. They share their passion. Managers control; leaders shake things up.
- The art of initiating and managing change. Anyone can manage the status quo, but it takes a leader to change things for the better.
- Organizing, inspiring, and driving a group to achieve results beyond their ex-

pectations. Combination of pragmatism and vision. Ability to quickly understand dynamism in the market.

- Motivating people to meet goals. Leaders help people believe in their goals and
  inspire them to deliver on their promises. Leaders instill a sense of purpose
  and urgency.
- At its core, leadership is the ability to inspire and develop others . . . to bring
  forth their fullest potential and highest capabilities . . . to encourage them to
  accomplish a mission as a team.
- Taking a group of people in a new direction or to higher levels of performance
  than they would have achieved without you.

Or consider the superficial, back-of-hand treatment of leadership published in, of all places, the official journal of the United States Chamber
of Commerce. Striking a tone much like a high school English essay, the
article proclaimed "three critical areas of leadership—Communication,
Accountability, and Trust," and concluded with this sweepstakes promise: "The advice of experts and the testimony of business people suggest
that if you develop CAT skills, there's a good chance you'll become ruler
of the jungle."[13]

As a final accumulation of the error of ascribing the same meaning to
two different words, J. Thomas Wren edited a little compendium titled
The Leader's Companion: Insights on Leadership Through the Ages.[14] Except
for his own preface, which contradicts virtually everything else in the
book, all of the essays are 100 percent about management. One is left
wondering how it is possible in an age that claims to be the most intellectually advanced in all human history that this kind of non-thinking
persists. If it were only an academic matter, it would amount to a mild
curiosity; as a practical strategic issue, it carries profound implications.

But the situation gets worse. There is another school of thought, led
by Professor Warren Bennis, that contends that management and leadership are exact opposites. In fact, the good professor took the time to
develop a point-by-point contrast.

But his philosophy is popularly reduced to an aphorism known
throughout Western civilization: "Managers do things right; leaders do
the right things." If only it were that simple! The confusion is much more
enigmatic than it may appear. The first problem is that his very attempt
to contrast management and leadership is an admission that they are, in
fact, items of the same class. It is a concession to logic that requires
comparisons and contrasts between or among things of the same classification, otherwise analogy is used. For example, it is impossible to
compare (or to contrast) a Volkswagen Beetle to a coconut, but certain
analogies may be helpful in making a point. In fact, the phrase Volkswagen "beetle" is itself an analogy, as are many other trade names.

Second, even Professor Bennis cannot escape the tentacles of science.

In his later works he admits a desirable, even necessary, connection between management and leadership. For example, he defines the "four competencies evident in every leader" as follows: management of attention; management of meaning; management of trust; and management of self. Furthermore, he goes on to say that in organizations with effective leaders, "empowerment" is most evident in four themes: people feel significant; learning and competence matter; people are part of a community; and work is exciting.[15] The language itself is of management origin. For example, "competencies," rather than characteristics; "effective," as in results, rather than anything qualitative such as being; and "empowerment," which is a tired ploy used by autocrats to bend others to their will. Moreover, all aspects of leadership are tied to work. But at least Professor Bennis strikes a blow for truth and justice when he admits that leadership cannot be taught.

The adverse consequences of this confusion are evident and incalculable. William Rees Mogg, the former editor of the *London Times*, recently declared, "The simultaneous collapse of leadership throughout Western civilization is not without cause."[16] The interesting thing about this observation is not the discussion of the cause(s), but that the collapse is a fait accompli.

It may be that same general sense of impending doom that has prompted the greatest outpouring of books on the subject of leadership during the 1990's than in the entire history of publishing up until that time. Book fairs at the conventions of professional groups proudly display an abundance of new titles each year, and as many as 80 percent mention "leadership" on their dust jackets.

But all of this literature is helpful in what is obviously an unintended way. Fairly and objectively, all publications on the subject, with perhaps two exceptions, can be arranged into four stacks—each representing a clearly distinct interpretation of leadership and each recommending its own method of "leadership development."

Stack #1

These books assert or assume that leadership is a set of *skills*. Leadership skills include all of the basic techniques required to do well in either standing out in a group or directing a group activity: communication, rational decision making, "consensus building," even the conduct of parliamentary procedure. One university-associated leadership training institute offered to test candidates for latent leadership ability. If the applicants achieve a passing score, which most assuredly they will, then the institute would issue them a large quiver, stated as a curriculum, and would then proceed to sell them an equally large number of arrows—skills that could be carried about and shot, at the appropriate times, to targets within any corporate system. Success was in knowing when and how to aim.

As if that were not superficial enough, leadership "skills" quickly became hardened into leadership "roles." Consider the following regrettable demonstration of popular misunderstanding:

Four Roles of Leadership*

Modeling. A leader becomes a model whom others trust and choose to follow.

Pathfinding. Leaders scan their environment, identify key customer and stakeholder needs, and develop a mission and strategy to meet those needs.

Aligning. Leaders align the systems and structure of the organization with the mission, strategy, and culture.

Empowering. Leaders create conditions within the organization where empowerment can flourish, creating results that meet customer and stakeholder needs.

Obviously, there is just enough truth here to keep a reasonably intelligent person willing to go along. The closest description to truth is the comment on "modeling"; but even this is explained, as are all the others, very overtly as organization skills. Yet the simple fact is that leading is not about doing but about being.

Stack #2

Leadership is a set of acquired *behavioral traits.* One typical quote says it all: "It is the manager's responsibility to choose the leadership style most conducive to getting work done by people." The "styles" supposedly range from the autocratic to laissez-faire—exactly the same as the styles of management. The obvious question is why and how the styles of leadership came to coincide with management styles. It seems that about mid-century, Professor James Cribbin, either in a state of confusion about the matter himself or wonderfully benevolent, wrote an essay in which he captured several "management-leadership" styles. The combination was forever fixed.

Then, Professors Paul Hersey and Kenneth Blanchard, seizing the moment, developed a whole enterprise around the concept(s). So the world was left with a rather strange pair of cognates (see Exhibit 1).

Appropriately, there were only two ways to deal with this duality: choose one over the other, or ignore both. Most serious-minded people choose ignorance. But the real issues here are about more than the confusion of leadership with management. There are two. First, "style" is

---

*Pilfered from a leadership seminar at Hofstra University. These notes were left by an anonymous teacher on the overhead projector.

Exhibit 1
Traditional Management/Leadership Styles

LEADERSHIP STYLES

AUTOCRATIC	PATERNALISTIC	DIRECTIVE	COLLABORATIVE	COLLEGIAL	BUREAUCRATIC	ACCOMMODATIVE

TRADITIONAL MANAGEMENT STYLES

AUTHORITARIAN	CONSULTATIVE	PARTICIPATIVE	DEMOCRATIC	LAISSEZ-FAIRE

invariably taught, and supposedly practiced, as habituated behavior. That is, the manager-leader has been conditioned through training, feedback, adaptation, and modification to have his or her behavior accommodate any situation. In fact, some theoreticians describe this as "situational leadership" or "situational management." In their world, such chameleon-like changeableness is a prized trait in one whose job it is to get work done through people. The second issue is obvious; that is, there is in the very suggestion that one might select suitable styles for given circumstances heavy overtones of manipulation. It cannot disguise its patronizing attitude, but leaders are never condescending.

Stack #3

Leadership is a set of *principles*. This theory is the most difficult to understand, ironically because of the nebulous nature of the proposition. The idea has esoteric appeal; it reverberates with moral tenor, yet, when pushed to specificity, it quickly evaporates into platitudes. The latest champion of this way of intellectualizing is Professor Stephen Covey, and his book *Principle-Centered Leadership* says it all. The only problem is that it does not say much at all. The book is, rather, a collage of speeches labeled with a catchy title for the marketplace—certainly it does not purport to be a well-reasoned thesis. The closest he comes to the subject is in a section titled "Leading by Compass."

> Correct principles are like compasses: they are always pointing the way. And if we know how to read them, we won't get lost, confused, or fooled by conflicting voices and values.
> Principles are self-evident, self-validating natural laws. They don't change or shift. They provide "true north" direction to our lives when navigating the "streams" of our environments.
> Principles apply at all times in all places. They surface in the form of values, ideas, norms, and teachings that uplift, ennoble, fulfill, empower, and inspire people. The lesson of history is that to the degree people and civilizations have operated in harmony with correct principles, they have prospered. . . .
> Principle-centered leadership is based on the reality that we cannot violate these natural laws with impunity. Whether or not we believe in them, they have been proven effective throughout centuries of human history. Individuals are more effective and organizations more empowered when they are guided and governed by these proven principles. They are not easy, quick-fix solutions to personal and interpersonal problems. Rather, they are foundational principles that when applied consistently become behavioral habits enabling fundamental transformations of individuals, relationships, and organizations.[17]

Almost, but not quite.
The key to understanding this philosophy, as well as its inherent dif-

ficulty, is in the last sentence above. Universal "principles"—natural laws—must be translated into "behavioral habits." The difficulty is this: one would expect that principles would be instilled through teaching and learning; only "habits" are formed by conditioning.

The real problem is a matter of credibility. Amazingly, in the book *Principle Centered-Leadership*, there is not a single principle of leadership enunciated. So the whole idea, while at first quite promising as an exploration of the universal, unchanging qualities of leadership, sadly dissipates into sermonizing and anecdote. The only attempt at principle is the old adage; "Give a man a fish and you feed him for a day; teach him how to fish and you feed him for a lifetime." But that is about teaching—not leading.

The real problem with principle-centered leadership lies in the assumption that those principles are "natural laws," which are translated into "correct principles." The question is, "Whose translation?" It is an extremely narrow-minded perspective that assumes that these natural laws will be translated the same way in every culture. Obviously, they will not. That is what defines culture. And no matter what the interpretation, any culture will still have leaders. Even if the laws are denied, the culture will have leaders. The fact is that leading is morally neutral. Evil communities, by whatever standard, have their leaders too. So to say that leadership consists of a set of principles defined by a certain Western perspective is somewhat arrogant. "True north" may be meaningful in one culture, "true south" in another, to say nothing of east and west.

Stack #4

This stack is without doubt the most perplexing, if not the most discouraging. So far this stack contains only one book; and if human reason and divine intervention have anything to do with it, there will be no more. The philosophy, if indeed it can be called that, holds that leadership is a "mysterious combination of chemistry, biology, physical appearance, temperament, and psychology."[18] The source of this off-the-wall thinking is Professor Howard Gardner, Harvard psychologist. The basic idea is that "leadership has far less to do with IQ, strength, aggressiveness or logical thinking than the right looks, good chemistry and the fuzzy, murky kind of decision-making we call common sense—even in monkeys." And it has nothing to do with character or values.

Speaking of monkeys, Gardner equates leadership with dominance—the "alpha male syndrome":

Having a head-of-state is merely one example of a behavior common to many primates: in chimps, monkeys, and baboons, there is an intricate pecking order,

known to all the animals in the group, and a top banana who lords over it all.
And rank has its privilege: top-ranking primates get first access to mates, choice
food, nice places to sleep and deference from those below. As a result, primates
continually fight, wheedle, cajole and jostle one another in a quest to sit on the
top rung of the ladder.[19]

But perhaps the most outlandish assertion is that physical appearance
is critical to leadership. In an example that recalls the morphe-typing of
nineteenth-century anthropology, Gardner displays the yearbook pictures of four West Point cadets from 1950 and asks the reader to judge
the faces for "leadership qualities" (does Gardner honestly believe that
people of all cultures would choose the winner, future General Wallace
Nutting?). The only validity in such an ill-conceived exercise is that it
does again demonstrate, quite dramatically, that "leadership" is a cultural phenomenon, not just a set of personal characteristics.

So the end to the matter of leadership is this: the inventors of words
may define those words any way they choose. And the users of words
may choose any number of variations, in kind or degree, whether or not
anyone else understands; that is the way of jargon. So it should not be
surprising that the only thing that can be known for certain about leadership is that it has nothing whatsoever to do with leaders or leading.

LEADERS

This is what is known, incontrovertibly, about leading, even though
in actual practice this knowledge typically is ignored or overridden.

(1) *Leading is not a matter of position; it is a matter of person.* Although
it may come as a shock to those who jealously attempt to parlay rank
and title into "leadership position," the truth is that leading (and leaders)
may occur anywhere within a group, *sine nobilitas*. In fact, leading is
inversely proportional to the presence of artifactual organizational constructs (i.e., authority). That simply means that, even in the traditional
organization, the real leaders are those who are actively involved in the
day-to-day social interaction, not those who are charged with the responsibility of strategy. The emphasis on the person as the basis for
leading is abundantly evident. Two recent surveys, conducted independently of each other, revealed the same attitudes among North American
workers—from executives to maintenance personnel. The question posed
was, "Who do you follow?" The intent was to shift the focus from theories about leadership to the validation of leading by following. If there
was any bias in the response, it was the prevalent influence of the general
views of leadership and the then-current sense of urgency for "excellence." There were four answers. The respondents said they followed
people who possessed:

- *Character* (truthfulness, integrity, courage, perseverance);
- *Competence* (the disposition more than the ability to do things excellently, if not magnanimously);
- *Commitment* (dedication in deed to the purpose of the group; the unwillingness to give up);
- *Concern* (empathy for all those joined together by a common undertaking; loyalty to them).

Overwhelming, the respondents confirmed, in anecdotes and by elaboration, that although they would obey the orders of those in positions of authority, that did not mean that they would actually follow the person. In fact, in many instances, the examples indicated that the more serious the issue was held to be the more likely it was that they would choose to follow the leader instead of obeying orders.

(2) *Leading is not a matter of authority; it is a matter of inspiration.* This thought raises a fundamental distinction between two quite opposite views of authority. On the one hand, there is the quality of authority that accrues to a person simply because he or she has experienced life at its most extreme high or low and has been personally victorious. That is commonly referred to as "moral authority," the person as "authoritative." He or she, therefore, can speak with "authority." Correspondingly, the word "authoritative" is used to describe anything that is beyond challenge. On the other hand, there is the quantity of authority delegated to each of the fixed positions in the traditional organization, usually by "level." Or the authority may be seized, by force or political manipulation, within or outside of an organizational framework. Whether in the context of hierarchy or personal force, this kind of authority is described as "authoritarian." And it is to this definition that this tenet especially applies. Authoritarianism by its very nature restrains, suppresses, and, in some cases, oppresses—but leading frees. The nominal meaning of the word "inspire" is "to breathe (life) into," a far cry from the cynical ploy of "empowerment" but a further cry from freedom as license. Aristotle said that freedom is simply "the prerogative to exercise one's full powers." Somehow it seems that leading is more letting go than holding on.

(3) *Leading is not a matter of command; it is a matter of example.* It is impossible to lead by mandate or directive. It is impossible to compel others to follow. The United States Army Infantry motto says it best: "Follow me." Me—not what I say (for actions often belie words), not even what I do (for imitation may not guarantee sincere, lasting motivation), but what I am. That is the highest calling of faith in another.

So that is what is known for sure about leading. Perhaps even more to the point of original question, we also know how and why leaders come to lead. And it is nothing like the loud corporation-tainted propaganda. For example, leaders do not exist *a priori*. They cannot be developed by training. They are neither made nor born. One does not become a leader by either aspiration or preparation. All of the so-called "leadership development" programs, courses, conferences, and workshops have yet to produce a single leader. The absolute low point in the current mêlée of "leadership development" is the LQ (leadership quotient) test by which one consulting firm promises to determine whether candidates have "leadership potential." If the test is positive, which most assuredly it will be, the same firm will enroll the leader-candidate in an expensive, protracted educational program, leading to a diploma and other credentials of, one surmises, a "leader at large."

The first thing one may be sure of is that leaders do not arise in a vacuum or float in the ether. Leaders presuppose community. Leaders simply do not exist outside of community—"community" by its original definition, that is, a place in which I see myself reflected back. That sameness may be physical, mental, or spiritual, or any combination thereof. But in every instance the ultimate mark of community is a common core of values—deep and abiding convictions that bind people together and to one another. These values are subject to no judgment except their own, whether good or evil is a moot question. Morality is perspective. Communities of evil may be as pure as communities of good. Gangs on the streets of Los Angeles have their leaders just as surely as the gangs in the Vatican. In a free, democratic society, even the vice and folly of government is a reflection of the values of the general population.

Second, there is a dynamic in all communities that is energized by the universal human need to see what is to be believed—idols, for example. So communities have a way of calling out those among them who best personify their values. And it is a calling—not an appointment. Leading is, literally, a "vocation"; it is not an occupation. It begins by the community's recognition of what is commonly referred to in today's idiom as "role models." While that idea is generally subverted into something vaguely resembling stock items from L. L. Bean, ordered to fill gaps in demographic types within an organization, it is fundamentally a natural process. A genuine role model is simply "someone in whom I see the *best* of me reflected back."

Third, leaders are role models raised to the highest power. They epitomize the community's ideals. A leader, thus, is "someone in whom I see my *highest aspiration* realized." In fact, the only difference between a leader and a hero is this: the leader is always present. One cannot lead *in absentia*. Heroes are symbolic, mythical. It is precisely for this reason that leaders are, and must be, called. They cannot be imported; it is impossible for someone from outside a community to lead that community. Furthermore, leaders cannot be hired, because leading is not a job, it is a relationship. And there are no professional qualifications, only the person. There are reasons other than financial for most corporate executives to refuse evaluation by subordinates within the corporation.

Traits of Leaders

Recounting the traits of leaders is dangerous business. Such a list immediately becomes an invitation for rationalists of every stripe, especially the amateurs, to rush out and develop a hopeless hodgepodge of curricula, processes, and programs aimed at mass-producing leaders for the *nonnes*, upon demand. It is a sad truism that misconception is a permanent affliction for which there is no cure. Nevertheless, the fact remains that all leaders are possessed of certain characteristics, not prerequisites for a job, but qualities manifest in their leading. All leaders have these traits; but possessing these traits does not make a leader. They somehow are more easily seen in retrospect. And while it is true that these attributes cannot be turned into a recipe for leaders, they can be reasonably infused into strategy. In fact, strategic planning (and strategic plans) will be successful only to the degree that they manifest the same four qualities.

(1) All leaders see in a special way. Absolutely nothing like the "visions" of futurism, the sight of leaders actually has the power to create reality. Especially significant, leaders never confuse that which is real with that which is reality. Pretenders mock one with the other by asserting that they are the same. They are so only to imbeciles and fanatics. Ontology and epistemology to the contrary notwithstanding, leaders know that the only reality we will ever know is the one we see. Furthermore, leaders know that what we see is completely a matter of our choice. But beyond all that, leaders know that how we see and what we see are exactly the same. Therefore, they move strictly by intuition, guided by reason. They are not bound by scientific methodologies, such as research, prediction, and extrapolation. It, no doubt, was to this kind of sight that Senator Robert F. Kennedy was referring in his now-famous observation, "Some men see things as they are and say why. I dream things that never were and say why not" (a paraphrase of George Bernard Shaw).

There are three dimensions to the sight of leaders: foresight, hindsight, and insight.

Foresight: The power, derived only from profound understanding of and deep commitment to certain ideals, to see future implications of even the slightest present "slices of life." As a creative force, its realization is not prediction, but possibility.

Hindsight: Respect, verging on reverence for the past, for the traditions, legends, and myths that constitute the fundamentals of a given culture. No leader can disconnect with that which called him or her to be a leader. But all leaders translate enduring values into new forms of expression.

Insight: Culturally centered invocation of each person's unique potential. This is how and why leaders free—calling others to be true to themselves. They attempt no imposition, exact no judgment. Leaders never expect. They live in a constant state of surprise.

Therefore, because strategy is all about creating new realities, strategic planning must deal first and last with sight. Reality is a matter of perspective. That which is seen as "unrealistic" is so only because of the impaired sight of the viewer. Reality, like beauty, is in the eye of the beholder. The greatest validation of any planning process is when those involved admit, "I'll never see the world the same way again!" But it must be remembered that sometimes eyes are not opened fully at once. Just as Jesus on one occasion anointed a blind man's eyes two times before his sight was restored, in many cases planners must learn patience and persistence. But the ultimate promise of strategy is true: believing is seeing.

(2) *All leaders are dedicated to a cause that transcends themselves*. They, therefore, are willing to subordinate any conflicting or inhibiting personal interest to that cause. The only explanation for that kind of selflessness is that the values or value system that they personify, that which made them leaders, is so intense or profound that values are translated into imperatives. Passion is subject to both degree and range. So it is possible to find within a group, or community, many leaders. All will be in harmony with the values of the group, but each may have a different relationship with the group. It is also possible for leading to be concerned with imperatives of widely varying significance—from building a better mousetrap to alleviating human suffering. Any human endeavor has the potential of creating leaders.

There is far more at work here than simple excellence. It has to do with the values themselves, specifically, the two kinds of values. First, those circumstances based on human need may serve as the context for leaders to appear. Assuming for the moment that Maslow's hierarchy is valid, it is completely plausible to suggest that crisis situations occur in each, whether in terms of an individual or a group. For instance, survival and security are the dominant motivations in physical catastrophes; belonging can be dashed by rejection or prejudice; self-esteem can turn to self-loathing with the slightest change of focus, threatening life itself; and self-actualization, with success, can quickly dissipate aspirations into despair. In each category, in any instance from everyday human experience, leaders are raised in the immediate cause, often anonymously. And then when the crisis is resolved, they are "disappeared." The extraordinary fades to the ordinary; intensity cools to casual. The need for circumstantial leaders passes.

But there is another more enduring dimension of practical imperatives. Any and all exigencies may be translated into causes; and causes may be magnified by ideas into crusades. For example, a near death experience with a dread disease often provokes zealous commitment to a cure; and the zeal to find a cure, fired by imagination, may become an all-consuming humanitarian movement. In either case, those who share the passion will follow. And the cause does not have to be dramatic, magnanimous, or altruistic. Any human passion—from acquisition of wealth to invention or artistry to athletic completion—may be easily transferred into a cause, sometimes a crusade.

It is in the realm of ideas that practical imperatives meet moral imperatives, simply because that is the domain of morality. Ethics are based on the human experience of getting along with others and, therefore, are subject to negotiation, "norming," and change. An idea of the 1960's, "situational ethics," still dominates relationships, whether personal or professional. The most definitive aspect of ethics is the question of fairness. Morals, in contradistinction, originate outside of human experience—almost always from a supernatural or divine source, although in modern times morality has also been sought in natural law(s). Interestingly, both the Hebraic and the Christian traditions hold that, because God created the world, there is no difference. A moral code was programmed into the physical universe. St. Paul often invoked nature, especially in the letter known as *Ephesians*, as validation of his faith. So morals become either commands or principles, doctrine or ideology, establishing right and wrong in human conduct. They are absolute. To cover them with relativism is to destroy the entire premise and eradicate order. The most definitive aspect of morals is the question of justice.

The idea of morals is fertile ground for the flourishing of causes and crusades. Fanatics and saints alike are impelled by uncompromising commitment to truth as it has been revealed or discovered. The Salem Witch Trials and the Emancipation Proclamation were demonstrations of the same kind of conviction. It is possible that both fanatic and saint are driven by either a tenacious fixation on a single moral tenet or a more universal commitment to the welfare of others—both with extraordinary results. In the first instance, righteous energy is channeled into impassioned advocacy, even confrontation with evil; in the second, the energy of righteousness sustains a whole way of life. With all respect, Martin Luther King, Jr. and Mother Theresa represent compelling contrasts. Or Mahatma Gandhi and Albert Schweitzer. And just as sure as such paragons of virtue are recognized as leaders by those of the same mind, they also are subjected to persecution and deprivation—even martyrdom—if not by the hands of their enemies then by their own neglect of self. The word "martyr" has a very significant nominal definition: it simply means "witness"—not in the sense of testimony, but rather that which one sees is of such transcendent importance that he or she will gladly sacrifice his or her life to it.

It is remarkable that of all the books ever published on "leadership," only two approach the subject from the moral point of view, and both are by the same author. These are the exceptions alluded to in the previous analysis of leadership theories. Mr. Robert K. Greenleaf makes a strong case for "servant leadership."[20] According to him, it is only through serving others that one is granted "legitimate" power and even greatness, not as a desired end but as a natural consequence. Resonating with Christology, from Catholic doctrine to the short stories of Hesse, these essays seem but elaborations on the eternal principles from the teachings of Jesus: "The last shall be first; the first shall be last (Matthew 20:16)." "Whoever wishes to become great among you shall be your servant, and whoever wishes to be first among you shall be your slave Matthew 20:26–27)."

It is not as if these paradoxical principles were new or unique to the Christian tradition; the essential idea is both ancient and of many cultures. But it is, nevertheless, a philosophy of leading and leaders, both new and unique. And it stands in stark contrast to all of the other notions of leadership. The implications are profound for all contemporary organizations, especially those constructed along the lines of the corporation model. For example, servants do not engage in competition, nor do they have any desire to win; they do not place personal or special interests above the common interest of the group. The corporation may be no place for such thinking, or for such people, simply because the idea is antithetical to the fundamental assumptions built into that system.

But it may be possible for altruistic organizations—typically in the United States, those with a non-profit designation or comparable status—to cultivate a value system of servanthood. For instance, in strategic planning for educational organizations, especially public education, the first question must be, "Are we willing to make all decisions based on the best interest of the student?" Public service companies, such as utilities, could easily ask the same question about their customers, were it not for regulations imposed upon them and the requirement to pay dividends; and, in point of fact, many corporations, sometimes despite bottom-line considerations, are turning more and more to an attitude of serving the public good. Admittedly, motivation is hard to determine, but sincerity is hard to fake.

(3) *All leaders live in risk.* At the risk of hedging, but strictly to clarify, three provisos must be made quickly about this very daring trait. First, the proposition. The phrase is not "at risk," as if some external threat had placed them in peril, but "in risk," a circumstance of their own

making. That is to say, risk is a matter of the leader's own will or, more accurately, disposition. Leaders consider risk their natural state. Second, it should not be inferred that risk means either recklessness or dependency on the fates. Leaders exercise reason, but never as a damper to creative energy. They are prudent, but so cautious that it diminishes their aspirations. They are circumspect, but never to the degree that it weakens their courage or resolve. Third, living "in risk" does not necessarily imply that leading is to be found in, and judged by, action. Again, leading is a relationship, a calling; so the quality of risk is a matter of essential character—of *being*, not *doing*. One simply does not "act like a leader" to attract followers. Rather, he or she *is*, and that fundamental nature compels others to follow.

Of all the attributes of leaders, risk most readily informs strategic thinking. No doubt that is the reason corporation and administration-model organizations produce no real leaders. That is not to say that there are no leaders in these organizations, only that they were not produced by those systems. Leadership training, so called, is the most effective known prophylactic for the prevention of leaders. The corporate-administrative mentality results in anti-leaders, those who by their presence, attitude, and activity suppress—or, in some instances, oppress—the authentic leaders among the social clusters within the organization. Anti-leaders dwell in risklessness, not as much a present state of being as a constant future pursuit. They do their worst to establish a completely risk-free environment, especially for themselves.

Of course, all managers and administrators must make some decisions. The very dynamic of organizational activity demands it, even though, in the age of computers, management has been reduced to choosing one of many options presented by various scenarios. Surely, all decisions involve some element of risk, but typically they are made on a case-by-case basis and range in methodology from seat-of-the-pants guessing to hyperbolic data-based conclusions, however tentative. But in every instance, the aim is minimum risk and minimum personal exposure. With leaders, action becomes not the consequence of rational decision-making processes or problem-solving techniques but the intuitive projection of self, a self charged with values and the certainty that they are right.

Managers and administrators have made resistance to change both an art and a science. Ironically, considerable artistry is manifested in the craftiness by which they block: stalls, hedges, alibis, favoritism, prevarication, stonewalling, studies—anything to quell the fervor of the new. But over the long haul, these techniques are irritants and not impediments. One of two things will happen to flush them out of the system: either the mad rush of daily events will overwhelm them, or they will mutually succumb to other challenges of the same kind. In a large organization especially, any given stall, hedge, or alibi always competes with several other excuses.

The science is another story. It is about science turning upon itself. The crisis occurred when observation (empiricism) became postulation (rationalism). In philosophy, the transition was made in the eighteenth century, primarily in England. In corporation-administration application, it occurred in the 1970's, primarily in the United States. In philosophy, it meant that the natural order could be overridden by human constructs. In the corporate-administrative mentality, it meant that the way to the future was in the past—in a word, precedence. That is to say what we or others have done previously, and reasonably well, is the only sure guide to what we should do in the future.

The origin of this idea no doubt comes from the profession of law, and there it is quite at home. Precedence in case law may simply be a matter of equal treatment or, perhaps, a stay against appeal. But in all other human endeavors, especially those societal, it is both an altar and an albatross, a seat of worship and an ominous portend of a dismal fate. No one ever worshipped precedence as much as the "quality" meisters of the 1970's, 1980's, and 1990's. For a while, annual pilgrimages led to Erie, Pennsylvania, and other centers of the quality movement, to revel in the revised doctrine of transubstantiation—the miraculous transformation of the quantitative into the qualitative through the intercession of operational research methodology. Actually, Karl Marx had ruminated on this possibility but, as one not especially keen on miracles, squashed the idea by refusing to explain it. And no one else could. But, lo and behold, the idea did not die; it only retreated, biding its time until the world was ready for its second coming.

And the timing was perfect. In the United States, a whole generation that had grown up with shoddy workmanship suddenly began to express, rather vociferously, its resentment, mostly by buying foreign-made products—most dramatically, automobiles; most specifically, Japanese. There was a national hue and cry for "excellence." It is understandable, then, that in the attempt to stem the tide of imports, American manufacturers would seek out and extol the supposed mastermind behind Japan's superior processes. Dr. W. Edwards Deming thus became the high priest of the quality movement. As popular as it was and is, the ideology has two serious flaws.

First, no one can question the resulting improvement in the technical features of American products, but the qualitative aspects suffered stultifying loss, otherwise why would Detroit keep trying desperately to build another 1965 Mustang or a 1955 Thunderbird? One has only to contrast the 1999 Acura and the 1959 Buick to see the difference between technicality and romance, between specifications and the imagination—

and, for that matter, between the Japanese and Americans. It seems that the United States succeeded only in trading one import for another.

The second flaw, and one from which no society can recover, was the extension of the principles of "quality" into the processes by which the products were made. There seems to be a natural law of correlation that any process of production takes on the characteristics of the thing being produced. Mechanical begats mechanical. So, as innovation was narrowed to refinements in products, creativity was replaced by improvements in the process. There are several problems here. First, no thriving organization or person has ever been efficient. Second, human beings are not "vital machines." Third, conditioning (and habits) can never replace motivation.

At about this time, the albatross began circling overhead, although few could see it in the glare; and still fewer understood that apparent good omens often turn into curses. Institutions, already given both to process and imitation of the corporation, rushed to embrace the vocabulary of "quality," if not the principles. Soon the worklike place was filled with chatter of:

- *Standards* (Ostensible indicators of excellence, but invariably minimums. There is no such thing as maximum standards.)
- *Benchmarks* (A curious but unintentionally appropriate metaphor taken from cartography, specifically the Transverse Mercator grid system; it refers to fixed geographical points that are usually marked by concrete posts—permanent, unmovable.)
- *Best Practices* (Purportedly, the formal accumulation, within a given industry type, of the immutable ways and means employed by the most successful organizations. In practice, the formal equivalent of a chain letter.)

Any immediate validation of these measures is lost in the broader application, because it is only here that the full implication of the ideas can be understood. For example, all are historical; that is, they attempt to project past experiences, that once were deemed successful, into the future. Also, these measures, by their very nature, strongly encourage uniformity even among competitors, so there is a general leveling of both expectation and performance. Furthermore, if followed as a matter of compliance, or if accepted as the limits of aspiration, these ideas become straitjackets that arrest the only potential any enterprise has of enduring success—uniqueness. Finally, they can easily become the insidious trap of doing the wrong thing well.

One of the favorite defenses offered by the advocates of precedence is the old saw, "There is no need to re-invent the wheel." Setting aside, for the moment, that in all probability the wheel was not "invented," but discovered (round objects roll just as sure as apples fall from trees) and that, logically, the argument itself is beside the point, the strategic reply is, "Yes, but there may yet be even mechanical possibilities beyond the many applications of the wheel that could move human civilization into entirely new experiences, maybe into new dimensions." Or, if that seems too philosophical, the question might be, "What do you do when the wheels come off?"

So what does all of this have to do with leaders? Simply this: Leaders resist the siren call of precedence and steer without a guide into uncharted water, reckoning by faith, not by old reference points. All leaders are explorers.

(4) All leaders live in a state of grace. Earlier in this chapter, it was suggested that leaders are called by the community whose values they personify. The obvious logical corollary is that they can also be "recalled" by the same community, not as an act of firing because they were not hired, but simply by the loss of will by others to follow. Those who formerly led have no continuing claim on affections; nor do they have recourse. Such a breach in the relationship is difficult to document in corporations, because no records are kept; but anyone who has ever worked in a corporation-institution organization could recount dozens of examples. And the more authoritarian the organization, the more pronounced any shift of allegiance for at least three reasons: in an authoritarian system, everything has a sharp edge; such organizations typically move in fits and starts; and such organizations are neither discreet nor subtle (what the "human resources" department does not tell, the grapevine will, and neither is distortion proof).

Perhaps the most illustrative, and certainly a highly publicized, rift in corporation solidarity occurred in the early 1990's at Alcoa. According to all reports, taken on their face, the company, which for almost three-quarters of a century had made its unique corporate system of values not only its signature but its driving force, abruptly, by board edict, went "outside" of the industry for a chief executive officer. That was a rather final answer to the question, "What is the primary responsibility: to turn a profit, or to build an organization that has the capability and incentive to produce profits?" The profits came all right—at least for the short haul—but the organization took a severe hit in organizational capability. There was an immediate exodus of senior executives who took with them most of the original culture, to say nothing of the company's intellectual capital. A parting comment was offered by one vice president as an explanation: "This is not our company anymore."[21] Of course, it is not uncommon in certain business groups for the senior staff to submit their resignations upon the appointment of a new CEO, simply as a matter of professional deference to the chief's prerogative of organizing; and it is not unusual for executives to resign over policy issues, or loss of career opportunity, or just plain sour grapes. But it is very unusual for the resignations to be prompted by a line-in-the-sand disagreement over values. One can never be sure exactly how pervasive the sense of rejection became throughout the company, but there is little doubt that the issue forced many employees to choose between financal security and conscience. The very last thing any organization should want is a situation in which employees sacrifice their personal values to economic considerations.

Typically, those who choose to work in corporations, either by disposition or conditioning, are more readily able to deal with the shocks and vicissitudes of conflicting cultures, and more likely to take drastic action, such as voluntary separation for employment elsewhere, than those who choose to attach themselves to institutional stasis. For the latter, security takes precedence over both financial gain and conscience. Furthermore, institutions have a built-in defense system to ward off serious change, to neutralize any and all threats against the status quo, and to maintain a risk-free environment. Administrators come and go, but the institution remains the same. Public school districts in the United States and Canada, local education agencies in Britain, and other similar quasi-political institutions are a case in point. Those in the United States are not quite as organizationally complicated, that is, bureaucratized, as the others, and thus provide the clearest example of misfits and false starts. There obviously is something terribly wrong with a system in which the average tenure of chief administrators is less than three years. How is it possible for such a deplorable practice to exist? The answer is twofold: first, school boards (the hiring authority) are, for the most part, totally oblivious to the implications of the values of the actual communities (not defined by geographical boundaries, but by value systems) within their jurisdictions. So, in an attempt to imitate the corporation model (many trustees are business types), they customarily seek, with all good intentions, to find an administrator outside of the local system to "lead" it. That cannot and will not happen. If polled, probably all trustees would reject as absurd the suggestion that, say, a Burger King manager could do well as a certificated superintendent of schools, but those same trustees will not recognize an even greater disparity between the district's values and the character of those who were not raised up by others of the same values. For example, it is virtually impossible for even a highly competent administrator from anywhere else to be a leader in Galveston, or Savannah, or Boston—or your hometown. Granted, some communities are more exclusive than others; but all are exclusive, nevertheless; it is the basic nature of community. What the corporate world holds as a deep secret is that everywhere the truly stellar CEOs have spent their entire career in a single company. A case-making example is that of Roberto C. Goizueta, the late chairman of the Coca-Cola Company, who began work as an entry-level chemical engineer in

Cuba in 1954 and eventually led his company to unparalleled success, financially and organizationally. Actually, the same principle is at work every day in the most successful educational systems.

Second, the traditional corporation-model organization is structured to prevent any intervention from the top, or interference from the bottom. There is a level spoken of (never to) only in hushed, reverential tones, but known universally as the "second tier." Those who are positioned here are the guardians of the way things have always been. They form a kind of Maginot Line, a bulwark against all invaders. So an incoming chief executive officer, flush with a new sense of challenge and a big raise, and armed with the board's mandate for "change," calls a meeting and begins hyperventilating about some rapturous "vision" of the future. And all of the second-tier blockers look at each other and gesture,* "Seems like we've heard this before. Let's see, this will be our seventh superintendent." How bad is it? Well, one school district on Long Island had fourteen CEOs within a span of twelve years, three on the payroll at the same time.

Although the allusion may strain credibility, much can be learned about leaders and leading from political systems, particularly those in which the general population has a voice—either actual free states or revolutions in the name of freedom. It is a fact that those who are elected most often reflect the values of the electorate. Free elections are always more values-driven than issue-driven. Evidently, both Plato and Thomas Jefferson realized that this was both the strength and vulnerability of democracy. Plato warned that democratic systems would fail when people realized that they could vote for themselves anything they wanted. Jefferson insisted on an "enlightened" citizenry as the only possible sustaining virtue of a democracy.

It is also instructive to note that in political systems, the "leader's" calling is not permanent. Because leading is a relationship and, therefore, subject to mutuality, either the follower or the leader may rupture the common bond; that is, leaders may violate the values implicit in the calling, and thus may be rejected; or the community may either re-form itself by an influx of strangers, who eventually become the mainstream culture, or it may undergo abrupt, fundamental changes in need-values, as in a catastrophe or a crisis. A contemporary example of community re-formation is the Cayman Islands. Giving in to the necessity for

---

*In extreme instances, they do more than gesture. When Mikhail Gorbachev attempted *Perestroika* in the Soviet Union, it was the second-tier officials who forcibly took over the legislative building and booted him out of government. At this writing, they are still in charge. Perhaps not as dramatic, but disconcerting, nevertheless, is a case in Colorado Springs in which a denizen of the second-tier orchestrated his own departmental "strategic" plan to counter the one approved by the board of the school district (District 11). He retired early.

expatriates to staff essential governmental and business activity, and accepting the massive immigration of Jamaicans, the country's original Caymanian population is now a minority; the entire culture is undergoing radical transformation: "He hath founded it on the sea" does not have much meaning for the new arrivals. As an example of the second, when Poland was struggling to overthrow communist rule, the nation enthusiastically followed Lech Walesa and his Solidarity Party to freedom. But when communism collapsed and democracy was established, he was rejected (narrowly) at the polls and sent packing his lunch box. He was the same person as before, but the need, hence the mood, was otherwise. All of these examples, as well as an abundance of corroborating anecdotal evidence, suggest at least three principles of leading that the modern organization, in its determination to impose constructs over formations, has swept aside. The first two are quite simple: leading is not a result of ambition or preparation; leading is not a career. The third requires some elaboration. Popular wisdom acknowledges that people cannot rise above their leaders; but not so popular is the converse truism that leaders cannot rise above their people. Why? Simply because leaders do not "empower" anyone ("empower" is a trick word used by authoritarian managers as a ploy to maintain their superiority). Rather, leaders derive their power from those who call them to lead. Theories abound, but in the final analysis, there are three kinds of power: the power of moral character—so strong that it transcends the person and becomes principle in human form; perverse power, which is authority without accountability; and the power granted by a group to those it follows. The latter is a state of grace.

Over the years, much has been made of *charisma*. And it has been assumed that this "grace" or "gift" had to do with personality—the manner, style, and attractiveness of the individual. Furthermore, it was assumed that those personality traits were universal. That is to say, the late John F. Kennedy would have been just as charismatic in a Bedouin camp as in Hyannis Port. Somehow, that defies both the law of probability and common sense. Charisma is not self-possessed. It is a vested quality, the spiritual extension of community into persons deemed worthy of the community's self. If the collapse of leadership is ever to be overcome, it will be because Western civilization recognizes, at last, the qualities of its authentic leaders and grants them chrisma by following.

- Leaders *see*, but only with the eyes of their community.

- Leaders *serve*, but only with the conscience of their community.

- Leaders *risk*, but only with the heart of their community.

- Leaders are blessed with *grace*, but only by the spirit of their community.

The implications of the authenticity of natural leaders within all organizations are profound indeed. It means that any process of planning, if it is to have any credibility whatsoever, must involve all of those leaders in an active way—not so much in methodology or representation but in their freedom to express themselves as they choose. It also means that the plan, the discipline, must be predicated on the common core of values that constitutes agreement; anything else will be rejected out of hand as a foreign import. Those values, far more than any other factor, impart both distinctiveness and energy to strategy.

Chapter 5

Arena III: Condition vs. Cause

If there is a critical stigma in the pathology of the modern mind, it is the remarkable inability to distinguish between cause and condition. The very question turns the mightiest intellects into ponderous blanks, and rationalistic eloquence into incoherent babble. The malady is frighteningly disorientating: everything is backwards, upside-down, and inside out. Even more frightening, while there are many notable individuals who are either immune or have escaped the affliction, it seems to have spread to almost every aspect of Western life, providing an overabundance of examples and case studies of human beings making less of themselves than they should. A quick glance at the gist of headlines and a little eavesdropping on popular wisdom should be enough to start heads wagging. They come from all categories of modern life:

Social

- Poverty is the cause of ignorance.
- Poverty is the cause of crime.
- Poverty is the cause of violence.

Education

- Prejudice by others is the cause of failure.
- Low self-esteem is the cause of underachievement.

Psychology

- Bad childhood experiences are the cause of most adult problems.
- Child abuse is the cause of psychopathic behavior.
- The cause of anything wrong is always outside of the person.

Business

- Lack of consumer confidence was the cause of a slump in retail sales.
- The closing of the military base was the cause of the store's going out of business.

Politics

- The economic policies of the president were the cause of the Great Depression.
- Slavery was the cause of the Civil War.
- Weariness over scandal was the cause of a low voter turnout.

Health

- Cigarettes are the cause of cancer.
- Stress is the cause of heart attack.

Mechanics

- An electrical fire in the cabin was the cause of the airplane crash.
- Airbags are the cause of injury and death.

Religion

- Temptations (trials) are the cause of my sin.
- Morality is the cause of intolerance.

Fast Food

- The hot coffee was the cause of my severe leg burns.
- The menu was the cause of loss of customers.

Environmental

- Aerosol spray is the cause of a hole in the ozone layer.
- The cutting of the rain forests is the cause of atmosphere catastrophes.

New Science

- The flutter of a butterfly's wings in Oregon was the cause of a tidal wave in Bangladesh.
- Social artifacts are the cause of human misery.

Only sports—namely, American football—get it right, sometimes: "The ground cannot cause a fumble." Surprisingly, that is the whole issue. Just what does that Olympian declaration admit that all of the other assertions miss completely? Simply this: in this world, there are only two kinds of causes; one is natural, the other human. Everything else *is* a condition. In fact, for the human being, natural cause and effect is a condition. To overlook that is to place all human beings in insurmountable hopelessness; furthermore, to put oneself and others in a situation where the human attempts to counter the natural is an invitation to unmitigated disaster. Almost no serious attention has been given to this subject in the modern age. There are only two possible causes of this uncharacteristic lapse of curiosity in the species: fear of the question, or fear of the answer.

The difficulty in making critical distinctions, at least at the first level of meaning, seems to lie in the fickleness of real definitions. It is especially tendentious that current English dictionaries agree with the use of the word "cause," as in the context of the foregoing examples, to indicate that the factor specified, in actuality, only "contributes" to the result. That is today's first definition; and, in the discipline of lexiconography, the order always moves from the most common (present) to the most obscure (past). Only the final entry links cause with effect: cause is defined as an "agent," the "origin or source of effect." If the most common definition is correct, ostensibly there may be (usually will be) any number of "causes," simultaneously or progressive, for any particular outcome. Post-result analyses lead only to vexing confusion and fallacious conclusions. Immediate, effective action is thwarted for lack of a point of entry into the chain of reactions. And the simultaneity of events and circumstances is an open irresistable invitation to attribute cause when there is only coincidence. This is the most serious flaw in modern research.

That is because the certainty and degrees of contributing factors are all but impossible to pin down; nevertheless, that inquiry is, in fact, the modus of contemporary research, especially in the rather nebulous soft sciences that can be made up as one moves along. Sociology and psychology seem especially suspect. Here the line between fact and fiction is not always discernable. If the answer is always in the question, as it surely must be, then that methodology begins with the conclusion merely by accepting the premise of multiple and progressive causes. The end is in the beginning.

Defining cause as "contributing" provides unlimited opportunity for analysis but offers little promise of resolution, responsibility, or action. And although that assumption may be tolerable in the several instances cited, if for no other reason than it may actually prompt some brief amelioration of the symptoms when carried into personal or organizational circumstance, it may be quite destructive. Solutions are impossible because problems are complicated beyond reason; and accountability of any kind is all but eliminated. Even worse, if taken as a personal philosophy, this definition is tantamount to denying or relinquishing control over one's life and yielding to "the fell clutch of circumstance." The most pathetic human state is to be blind to the cause of one's own troubles.

Etymology reveals more about the evolution of perspective than about the historical development of word usage. When the word "cause" came into the language in the thirteenth century, it was defined strictly as "that which brings about effect or result," or "the reason for action." Life was simple. It was not until the next century that "cause" became a verb, transitive. Life became simpler. Of course, it may be only coincidental—and to even raise the possibility of a connection may be unreasonable—but during the same period, there occurred a radical shift in attitude from that of the Middle Ages, during which people were acted upon, to that of the Renaissance, during which even ordinary folk realized that they themselves could act. Their inspiration, of course, came from the discovery of ancient thinking, primarily Hellenistic. Renaissance humanism exalted the individual by focusing attention on the innate powers within each person both to be and to do. An unparalleled era of creativity, invention, and exploration was ushered in throughout Western civilization. Some mildly jaded wags have suggested that there has not been much new or exciting since then.

In fact, that same expansive view of the human spirit, and even the visionary ideas of that time, continue to spark whatever genius of creativity is left in the modern age. Only now that bright and shining spirit is diminished, its existence isolated, sporadic, suspect—always outside of the established system. Romanticism is now woefully out of fashion; thinking is too dangerous. There is nothing on earth as intractable as a human system in place, especially an intellectual one. So, during the intervening centuries, the flame has been virtually extinguished as, little by little, Western institutions devolved back into benighted authoritarian orders even more suffocating than those of the Middle Ages. The latter end was worse that the first. It may be only talk-show fodder, but in 1998, Gerry Spence, the buckskin-clad lawyer and frontier *bon-vivant*, whose primary credential may be that he thinks in unusual ways about unusual things, had the audacity to argue that contemporary human beings, Americans specifically, were nothing more than "slaves" to those orders—political, economic, religious, social, intellectual.

Quite in contrast, Aristotle defined freedom as "the prerogative of exercising one's full powers." What amazing implications! That concept was the epitome of the Renaissance—its driving force. It is tremendously significant that for those incomparable artists, inventors, and explorers of that epoch, even though their imagination was often in thrall to the institutional church, and although they themselves were often treated like slaves, it was not the Church that propagated or controlled their creative spirit. Paradoxically, it was the dynamic unleashed by the thinking of an ancient pagan world, newly discovered like manna in the wilderness.

However, during the intervening dreary centuries since the Renaissance, Aristotle's majestic definition of freedom has suffered two nearly mortal blows, both ironically celebrated today throughout Western society as milestones in the development of that civilization. The U.S. government has even taken to legislating and memorializing the loss. But civilization has never dealt kindly with human values—especially those matters of faith that spur unconventional thinking and personal freedom. Civilization always subordinates culture. The more variegated the society, the more intense the subordination, until cultural values disappear altogether, and the civilization loses not only its identity but its intrinsic spirit. It becomes a hollow shell. In any Western nation today, the prerogative to exercise one's full powers flies directly in the face of the systems and institutions that supposedly are the visible manifestations of that civilization.

The first blow was Martin Luther's compromise with what was arguably the most tyrannical religious system the world has even known. Wealthy, arrogant, diabolical, the ecclesiastical order held a life-and-death grip on everyone within its domain, even the nobility. Luther learned from earlier heretics like Hugh Latimer and John Wycliffe that the displacement of the established church in favor of a religion more closely resembling the simplicity of the teachings of Christ, without ecclesiastical shackles, was impossible. "Upon this rock" was both less and more in fulfillment than it was in prophecy. So Luther hit upon the idea of a compromise; that is, "reform." His legacy became not merely the great religious Reformation but the genesis of the reform mentality itself. And although he was severely punished for his impudence, however deferential, he actually inadvertently gave the Church a blessing: specifically, permanent leverage against all who would challenge its relevance, validity, and veracity. "Thine is the kingdom and the power, forever. Amen."

Reform thus became a sop to all who would betray. For five centuries, the promise of reform has guaranteed the perpetuation of systems long after they are obsolete, long past any human benefit, long past any notion of why. Yet there is no instance on record in which any attempt at reform succeeded at anything other than producing the result that was the *exact opposite* of the original intent. For example, the 1832 Reform Bill in England was intended to reduce the appalling rate of poverty at the time; but within ten years, poverty quadrupled—according to most historians, as a direct result of the measures in the bill. Cause and effect may be difficult to understand in the abstract, but this one thing is abundantly clear throughout the world: reform always produces the perverse effect. The road to progress is littered with the bones of programs, projects, and schemes that promised to rectify the existing order of things. In the late twentieth century there was a mad rush to salvage all of the remaining constructs of Western society; the buzzwords became "re-engineering" in manufacturing, "reinventing" in government, "reform" in education and health care, and all of the above, plus "reorganization," in business (the first order of busyness for any business in trouble was to "reorganize"). In almost every case, the promise, if not the effort, was welcomed by all those in existing systems as tacit affirmation of their continued viability and as a gracious grant of a stay of execution. But in no instance did the result come close to the announced intent. The attempt, however sincere, only compounded the dysfunctionality, yet the system survived.

The second blow actually was two blows, a one-two punch that sent the human opponent reeling. The setup was Francis Bacon's *Novuum Organum* (1625) which, although its title harkens back to Aristotle, was not as much formula as postulation. Specifically, it advocated that human observation, combined with reason, is the only way to knowledge and thus the only hope of bringing the kingdom of God to Earth. This idea, whose time had obviously come, provided the foundation for modern empiricism. There are many currents in the stream of Western thinking, but the channel of empiricism is easily discernible and readily traced. Exactitude, after all, is that philosophy's inherent characteristic.

The bell-ringing stroke was delivered by Isaac Newton's *Philosophiae Naturalis Principia Mathematica*, which portrayed the universe as a gigantic clock, mechanistic and mathematical, characterized by *process, uniformity*, and *precision*. Furthermore, in this exactly ordered world, time is inconsequential—the past and the future are equally detectable and interchangeable. Whereas Bacon's doctrine was more instinctive than intellectual, Newton's was intellectual to the exclusion of the intuitive. Empiricism advocated observing to discover the truth; rationalism asserted selected hypothesis as truth. Together they succeeded in accomplishing what Luther could not: they displaced the religion of faith with the religion of science.

Newton's theories provided the basis for the development of rationalism—generally described as related systems of thought (philosophical, scientific, religious), which rest upon the authority of reason rather than sense-perceptions, revelation, or traditional authority. Although Newton himself was a "supernatural rationalist," believing in an omnipotent God and viewing the universe as His handiwork and, therefore, as proof of his existence, it was not long until "natural religion" replaced the traditional Christian religion. The new doctrine held by Deists rejected divine revelation and subordinated the God of the Bible to nature (as in "nature and nature's God"). Natural religion stressed human reason as the only guide to truth and good conduct as its effect. When God is removed from the universe, it seems that all things are possible. Interestingly, in the eighteenth century, rationalism took two distinctly different paths. On the one hand, it became an ally of neo-classicism, which emphasized logical form over actual substance; on the other hand, it was transformed into an early type of romanticism that extolled the goodness of human beings, if not their individual originality. However, before the end of the nineteenth century, "religion" had been dropped completely from the Western world picture and "naturalism," devoid of any supernatural element, became the dominant philosophy. When public education systems began placing primary emphasis on math and science, the human being grew up as a statistic, not as a creator, and as an accidental formation of protoplasm, not as beings made in the image of God. Religious doctrine aside, the shift all but eradicated the *being* in human.

Naturalism, in its simplest sense was (is) the application of the Newtonic principles of scientific determination. According to this philosophy, everything that is real exists in nature. Nature is defined as the world of objects, actions, and forces that yield the secrets of cause and effect only to objective scientific inquiry. The fundamental view of human beings is that they are animals in the natural world, responding to environmental forces and internal stresses and drives, over none of which they have either control or knowledge. The human being is a victim caught in a relentless struggle for survival but is unable to save himself or herself from whatever is determined by environmental, social, or economic factors.

Rationalism had three intellectual manifestations, each significant enough to provide the basis of a distinctive philosophy, yet all convergent upon the human being: *predictability, determinism,* and *freedom.* One became the stuff of physical and behavioral science, another the germinal idea of dominant socioeconomic theories, and the other the primary motivation in political organization. In every case, the human being was confronted with forces over which he or she had no control and could not fully understand. For the serious-minded person, life became an endless struggle to maintain some kind of balance while trying to comprehend what was happening. Those not as serious learned, as Joseph Conrad put it, to "skim over the surface of life." Empiricism had declared that one could discern truth by looking outward; rationalism sought to codify that which was observed into "laws"; neither looked into the human being. So gravity was made a law rather than a condition. It has never been repealed. No one knows how.

Predictability was intended by Newton to be evidence of a God who could create and sustain an orderly universe full of precise, consistent phenomena. It was to be the proof that lends credence to faith. If indeed the physical cosmos is clockwork, as Newton surmised, then the movements of all of its parts are exactly calculated and mechanically integrated. Cause and effect are built in. That means, in effect, that the person is dealt out as a causal agent, dealt in only as an observer, rendered ineffectual in bringing about results and circumstances. Human intervention is limited by impossibility to merely "shaping" or "influencing," never creating and controlling. The ultimate human action is the application of some formula or process gleaned from nature through diligent inquiry, experimentation, or the experience of others. For the human being, cause and effect—as it had been before rationalism—became, in practice, affect and condition. That is to say, one could affect

conditions, but not affect a result. The implications of this way of thinking are terminally debilitating: rather than imagining a future and bringing it about by dint of one's own efforts, human beings can only make
the best of existing circumstances—present and future—which are suppose to be the only causes. Even for those bold visionaries who somehow
see themselves as "change agents," predictability is a trap. If its implicit
chain of cause and effect is accepted (A → B, B → C, C → D, etc.), and
if causation is contingent upon finding the right link at which to enter,
then the aspiring agent of change has already conceded opportunity as
the power of creation.

As an indication of both how and why this philosophy became so
pervasive in Western society, systems of education institutionalized their
tenets in curricula that defined higher-order thinking skills as "critical
thinking"—not creative—and teaching methodologies that were aimed
at conditioning—not learning. Imagination was taboo, but at least students learned that almost all predictions are self-fulfilling.

There is another even more curious aspect of predictability. If time is
factored out of the occurrences of natural phenomena, then the processes of cause and effect may be as easily reversed as forwarded. Re-
construction is as possible as construction. The effect becomes the
cause, the cause becomes the effect. Admittedly, this kind of "Alice in
Wonderland" abstraction is difficult for time-bound beings to understand fully, but when viewed in the perspective of practical, everyday
events and situations, from personal to societal, the implications of
this kind of thinking begin to sink in. Take, for example, any common happening—say, an automobile accident—and watch as investigators begin to meticulously examine the cause. Since, in every such
case, there were multiple progressive actions (or actions) and circumstances preceding the crash, when the "cause" is finally identified it
is actually the effect of post-accident perspective. In matters of personal behavior, this kind of rationalization becomes the grounds for
alibis and accusations and miscreant behavior. The same is true of
any social, political, or economic phenomenon. That is why the recon-
struction of history is so urgently the first priority for any successful
revolutionaries, or for any who fancy themselves so. For example,
radical changes in government as in the Soviet Union and South Af-
rica are immediately attended by the appointment of "truth and reconciliation" commissions, with the full force of law. In the United
States, reparation became a *cause celebre*. This is as close as rationalism
comes to creativity. Obviously, history is written and re-written by
the winners.

Determinism did not originate with rationalism, but it was given
respectability by that science. In fact, modern determinism is little more
than scientific versions of old superstitions about fate or, more accu-

rately, the fates. Whereas predictability is about action—mechanical, logical, mathematical, fate is about the force—impersonal, irrational, unalterable—that determines in advance what happens. Destiny is fixed and inescapable. No one knows for sure just how and when the notion of fate became such an overwhelming influence in the lives of human beings, but by the time of Greek and Roman civilizations, the mythology about the fates was fully developed. Clotho, Lachesis, and Atropos were considered goddesses long before there were gods. Together they decided in advance who would be born where, whether and how much good or bad luck he or she would have, and when the person would die. Whatever they decided would happen, happened. Not even kings or gods could escape their destiny decreed by the fates.

Nor was the philosophy of fatalism exactly new or Western. From all indications, the belief that everything follows an unchangeable plan is both ancient and universal. Many Eastern religions are based on this idea, and kismet is especially important in Islam. All fatalists have this in common: they are convinced that the actions of human beings cannot alter one iota the events and circumstances of their lives. They are fated to do exactly what they do. Strangely, some Christians—ostensibly a religion based on the free will of humans and the grace of God—believe in fatalism, with a twist. According to them, God is both omniscient and omnipotent; therefore, He must have predetermined before the beginning of time not only world history but also the life and final destiny of each person. It is especially comforting to note that most of those who hold this view believe that they are the ones predestined for eternal salutation.

One of the strangest poems ever written was William Ernest Henley's desperate, defiant *Invictus*, a work generally considered Christian, despite the fact that all of its language and allusions are as pagan as the runes.

> Out of the night that covers me,
>   Black as the Pit from pole to pole,
> I thank whatever gods may be
>   For my unconquerable soul.
>
> In the fell clutch of circumstance
>   I have not winced nor cried aloud
> Under the bludgeonings of chance
>   My head is bloody, but unbowed.
>
> Beyond this place of wrath and tears
>   Looms but the Horror of the shade,
> And yet the menace of the years
>   Finds, and shall find, me unafraid.

It matters not how strait the gate,
    How charged with punishments the scroll,
I am the master of my fate;
    I am the captain of my soul.[22]

Those sentiments and their righteous approbation are a glaring reflection of the influence of scientific determinism on the thinking of even those who claimed to worship a God of justice and mercy, a God who had made them in His own likeness, a God who died to save all humankind.

Determinism was no passing fad. It was a tectonic shift in the way human beings viewed themselves, the world, and other people. Yet the degree to which it permeates all modern thinking is either ignored or underestimated. It is not a school of thought, as are so many other categorical philosophies. It is, rather, a lens through which every aspect of human life on this planet is viewed. Consider how that view has pervaded Western thought. *Mechanistic* determination was Newton's perspective; Darwin could see only *biological* determinism; Karl Marx, *economic* determinism; Sigmund Freud, the determinism of the inner and subconscious *self*; Comte, both *social* and *environmental* determinism; Thomas B. Watson, *behavioral* determinism; and Taine even viewed *literature* as the product of determinism. With this kind of barrage from every direction in the nineteenth and twentieth centuries, is it any wonder then why the human being either forgot or never knew what dangers lay within?

The loss of personal power would have been bad enough, but it was not all that was lost. If, in fact, free will is removed from human action, then there is neither individual responsibility or accountability, nor private or public morality. The world becomes, at worst, to use Darwin's metaphor, nothing more than a "lawless jungle"; or at best, as Marx put it, a "battleground." The human being was out of control, in more ways than one.

Rationalism also brought a new meaning for *freedom*, not necessarily better, but much different from the political concepts of Solon and Plato, and diametrically opposed to Aristotle's definition of personal freedom. No one had yet even dreamed of economic freedom.

At the time rationalism appeared on the scene, democracy was only a footnote to ancient history. Solon had actually instituted in Athens a radical form of government based on promoting general egalitarianism almost 200 years before Plato started dialoguing about it. His bold experiment was motivated not as much by philosophy or altruism as by the practical circumstance of the increasing economic equality among the residents of the city. Trade, commerce, and crafts had made the previously disenfranchised commoners quite wealthy, in some cases even wealthier than the nobility. But, alas, the scheme came to an inglorious end when the ingrained class system refused to yield. The people proved unable or unwilling to rule themselves, and the affairs of the city-state degenerated into raucous clamoring.

So Solon, ever the innovator, conceived the idea of a representative democracy, filtered through the semi-porous wisdom of the electoral process. Eventually he structured the government with three interrelated parts: a congress, a president, and a nine-member supreme court—so much for political freedom. When the nation of Israel in the seventh century B.C. had demanded of their God that He give them a king, they were warned by the prophet Samuel about what such rulers would bring to bear upon them: levying of taxes, conscription of military service, and abduction of children to work in the king's enterprises; all seriously compromised or eliminated the freedoms they had enjoyed in a theocracy. Democracy proved to be little different.

Evidently, Plato learned from Solon's experimentation that idealism, from time to time, must be tempered with reason, if not prudence. Perhaps the bite of sarcasm is all too sharp when he remarked, "Democracy is a form of government in which unequals are treated equally." So democracy contracted and remained severely limited to only a few, the upper class. In the golden age of Athenian democracy, the city had a population of 450,000 (half of which were slaves), but only 30,000 were actually citizens who had the right to vote. It is discouraging, and a bit deceptive, that the framers of the U.S. Constitution adopted that model of liberty.

It seems that all revolutionaries replace the old system, no matter how oppressive, with a virtually exact replica. Those who rule may change, but there are still rulers; the criteria for social class may change, but rank order still exists; the grant of privilege may change, but it is still hauteur.

The story of twentieth-century Russia illustrates this point. Who would say that freedom was enhanced when the czar was overthrown and replaced by a dictator, or when dictatorship was abandoned in favor of a mock democracy, characterized by social depravity and economic ruin? On a smaller scale, but equally poignant, when the Saskatchewan Indians gained autonomy over their educational and social systems in the late 1980's, they set about to build their own indigenous versions; but they succeeded only in establishing a veritable duplicate of the abhorred provincial systems.

The various experiments with democracy from the beginning, and throughout the twentieth century, have produced two lessons: first, democratic systems go from bad to worse to worst; freedom becomes an impenetrable morass of laws, rules, and regulations. The more freedom, the more control over those who think themselves free. Second, personal freedom, eventually gives way to license and mediocrity. Contrary to

myth, there is nothing creative about rebellion, anarchy, or even revolution; all are fundamentally destructive. Creativity may require the destruction of old orders, but it simply cannot occur without the tension
provided by some moral discipline with implicit ideal purpose. And
egalitarianism is achieved only at the lowest common denominator; true
excellence is achieved only at the highest. That way of thinking transcends human nature, but that is the real *Novum Organum*.

According to the Scriptures, God finally allowed Israel to have a
king—his king, but democracy was out of the question. (Manfred Dav-
idmann has argued that the Torah was essentially a guide to freedom,
but it would never survive a referendum.)

As bad as they are, perversions of political (social and economic) freedom are not nearly as repressive as intellectual systems that restrict or
suppress freedom of thought. One can be personally free, though a slave.
But if that person thinks like a slave, then slave he or she will be, even
though "free." Maybe Gerry Spence is correct.

There are at least four assumptions, or implications, in Aristotle's definition of freedom: (1) all people inherently have "full powers", that is,
immeasurable capacity; (2) those powers can be developed only by the
individual; (3) the exercise of those powers is a human right; and (4)
genius lies in the uniqueness of each person.

The place to attack may always be the enemy's weakest point, but the
place to undermine is in the enemy's strength. Cynically applying the
principle articulated best by Jesus, "As a man thinks in his heart, so is
he," rationalism declared victory over the human mind when education,
like manufacturing, was "rationalized." In the United States, and in all
other modern democracies not dominated by the Church, rationalism
preceded the institutionalization of education. Much has already been
made of Thomas Jefferson's insistence on an enlightened citizenry, yet
that phrase is popularity rendered in a more favorable light than its
original intent would merit. Jefferson's world was one that had given
itself the self-congratulatory designation of "the age of enlightenment."
Although the light motif was probably of Eastern origin, the definition
was purely Western—thoroughly scientific, predicated on the natural
philosophy of the seventeenth century. But he never imagined that the
masses could be so enlightened as to govern themselves or, for that matter, to take care of themselves. Enlightenment was only for the refined
aristocracy, the intellectual elite, the financially mature.

But in the middle of the nineteenth century, any classical notion of
learning or democracy was quashed by the advent of a system of public
education that was both institutionalized and rationalized. The rationalization was not after the kind Jefferson would have known. It was not
founded on philosophical tenets but on the rationalizing of industry,
commonly known as the Industrial Revolution. That is to say, education

was assigned the role of serving industry—of training competent workers, of insisting on an attitude of compliance, and of teaching consumption of goods and products. The original idea of citizenship, if taught at all, was subordinated to any number of job and career training programs. By 1910, although the purpose of education was never formally or legislatively stated, the die was cast for virtually all education systems of the twentieth century. Almost a century later, nothing substantial had changed. The systems of the United States and Canada, as well as those throughout the West, were predicated on the principles of industrialization. They became in philosophy and practice the repository and propagator of the industrial mentality. The characteristics of that way of thinking were the reason for the failure of public education and, ultimately, its demise: data based, research driven, analytical, operationally focused, specialized and departmentalized, agnostic, and inhuman. As an indication of the permanence of this disposition, in the 1990's something called "outcomes-based" education swept the country, provoking all kinds of controversy fomented by religious parents and special-interest groups who objected to public schools teaching values. Part of the recommended curriculum included instruction in something called "adult life roles," two of which consigned the individual to a very limited existence as "worker" and "consumer," as if this were the substance of life. As late as 2000, the SCANS (Secretary's Commission on Achieving Necessary Skills) report constituted the curricular template for America's public schools, and the very popular "school to work" initiative became manifest evidence of the nation's lack of aspiration for the rising generation or the impossibility of educating them. "Tech prep" was for the really advanced students.

To make matters universally worse, the national system of education itself was rationalized; that is, permanently institutionalized. There was no other choice: if, in fact, education was to be made available to the masses, then it had to be dealt with as any other mass-produced commodity: efficiency, standardization, and monosystemization. The exact purpose of such an education is still unclear but is based on the thrust of even contemporary curricula. The primary oft-repeated incantation is "to provide the skills, knowledge, and ability to be productive citizens." To do so it adopted the principles of industrialization: process (linear, sequential); uniformity (measured, standardized); and precision (interchangeable parts, graduated). Each aspect demanded and rewarded conformity in both conduct and thinking—same problems, same answers, but the expectation was that things would get better. They did not, because they could not. By the end of the twentieth century, the public system of education was under attack on all sides. Consequently, "alternative" systems sprang up—charter schools, home schools, distance education, contract-managed schools, commercial schools. But none of these "radical" approaches changed institutionalized education. In fact, they only reinforced that system by attempting to do it better. What a chance missed!

While the purpose of education remained unstated, the continuing result belied any pretense of citizenship or personal freedom. Generations of people, who although constitutionally free, were captivated by a slave's mentality. Specifically, that meant:

- Acceptance, rather than inquiry;
- Rather than the causal agent, perceiving the human being as one of many factors;
- Reaction, rather than creation;
- Confusion, rather than certainty;
- Fear, rather than confidence.

It is no wonder that the truly significant inventions and discoveries, and all great art, have come from individuals who made a dramatic break from institutionalized, rationalized education. Nor, ironically, did business and industry do much by way of capitalizing on human potential. Quite to the contrary, industry demanded that the person conform to an oppressive, unnatural environment that neither recognized nor enhanced human capacity. When Henry Ford remarked, "There is nothing a person cannot do," he was not espousing a noble humanistic philosophy but the rationale for pushing people to maximum productivity. Significantly, he did not say, "There is nothing a person cannot *be*."

By 1908, "scientific management"*a la* Frederick Taylor had become the order of the day. Human beings were unequivocally declared "vital machines" and, consequently, they were treated as such. Even though business historians may trace the fitful evolution of management from scientific to social to humanistic to contingency, the science and its practice never overcame the original blight. Even today, in any manufacturing operation, industrial engineers still consider human beings in strictly mechanical terms: workers are measured by "specifications," "standard efficiencies," "standard deviation," "tolerance," and by other machine "functions." When the great economic transition from manufacturing to information-service occurred in the 1970's, the new enterprises, rather than creating new systems with human vocabularies, true to form tenaciously held on to the structures and concepts of the past. Of course, that should not have been surprising; the engines of the most advanced twenty-first-century automobiles are still measured by "horsepower," and "manu"facturing is still the word for making things, even though hands are seldom involved. Banks and burger stores—all continue to accept the traditional definition of "management," that is, "getting work done through people." They all operate in the same organizational design and with the same attitude toward people, that is to say, they subscribe to the same principles of management that were codified in 1926 by Henri Fayol: *planning, organizing, staffing, directing, controlling,* and *evaluating.* Characterized by command and control, modern organizations have little chance of enhancing or releasing the full power of the individual. It simply is not profitable. Those persons who serve such systems consign themselves to an anemic existence—the product always determines the nature of production.

Without doubt, the mentality of dependency fostered by both education and business is the most serious impediment to strategic thinking. True enough, education, from time to time, will attempt "creative thinking," but that is quickly forced into a rigid prescription and limited to one of sixteen or so formulas. Business mindlessly repeats the tattered cliché, "Think outside of the box," yet the box is always there. Two of the most intractable boxes are the requirements that all decisions be "data driven" and all action "market driven." The truth is that anything data driven will be based on the past; anything market driven will be too late. So when solutions are required or opportunities are to be seized, the answers become merely extensions of the problem, and opportunities quietly pass by.

The most tragic examples of non-strategic thinking and the two with the most far-reaching implications for both the person and society are "critical thinking" and the application of technology. One destroyed the notion of absolutes—hence, people become flotsam and jetsam; the other makes the systems of the past obsolete, so people are trapped in the dilemma of doing the same thing over again and expecting a different result. One turned the brain into a computer (vital machine); the other computerized the brain with bytes, protocols, formats, modes, and programs. Both established the limits of the human mind; only the illiterate had any possibility of original or sustained thought.

Sometime in the mid-1970's, Western civilization came to the threshold of a new world. Education had the epochal opportunity of redefining knowledge and, consequently, its own purpose. But faced with such a daunting challenge, education professionals, acting out of habit, did an about-face and chose the diversionary tactic of redefining the *process* of learning. Completely ignoring the fact that the processes one learns and what one learns are the same, educators tried stressing the how of right thinking rather than the accuracy or sanity of the result. That is to say, it makes little difference whether answers are right or wrong. The only thing that matters is whether the process by which they were produced is correct. There naturally ensued a double loss: self-confident thinkers, who were satisfied with any answer. The greatest danger in thinking is not that it be radical but that it be radical enough. So from taxonomies of learning styles to brain compartmentalization to multiple intelligences, analytical process-learning replaced thinking. Behaviorism had at last penetrated the defenses of the mind and had claimed victory.

Technology, which so proudly we hailed at the dawn of the age of information as a clean break with the industrial age, proved itself a disappointing, even counter-productive force in three ways. First, it was given not to creating new systems—not even those of information—but to the unending and highly profitable task of retro-fitting every existing system on the planet, including those systems that were already obsolete. The world became one gigantic oxymoron: "computerized classroom," "electronic mail," "cyber office," "virtual corporation." Evidently, the idea was that technology could restore relevance and vitality. There is one thing more ludicrous than beating a dead horse and that is feeding it, hoping to detect a twitch or perhaps a pulse.

Second, technology purveyors cunningly spun a world of delusion about the evolutionary spiral of technological advancement. The "cutting edge" was always just out of reach. It was simply the computerization of the old incitement to frenzied consumption known as "product obsolescence." The basic assumption seemed to be that the faster and/or more complex any process can be made, the better the result. The difference between optimal and maximal never occurs to those who live in a constant state of technological neurosis. So capacity is burned. They are afraid to ask questions like, "Is the technology of Mercedes-Benz more advanced than that of, say, Volkswagen?" or "Do we really need all these bells and whistles when our business isn't even sound?" No wonder technology was the greatest commercial success of the twentieth century.

Third, the real catastrophe is that technology destroyed the need and ability of the human being to think. This issue is not as simple as the use of computers on algebra exams. It is about language itself. There is sufficient evidence, including common sense, to support the proposition that language and intelligence are inextricably connected. Language is the infrastructure of reasoning, of critical distinctions, of imagination, of values, of truth, of culture itself. It is through language that human beings order their lives, their worlds. Technology has all but displaced meaningful words with visual symbols that have no significance beyond themselves and that evoke visceral reaction rather than intellectual comprehension. Paradoxically, Anthony Burgess (1917–1993) pointed out in those early halcyon days of modern science that the scientific approach is not really appropriate to states of "visceral anguish." Probably the most original thinking during the past half-century was that of Dr. Leonard Shlain, who suggested that the graphic symbols so dramatically generated by technology provide dimensions of communications that are not just beyond words but beyond the alphabet. Basically, the alphabet is portrayed as the gene of retardation. Language, as it has developed over the centuries, especially that of the Indo-European family, is therefore—literally—a kind of interlude between pictures on the wall of a cave and pictures on a screen. Ironically, but fortunately, the good doctor communicated his own ideas through common graphic symbols, the alphabet.

Chapter 6

Arena IV: The Nature of Systems

Systems have remained a constant source of both fascination and frustration for the human mind, whether in the particulars of an actual system or in the abstract speculations about the wondrous workings of quanta, cybernetics, and chaos. Pythagoras enjoyed the same pleasure and pain. Not surprisingly, quite often the particulars overlook the systemic implications; and sometimes the speculation is relevant to nothing in particular. Yet it must be within the realm of reason to know about systems—their kinds and, perhaps, their common critical attributes that identify them as systems.

There are two kinds of systems: natural and artifactual. Some would suggest that there are three, the third being spiritual; and there is much to be learned here. To begin with, whether the concept of system is real or metaphorical in the context of that which is spiritual would make for lively debate among metaphysicians. The basic propositions deserve resolution. Is it not true that all religion is predicated on spiritual systems, that theosophy is a system unto and within itself, and that the occult presumes to tap into a system beyond human understanding? But there is another very intriguing aspect of spiritual systems that has significance to those natural and artifactual, that is, the question of systems within systems—like Ezekiel's wheels within a wheel. Because of the modern atomistic predisposition, human perception orders complex systems into ever smaller and smaller sub-systems, from galaxies to microbes. During the Middle Ages, analogy was the logic by which these systems were correlated, hence, concepts such as "microcosm." But in the analytical modern age, the tendency is toward the superimposition of a higher order. The assumption is that the particles and pieces have no identity, no meaning, and no energy, except in the context of the larger system.

However, it may be that the old idea is closer to the truth, imminently so; that is, even the tiniest systems are complete and distinctly identifiable rather than just things that gain identity only by being arranged within something else. They may simply converge naturally in various composites because they have harmonic critical features, modulate along the same frequency, or possess some other kind of mutuality. What was seen in the Middle Ages as "spheres," in which each system naturally existed, is viewed in the contemporary age as single systems with dependent, perhaps interchangeable, parts. The industrial mentality's affinity with machines blocked any sight of the essentiality of systems. Ironically, it has taken the very highest technology to open the eyes of those who could already see. Virtuality is the entrance to the spiritual.

But, alas, as enticing as the subject may be, the spiritual (including the moral) is not amenable to strategy, at least not in the same way as the other two. Natural systems are those that exist in a state of nature. Artifactual systems are those invented and constructed by human beings. They range from the physical (utensils, habitats, transportation, communication) to the sociopolitical (government, economies, religion—the family is a natural system) to the intellectual (philosophy, knowledge, ethics). All artifactual systems have two inherent characteristics, either of which makes the artifact immediately susceptible to and dependent upon strategies: (1) they each and all are created for the same basic purpose, that is, to serve only those people who create them, so they are basically expediencies, therefore, expendable; (2) irony of irony, they are subject to natural conditions, known popularly as natural "laws." Sooner or later, all human system must confront the strategic implications of these two certainties. Either is sufficient to eventually force every human system to choose between strategy or extinction.

In the first case, expediency, suppose a group of people comes together to create a particular system—say, some political or social order or process—that is intended to serve its purposes. And say it does so, exceedingly well. Suppose, then, that another group of people enter the scene— people who had nothing to do with creating the system and who are, in fact, not being served by it, perhaps maybe even harmed by it. Sooner or later there will be serious conflict. Is this just academic speculation? Hardly. For example, the illustration on the following page is a real-life, present-day situation of inestimable proportions.

It just so happens that over 50 percent of the U.S. population lives within 50 miles of the coastline (Great Lakes included). Within this ribbon, because of the accumulating influx of immigrants from non-European countries, almost everything about traditional American democracy, that which is inherently Western—democracy, culture, eco-

nomics, and society—is being ignored, challenged, eroded and, in some instances, intentionally abandoned. As a result, strange as it may seem, the meaning of "liberty and justice for all" is being seriously reconsidered by conservatives and liberals alike. So is the idea of personal freedom. So too is allegiance, not only by individuals but by major corporations. Democracy may actually turn against those who invented it. And the uniquely capitalistic-socialistic, free enterprise-welfare state, jury-rigged, pseudo-system that was already having some difficulty passing for social order is being laid waste by the frantic attempt to administer laws, regulations, and programs contrived to hold things together in some approximation of normality one more day. Only one fact is certain: if the U.S. Constitution were being drafted today, it would bear little resemblance to the one adopted in 1782.

In the second case, natural laws have even more profound implications. They have to do with the nature of systems themselves—as it turns out, both natural and artifactual—but these implications are especially critical to the artifactual. This is the realm of the strategic. Actually, nature seems to pretty much take care of itself, contrary to the opinion of professional environmentalists who think they are the nursemaids of the world. The optimistic message from the natural world is one of continuous renewal and inexhaustible energy: the sun comes up each morning; the land and sea always reclaim themselves; children are always smarter and better looking than their parents; and everything that has a beginning has an end, which may be a beginning. For the human being, and for human systems, creation is the juncture of the physical and the spiritual.

All systems, whether natural or artifactual, have only four qualities—

the same four qualities. No system is exempt from these qualities, not even sub-atomic systems. Corroboratively, all exposition and analysis of systems must acknowledge and deal with at least one of these features: *control, life, definition,* and *motivation.*

CONTROL

Control is the primary factor in all systems. In fact, it is arguable that control is implied in the mere idea of a system; that is, control is system and system is control But the strategic question is whether the control is internal or external; that is, does a system control itself (active) or is it controlled (passive)? And while the answer may depend on many variables, in any given system, "both" is never the correct answer.

The locus of control is a life-or-death issue for all systems. The reason is an exhilarating paradox: quite simply, control determines capacity. So the critical question is, "How does control produce capacity?" The operative force in control of any kind is power; and the relationships within thriving systems are always reciprocal. In inert or waning systems, there is no reciprocity; control, like all other aspects, is absolute. But in vital systems, the application of power in the form of control, whether internal or external, is always at least equalled by contravening power, as in resistance; or it is exceeded, as in release. The release is either creative or dissipative. If it is true that nothing creative ever happens until energy is forced into a discipline, as surely it must be, then creative capacity is always a direct result of control within or upon the energy of the system. In a human system, control is not a matter of constraint versus freedom; it is a matter of creation versus dissipation. To insist on total freedom is to forswear creativity or productivity. Freedom is always a means, never an end. Thus, the whole purpose of control in any system is to expand capacity, and increasing capacity is tantamount to increasing performance. Control that restricts or reduces capacity is probably the single greatest perversion of natural law and the most debilitating condition for the person or system. Unfortunately, management, as a science, is the most omnipresent and pervasive of all such controls. When controls are exercised as the discipline required to generate creativity, there is naturally no limit to a system's capacity within its kind. But when so-called control mechanisms restrict or prevent the continuous expansion of capacity, the release thus engendered is in the form of waste.

One would be tempted to quickly conclude that external controls are always more onerous and counter-productive than those internal, therefore, more restrictive and threatening, but that is not the case. While it is true that internal controls are more likely to positively affect the vitality of the system, internal, self-imposed controls can effectively destroy a system by stifling its creative energy. There is hardly anything more ironic than a system that unwittingly self-destructs.

The practical significance of all of this is that the locus of control is the factor that determines whether the system is indeed strategic. This is the fundamental question, because only strategic systems have the prerogative (and responsibility) of strategy. Contrary to popular opinion and the counsel of management gurus, strategy is not some kind of optional accessory; that is, it is not an exercise universally available to any and all organizations. As a matter of fact, it is so exclusively a part of strategic systems that they all necessarily engage in strategy, even in refusal. But foolish endangerment and severe embarrassment attend those who presume to heedlessly appropriate strategy to non-strategic systems. The results are disastrous: promises are not kept, expectations are not fulfilled, and good faith and good will are lost.

There are five essential aspects of strategic systems. The first is *autonomy*. Strangely enough, of all these characteristics, autonomy is the must misunderstood. The very idea seems completely foreign to the modern mind. Or perhaps it is often deliberately confused for advantage—strategically. Generally speaking, careless use has made the word meaningless and rendered contemporary organization all but dysfunctional. The meaning can be found only in the nominal definition. Evidently, the ancient Greeks did not favor prepositions, or merely assumed that they were unnecessary for logically thinking people. They had the very annoying habit of joining two words, or morphing, without providing exact clarity of their relationship—for example, "democracy." It is still unclear, despite President Lincoln's inclusive interpretation, whether it is rule "by," "for," or "of" the people, or all three. Autonomy seems, by comparison, rather clear: literally, "self-law" (interestingly, "autocracy" is translated into a "one" person "rule"), but it is in application that the meaning is skewed beyond all recognition.

First, it must be pointed out that the word "logically" will bear no modifier, except one indicating time or place. That is to say, there is no such thing as "delegated autonomy," "relative autonomy," "shared autonomy," "limited autonomy" and, most assuredly, no "quasi-autonomy"—all very common terms in modern bureaucracy-speak. Autonomy is by either grant (usually by national or state government) or seizure (that is, by force or capitulation); it is never assigned; its authority is never compromised by relationships with other entities.

Second, *nomous* (law) signifies both the prerogative and the wherewithal of directing oneself, whether individual or corporate. Obviously it does not mean control over all external conditions. Even autonomous systems are subject to natural law and to the rules and regulations of human authorities within the context. For example, banks are extremely regulated, but they are nevertheless autonomous. Their boards of governors (directors) have the latitude to decide which kind of bank they will rule, where they will operate, how large they will grow, and with whom.

Third, autonomy is more than just a matter of charter. Perhaps the true meaning is realized only in the psychology of the person or system, that is, mental autonomy. It is possible for a system to be autonomous *de jure*, yet be coweringly subservient *de facto*. The reverse precipitates seizure of authority.

Fourth, autonomy always carries with it a full measure of responsibility. Perhaps that is why people and systems shy away from it. As long as the locus of control is outside, there is always someone or something to blame; but once it moves inside, there is no possibility of shifting accountability. Just as a note, in the mid-1990's, a new word entered the English language; not surprisingly "victimhood" captured the mood of the bureaucratic age.

Fifth, so far this discussion has dealt with the second part of the word, *nomous*; however, although usually disregarded, the first word, *auto*, is profoundly significant, especially for organizations that would attempt to act as if non-strategic systems are, in fact, strategic. "Self" can mean only one thing; that is, the system in question has sufficient critical features to constitute its own separate identity. Disguises will not work, nor will semantics. The corporation-model organization, just as the process continuum, relegated all of its parts to only that, part of something else. And none of these can ever move as a self-contained whole system. If, for example, a business should declare a particular department autonomous, or a school district a school, and even if in each instance either were to install "governing" boards, still neither would be autonomous because they have no distinctly identifiable self.

The four other aspects—identity, resource, culture, and scope and range—are actually the practical dimensions of autonomy, yet each is so essential to strategic systems that they require individual consideration. *Identity* is much more than the possession of specific kind and critical attributes; without that, nothing would be distinguishable. It is, rather, uniqueness—that original combination of kind and attributes that makes the system one of a kind. That is an especially critical question for all human systems, from the individual to global enterprises. It is not about identification. Identification is for bodies washed up on shore and for washed-up organizations. Identity is about the very life of a thing, whether it has meaning, purpose. It is the only justification of existence. Uniqueness does not mean that the system is in every respect unlike any other, but that it is immediately set apart from all of the others, and that has a threefold significance. First, uniqueness invariably correlates with strength. Any organization that fails to capitalize on what it does best quickly loses its identity. Second, uniqueness is the ultimate means of overcoming competition; competitors are eliminated by definition. Third, uniqueness demands concentration of effort. It is only by this discipline that any system becomes and remains truly superlative.

Resources not only sustain a system, they also provide the capacity for growth and/or change. Strategic systems inherently have the obligation both to ensure the adequacy of resources for achieving the stated purpose and to appropriate the resources within the system for optimal results. Regrettably, this has proven to be an unbearable burden for many organizations, especially in a capitalistic society where there is never enough. Here, although resources are typically categorized as financial, physical, human, and intellectual, almost everything begins and ends with economics. So corporations, while they will invest in physical capability—if for no other reasons than to qualify for a tax break or to remain competitive—are reluctant to reduce the bottom line by direct expenditure for acquiring or, even more crucial, developing human or intellectual capacity. "Downsizing," the black plague of contemporary organization, is not a growth strategy. And public systems, which live by proration and priority, seldom are able to fund the last few items in the budget. The average investment in human capacity is less than 1 percent of the total revenues. Most modern organizations, therefore, are seriously incapacitated; even the routine business operations are marginal. And, worse still, there is no capacity for expansion. Quite often the impetus comes form misguided management practices. An overemphasis on efficiency, a term borrowed from manufacturing, not only prevents current effectiveness, it also forecloses any hope of future development. In extreme instances, the depletion of capacity is equivalent to self-cannibalization. There are two immutable strategic imperatives in the matter of resources, both of which will be explored fully in the section on strategic action: (1) capacity exists only in excess; and (2) capacity is always developed outside of the current context. Only truly strategic systems have the capacity to understand that.

Culture is the form of values. The formation is either an accidental accumulation of human debris or the deliberate cultivation of beliefs, conduct, language, art, expression, and impression. Although culture is the one quality both intrinsic and extrinsic in all systems, only strategic organization holds the agency of intentional formation. Culture is to organization what character is to person; both are based on either intellectual discipline or moral imperative. Of course, that is not to say that all strategic systems are moral in the sense of being good or even positive. Evil systems have their ethos too. Culture is, in effect, the quality of being. As such, it is any organization's most valuable asset, not just because it asserts some kind of presence or creates impetus for action but because of its sheer practicality.

First, culture determines whether the system needs continuing reha-

bilitation, as in training, or constant direction, as in policies and procedures. Typically, both natural and artifactual systems require initial input
that in one instance overwhelms or in the other exceeds the immediate
benefit, for example, the proverbial flooding of the Nile River and the
common business experience of "initial investment," "start-up costs,"
and "development expense." But if any human system is to thrive, the
culture itself must advance the enterprise; it is tantamount to moral imperative. The reluctant philosopher and inadvertent prophet Antoine de
Saint-Exupéry was right on when he contrasted two organizational cultures: "If you want to build a ship, then don't drum up men to gather
wood, give orders and divide the work. Rather teach them to yearn for
the far and distant sea."

All of the training, reward and punishment, and repair and maintenance in the world are but a poor substitute for commitment to ideals.

Second, culture is the only source of leaders. It has already been
pointed out in this book that leaders are not produced by promotion
through the ranks of the corporation-model organization. Rather, leading
is a relationship. Leaders are naturally called because they personify the
values, perspectives, and highest aspirations of those who choose to follow them. So leaders may be either pied pipers or dedicated servants,
depending on the culture. Healthy, prospering organizations do not dictate "leadership"; they are much too busy nurturing real leaders to be
distracted by pretense or manipulation. How do they do it? By identifying clearly articulated values, by uncompromisingly practicing the
principles derived therefrom, and by constantly reinforcing and reward-
ing those persons who exemplify them. Like it or not, believe it or not,
all strategic systems necessarily grow their own leaders. Even if they
resort to the open market and import "leadership," the leaders are already at home. There is simply no escaping culture. The wisest course
is to make the best of it.

Scope and range are, quite simply, basic features of any system. Perhaps
that is the reason they are overlooked by human organizations characterized by complexity, superficiality, and extravagance. Ignorance is a
self-made booby trap. For strategic organizations, scope is full and range
is endless. Regarding scope, all decisions and action—and even lack of
decisions and inaction—involve the total system; nothing can be piece-
meal; everything has holistic implications. The slightest strategic sound,
light, or heat reverberates throughout the system. The absolutely worst
imaginable situation is an organization whose prerogative and responsibility of creating strategic context is abandoned in a vain attempt either
to look after all operational details or to treat its various components as
separate, freestanding units, cobbled together by the exigency of the moment. Nevertheless, governing boards, when they do not know their own
job, will invariably try to do the work of everyone else. Range has to do

with the influence on, or even the determination of, the future of the organization. Just as scope embraces the whole system, range comprises the entire future of the system. The corporate graveyard is a sobering warning that one seemingly incidental decision has the potential of establishing an irreversible course. On the other hand, honed intuition, charged with judgment and daring, can vitalize a system, generation after generation.

The issue of control is the reason so-called "long-range" planning is not, and cannot be, strategic. Yet, at least 95 percent of all corporate planning, although labeled "strategic," is in actuality nothing more or less than sophisticated prognostication. The definition of long-range planning, although sometimes difficult to come by, is really quite simple. While there is no single source and no definitive explanation that defines this concept of planning, and while there is no specific protocol, the key to distinguishing one kind of planning from another is this: all planning is based on assumption. The assumption made in long-range planning is that all things work in a predetermined way toward a predestined end, and that human prediction can be unerringly accurate. An easy example of this kind of thinking is the admonition commonly offered to schoolchildren; they are told, "Prepare yourself for the future!" The tacit presupposition is that human beings can know exactly what the future will be—that it is already "fixed." So planning begins by conducting an "environmental scan" or a "market survey," extrapolating existing circumstances into future "intersections." In every instance, long-range planning ends and starts at the same place. Nothing can exceed the promise of its beginning. The necessary implication is that the system or the person is reduced to reaction or passivity, struggle, and eventual decline.

But strategic planning is predicated on the assumption that people can prepare the future for themselves, and that successful businesses create their own markets. This is the ultimate control.

LIFE

The life of any system consists of duration and quality. Nothing better illustrates both and their symbolic relationship than the ancient and universal principle of the life cycle. Diagrammatically, it appears rather simple (see Exhibit 2).

And, in fact, in the earlier days of corporate strategic planning, the 1960's, the intellectual basis for strategy was the answer to the questions posed by three successive possibilities: is the organization *emerging, growing,* or *mature*? The states were posited along the upward curve (0, 5, and 10, respectively). Then a somewhat elementary matrix was developed by asking the same question about the industry in which the enterprise was or intended to operate. And while being an emerging business in an emerging industry might carry tremendous risk, that risk is usually offset by opportunity. On the other hand, a mature business in a mature industry faces the unhappy prospect of intense competition just at the point where it is most susceptible to entropy. That kind of analysis is meaningful, as far as it goes. But that is the problem: it did not go far enough. Although it was never stated in so many words, there was a popular notion, perhaps more wishful thinking than theory, that perverted the whole concept of the life cycle. The tacit assumption, even in strategic planning at the time, was that once a system reached maturity it could exist in perpetuity in a kind of homeostasis. Strategies were aimed at stabilizing and maintaining the system. So, in actuality, the diagram evolved (see Exhibit 3).

Exhibit 2
The Life Cycle

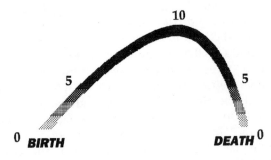

Source: Author.

Exhibit 3
Crisis

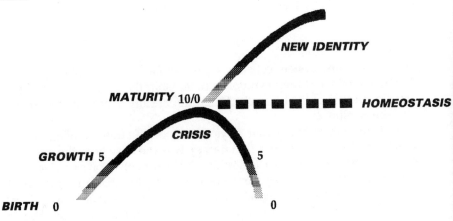

Source: Author.

Unfortunately, and to the unmitigated chagrin of all who heeded that advice, this proposition was not only false it was also completely oblivious to the truly critical aspects of the life cycle. Without doubt, the most critical stage is the inevitable state known historically as "crisis" (10). In fact, this word is so significant that it is never translated in European languages; it is always transliterated. Even today, crisis is the point between life and death. That is the natural law from which no artifactual system is exempt: sooner or later, all reach the point of obsolescence.

Obsolescence means that it is costing more, by whatever measure, to support the system than the system is capable of producing, by any measure. The artifactual expedient has run its course. So, if the system continues, it is only because of a paradoxical inversion of roles: specifically, those who were once served by the system agree to serve it. That is the most pathetic kind of dependency, or perhaps it is an addiction. There is a strange myth popularly associated with obsolescence. The belief is that since progress, as defined from the nineteenth century on, is incremental—as in continuous improvement—then the same must be true of regression. That is, obsolescence, when and if it happens, is gradual, with sufficient indications of decline to allow the wary to either arrest it or adjust to it. However, that is not the case. Obsolescence is like falling off a cliff; there is no recovery, no forgiveness—just a slam. So the life cycle is not a curve at all, it is more like a crash (see Exhibit 4).

That is precisely why the idea of cycles was rejected in the earlier discussion of predicting "futures." What goes around does not come around. Its course is rudely interrupted by the perpendicular. However, crisis itself is not final. There is within it the opportunity for the creation of a completely new system. This is the heart and soul of strategy. It is the rarest of all human experiences, yet probably the most desired.

The ancient Chinese uniquely captured the spirit of this dual human phenomenon. Their symbol for crisis is composed of two characters: *wei,*

Exhibit 4
The Effect of Obsolescence

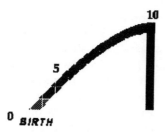

Source: Author.

or danger, and *ji*, or opportunity. Although crisis is a time of great danger, it also contains potential opportunity. The effects of crisis situations can be devastating or debilitating, a time of creation.

Aristotle's word for this process creation was *metamorphosis*, as in butterflies, rocks, and Franz Kafka. The word literally means "next form"; it does not mean, as some have implied, "higher" form. But the word is significant beyond itself. Aristotle knew two words for which is rendered "form" in English, and his choice presents a dramatic contrast between the two. *Schema* also translates "form"; however, the meaning of this word is limited to external appearances—specifically, to the shape of the object. But *morphe* speaks to the essence of the thing itself, its fundamental and thorough nature. Therefore, mere refurbishing, restructuring, transforming, or even re-creating does not capture the original idea. Refurbish means to fix up; restructure means to reinforce that which is about to collapse; transform means to move from one form to another like form; re-create means to disassemble and assemble again in a different way. Metamorphsis is actually a new birth. The old is completely displaced. Nothing of it remains, except the life force itself. In the caterpillar's cocoon, for example, the previous system is completely liquefied, and the emerging system is a completely different kind. In that case, it is the other side of life. The portrayal of the traditional life cycle thus should be modified (see Exhibit 5).

How appropriate it is that even today failed or abandoned businesses are "liquidated." Any planning exercise that does not call for and inspire metamorphosis is not strategic. Exhibit 5 clearly suggests that there are two kinds of change. In fact, it is instructive to note that psychotherapy, among other disciplines, recognizes two "levels" of change. Level I is the change that occurs within an existing system. That type of change is deceptive because it is attended by the sensations of velocity, disequalibrium, and stress—all of the factors that one would experience in the creation of a radically new order. But, despite all of the symptoms, the system is still basically the same, only it is speeding more merrily toward

Exhibit 5
Metamorphosis

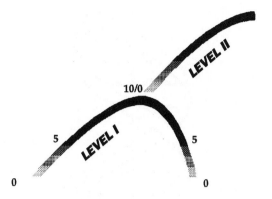

Source: Author.

perdition. But level II change is a completely new reality, *beyond* the previous system. Everything in or about the system is different in kind, not merely in time.

Now, all of this is the truth, but it is not the whole truth. And if the discussion were to end here, the impression left would likely be that the life of any system is a series of plateaus and valleys and that, consequently, strategic planning should be correspondingly serial episodes, usually taking place in the valleys. So, after the term of any plan—say, five years—the system would be expected to "start over" because the plan had expired. That is a very naive and dangerous interpretation. Extinction does not wait for planning. If strategy is properly understood and applied, it recognizes that all healthy systems actually live in crisis and, therefore, must be engaged in the perpetual creation and constant emergence of new realities. Thriving systems continually force crisis through strategy.

The best graphic illustration of all of this is a helix. As a mater of fact, the helix is far more than a convenient figure of speech, a simile, to convey the duration and quality of life. It is the basic design of life. In 1953, James Watson and Francis Crick suggested for the first time the now commonly acknowledged "structure" of deoxyribonucleic acid (DNA), the rather complex molecular composition that is the essential constituent of genes. They even noted, almost as an aside, that "It has not escaped our notice that the specific pairings we have postulated immediately suggests a possible copying mechanism for the genetic material."[23] Their description of the structure of DNA, and their accompanying analysis, had significance beyond the biochemical specifications (see Exhibit 6).

There is something especially intriguing about this structure. Its pro-

Exhibit 6
The DNA Double Helix

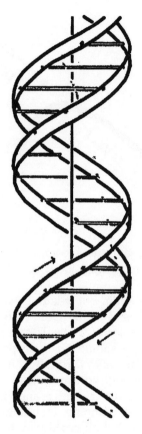

Source: James Watson and Francis Crick, "A Structure for Deoxyribose Nucleic Acid," *Nature*, April 2, 1953. Reprinted with permission.

portions and patterns are those of the famous "golden mean," the magic ratio that occurs throughout nature, from the circular arrangement of seeds in the pistil of a sunflower to galactic spirals. Aristotle, who unwittingly gave his name to the phenomenon, emphasized the constancy of its dimensions in human art (statues) and artifacts (the Parthenon) and, by analogy, even in human behavior. The latter is the current real definition—"moderation in all things." But through his famous rabbit riddle, Fibonacci reduced it to numbers: 3, 5, 8, 13, 21, *et cetera*, ad infinitum. As fascinating as the sequence may be, it is the ratio (.618034) that may be the key or code to any kind of life, and to any aspect of life— physical, mental, and in the case of human beings, spiritual. Although it is obviously manifested in the bodily proportions of all species, and most charmingly so as human beings observe one another, exactly what it means in the quality and duration of the physical is not yet clear. Nor are its mental and spiritual implications. For example, could it have something to do with physical longevity, with cognitive faculty and emotional stability, or with eternal juvenescence? Or could it have something to do with the ratio between the amount of energy (resources) required by a system and that which the system produces? The answer to all three is unhypothetically "yes," but it begs authentication as yet not known. When that knowledge is discovered, it will profoundly change the human perception of all systems; and that reality will usher in a new age, likely the ultimate age, of strategy. Contrary to Disney's grotesque Wild Kingdom interpretation, this is the real way to the "tree of life."

These facts of life are the reason that the exercise popularly called "comprehensive planning" is not, and cannot be, strategic. Yet 95 percent of all public sector planning, even though referred to as "strategic" in legislative mandates and the like, is nothing more than comprehensive planning. Unlike long-range planning, which has no set format other than beginning with analysis of the environment, this approach has many protocols, as many as the institutions that use it. In fact, comprehensive planning is tantamount to institutionalization. No matter what the specific format, this kind of planning is always based on two assumptions, both of which are false: (1) all human systems can be perfected; and (2) all human systems deserve to be perfected. In the first instance, comprehensive planning preaches the bogus doctrine of improvement, "incremental" and "continuous." In the second, it practices the unnatural rite of attempting to reanimate dead bodies.

What is needed is some credible way of conceptualizing and committing to a future of one's own making. In the simplest terms, planning deals with three explicit questions and one implicit question. It is the order in which these questions are addressed that determines the kind of planning—long-range, comprehensive, or strategic. Their order reveals the basic assumption; the assumption establishes the context; and the context determines the outcome. The three questions are: (1) Where or what do we want to be at some time in the future? (2) Where or what are we now? (3) Where or what would be at that time in the future if we continue without intervention? The implicit question is: (4) What will it take to close the gap? A depiction of the issues is shown in Exhibit 7.

Recalling, for the moment, the previous discussion on the nature of systems, this graphic illustrates the fundamental distinctiveness of strategic planning. Long-range planning would begin with question 3—that is, some rational prediction about the future; and then the plan would be aimed at adapting to that future or responding to that circumstance. Comprehensive planning begins with question 2—that is, the current situation; and, therefore, vast quantities of research data would be ac-

Exhibit 7
Questions and Answers in Strategic Planning

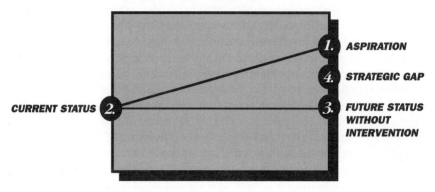

Source: Author.

cumulated to provide the rationale for the plan's ambition, which in no case will exceed the capacity of the existing system. Strategic planning, however, begins with question 1—that is, it is the aspiration, not the circumstances or predictions, that determines the result. The baseline is drawn from that perspective, and the strategic gap always greatly exceeds the present capability of the system. If a plan can be accomplished by the organization that developed it, then the plan is not truly strategic. It is only in creating the capacity to realize the plan that the new creation occurs. The challenge, therefore, in strategic planning is to build a plan that is at once systemic yet organic, rational yet intuitive, disciplined yet creative, and practical yet imaginative. The basic assumption is simple: human beings can see the future they want with such clarity that they can write specifications for it, and then by dint of their own effort, can actualize even more than what they see.

DEFINITION

The definition of a system is the most confounding technical difficulty in the application of strategy. The problem seems to arise from the fact that since the anti-establishment fever of the 1960's, especially in the United States, there has been a persistent, insidious breakdown of order, both public and private. Protest is the state of the union. Rule of law is, at best, suspect. Any idea of order has become blurred, its recollection hazy. So the definition of order required by—indeed, inherent in—a system may be beyond the intellectual and emotional grasp of contemporary generations. And the incapacity is, in fact, cross-generational. One would expect the rising generation (Generation Y) to be influenced by the disposition of the older so-called "boomers," but, amazingly, the most senior generation sometimes is more vociferous and active in its opposition to existing systems than either of the others. It is interesting that many sociologists now believe that the cataclysmic thinking of the 1960's was actually fostered by the pent-up anger, frustration, and want that these seniors endured when they were struggling young parents in the post-depresion era. One of their own, Dr. Benjamin Spock, wrote the bible on child rearing and forever changed what previously had been known as discipline. That regrettable condition portends an uncertain future for systems of all kinds. Not only is there a pronounced aversion to both the logical and natural principles of organization, there is also, much more dangerous, a general predisposition toward systemlessness. From that point of view, the only good system is an anti-system. It is little wonder that the contemporary intellectual passion is looking for order in chaos.

As evidence of what may seem at first thought an unjustified assessment of popular attitude, there is no better example than the Internet, although politics—which overrides the order of law, and law—which prostitutes principle to undue process, and religion—which makes sacraments of self-worship and material wealth, all come close. The Internet is, by its very nature, disorder; even the most powerful government in the world admits that it is beyond control. Information, and moreso data, is always counter-system. And while real information has some semblance of form, even it provides only a limited interpretative context; that is, it has no meaning outside of itself. Data is even more problematic. Since it is random, it has no meaning at all, until and unless it is subjected to interpretation by which it is translated into information. Paradoxically, when information is accepted as reality, in fact or aspiration, it inevitably destroys the system that produced it. That is devastatingly true with authoritarian systems, such as governments and corporations. Control is met with equal and opposite force.

The wasting of politics, law, religion, and all other rational artifactual systems is always strictly a matter of human will. After all, that was the source of their creation.

The general proclivity to disorder may be explained in three ways, each of which epitomizes fundamental conflict: (1) reaction to authority; (2) moral schizophrenia; and (3) epochal disequilibrium. The first, and the most common explanation, is the rather simple proposition that the disorder was the reaction to authoritarian regimes that had dominated the previous three decades, especially the 1940's. That decade imposed the most rigid order in modern times on every aspect of the lives of the citizens of the United States. The 1950's rendered them virtually inert. But with the elimination of the threat of war, and with at least the prospect of affluence, the natural human propensity for personal freedom exploded into sometime violent opposition to the existing orders—from civil rights to a God-is-dead theology, from the Rolling Stones to space travel, from communes to riots in the streets. The greatest threat in rebellion is not that it overthrow existing orders, which usually deserve no less, but that it destroy itself in the process.

The second explanation, while admittedly somewhat esoteric, is nevertheless compelling. Western society, especially the United States, from its very inception, has been torn between conflicting moral imperatives arising from its religious heritage and the personal liberty implicit in democracy. The dilemma was solved historically not by choosing one over the other but by acceding to both. Only rationalism could have reconciled these inherently opposite philosophies. There is no more poignant example of this kind of contradiction than capitalism, an economic system based on scarcity, greed, and competition, yet upheld by religion and pursued as being righteous. Andrew Carnegie's famous "American Beauty Rose" dissertation, in which he lauded the rich and heartily condemned the poor, was delivered first to his Sunday school class. And while that philosophy evidently appeased the collective consciousness regarding the unfettered pursuit of wealth, it did not altogether assuage the individual conscience in the violation of other, perhaps more personal, moral precepts. That is, individuals might choose to do wrong, even that which is deemed sinful, but they would expect and feel guilt. Thus gratification and conscience came to co-exist: one was the price of the other. That is the only way perpetual license is possible.

The third explanation is based on the upheaval that occurs between epochs. Time may be measured by the accidental, purely linear Western calendar, but human history is not. That which serves to date contracts, to take the span of life, or to mark significant events in a certain culture's experience does not tell human beings *when* they really are. So much for the idea of progress. The when of human existence is determined only by first examining the ebb and flow of human life on this planet, and then qualitatively relating one period to the others. Epochs are those extended periods, usually 300 to 500 years, during which the single life cycles of expansive human systems are played out from birth to death. Almost all ancient civilizations are dramatic evidence of this phenomenon. All are precipitated and attended by a certain worldview and by the creation of artifactual systems consistent with that view, which is, in effect, a world picture.

When that view is through a single, narrow lens, order is immediately perceptible and sure, but when that lens becomes so intensely focused that it precludes any new awareness, the system disintegrates because of its own rigidity. The end of all epochs is marked by occlusion of sight. However, when the lens is widened, or when there are multiple lenses, although order is much less certain, a new vista becomes possible. The beginning of epochs is always signaled by a new lens—unfocused, perhaps, but the prospect is exhilarating even in its initial obscurity. That is precisely where Western civilization was while it was being distracted by a coincidental calendar turn of the millenia and its attendant paranormal activity. Technically, the interval between epochs is a cusp between two orders. In this instance, the old order had dominated and constrained human life for almost 400 years; the new, an emerging system of relationships, patterns, and designs eminently conducive to the fullness of life and human freedom.

System definition is an ancient question, but only in modern times have the answers drawn such a sharp contrast between two possibilities. It seems ludicrously unlikely, but in the mid-nineteenth century there was no more popular topic, especially among the curious and bored. Long before television and other scintillating diversions, one of the most popular forms of entertainment was the public debate. Enter the Chautauqua society, for example. The subject that always drew standing-room-only crowds was the nature of systems; specifically, whether they were "atomistic" or "organismic." Even that specific question was not new. Aristotle had argued with himself about it, and lost. For centuries the whole matter had been relegated to the ring of academic sparring and had not impeded the course of civilization, at least as far as anyone knew. But the accumulation of events between 1770 and 1840—individual, political, social, and intellectual—forced an answer, once and for all.

The settlement of the argument occurred gradually, although sometimes tumultuously, but the outcome was hardly ever in doubt. Not since the convergence of ecclesiastical authoritarianism and secular feudalism had there occurred such a coincidence of philosophy and socioeconomic practices. Both were thoroughly "rationalized." Rationalism became the defining context for all systems in the society. As Locke was to political systems, Newton was to science, Darwin was to society, Malthus was to demographics, Marx and Adam Smith were to economics, and Descartes was to the fundamental construct of intellectual artifactual systems. His formula, mercifully reduced to four steps from the originally intended 36, was simple and direct: (1) accept as true only what is apprehended so clearly and distinctly that you cannot doubt it; (2) break up each problem into as many parts as it will yield and tackle these in turn; (3) observe an order in your inquiry passing from the simple to the complex, from what is easy to understand to the more complex; (4) make sure of covering whole ground. It is rather amazing, even to a rationalistic mind, that these rules survived through the twentieth century as the cardinal principles of "critical thinking," as the basic model for problem solving, as the fundamental design of production activity, and as the intrinsic principles of organization.

Atomistic systems, by definition, present two serious problems, serious because they are unsolvable dilemmas, and because either of which has the effect of tying the system in knots—Gordian knots. The first is fragmentation; the second is dichotomy. One is simple, almost mathematical; the other is somewhat more difficult to measure, but equally destructive. Fragmentation is based on the industrial notion that all systems are made up of a collection of preferably interchangeable parts, as a machine. Scientific organization, necessitated by scientific management, laid out the work on the factory floor and divided it into pieces according to task grouping. It was termed "division of labor." This is the arrangement reflected in the traditional organizational chart—line and staff, and, of course, top-down. The intent might have been control in order to achieve efficiency, but the effect was fragmentation and the subsequent isolation of the parts, each spinning in its own orbit or moving at its own speed. Communication was impossible; strategy was unthinkable. The only interaction was in the form of competition or sabotage. Management by objectives actually encouraged this kind of internecine warfare.

Regarding the dichotomy of systems, as management was forced to seek relief from the counter-productive influence of autocracy, control (ostensibly, and usually with much fanfare) was shifted to the parts, at least to the most important parts, those nearest the headquarters. This process was referred to as "decentralization" in the corporation and, later, as "site-based management" in the public sector, especially in education. But this vain attempt did more to highlight the tension that already existed in the conflict between the whole and its parts. The promise of decentralization was impossible to fulfill. The very word "decentralization" presupposes "centralization"; and there is good reason to believe that that is exactly what the autocrats wanted. The idea of decentralization was a ploy to extend the nexus of control further down the organization. The ultimate extension came to be known as "micromanagement," and that phrase also plainly speaks to the extent of particlization.

But, to the contrary, the sub-divisions in many cases took full advantage of the offer of independence and immediately set about building their own empires. There are instances of businesses in which departments gradually overwhelmed, financially and in size, the rest of the corporation, defied the board, and bought themselves out. Decentralization is particularly confusing in the bastardized corporation-model organization used by public institutions. For example, the school district of Edmonton, Alberta, Canada, if not the first to experiment with site-based management, was the first to push the concept to the point of diminishing returns; eventually, it became not a school system but a *faux* system of schools, and that became the *modus operandi* for most districts. In fact, there was one case in Florida in which a school sued its own district because it disagreed with the system's mission, and the state Department of Education filed an *amicus curiae* brief on behalf of the school. It should be pointed out here that in departmentalized organization, planning by the components is, in fact, a legitimate, even necessary, exercise. But this kind of planning is not, under any circumstances, strategic. It is, rather, the kind of planning that was always stated as the first principle of management—job planning, task planning, program or project planning. In fact, the latter two (program and project) are so practical that they have their own disciplines.

Program planning is the process of creating a grand design to make a concept operational. This type of planning is usually conducted within the context of a larger organization and, in fact, is typically assigned by or derived from the initiatives of that larger organization. Exploratory by its very nature, program planning becomes a kind of evolutionary process. Its purpose, quite simply, is to take a single idea, test it against the real conditions and circumstances, justify it by intended outcomes, and describe how to make it work. In the end, the emphasis is on sustaining functions, relationships, and results.

Usually this kind of planning follows a predictable, although somewhat flexible, pattern: identification of the subject, sometimes in the form of a hypothesis; assessment or evaluation of need; analysis of information regarding the current status of the subject and surrounding conditions; verification of the need for the program; establishment of goals and objectives for the program; an extensive, detailed design of functional relationships, accountabilities, and outcomes; a description of the system to be set in place for monitoring and controlling the program; and, finally, specific standards and methods of evaluation toward improving or refining the program.

Program planning is typically employed for undertakings such as awards or employee recognition, public relations, employee benefits, marketing and advertising—anything that lends itself to being systematized and put into place as an ongoing plan of action. Some strategic planning disciplines actually include "programs" as the immediate context for strategies, that is, the strategies are considered a sub-set of programs.

Project planning, as the term implies, is the logical, sequential process of the advance design necessary to carry out any significant task to accomplish a specific purpose. The next step is implementation. Typically, the initial steps used in this process are the same as those in rational decision making:

1. Identification of the task
2. Analysis of status and/or situation
3. Establishing the project's objective
4. Identification of alternative (possible) courses of action
5. Analysis of the obstacles and adverse consequences related to each possible course of action
6. Decision regarding the course of action to be taken

When the course of action is decided upon, then detailed plans for necessary management activities can be developed, such as basic tactics, sequences, and timing; organization; allocation of resources; staffing; directing and controlling; evaluation; and, if appropriate, provisions for recycling the project. The project planning process is used to accomplish initiatives such as building construction, campaigns of all kinds, and any other stand-alone action with its own budget.

Likewise, departmental or site planning is necessary, but only in a strategic context. This will be discussed fully in the chapter dealing with the strategic planning process.

Organismic systems do not solve the problems of atomistic systems; they preclude them. "Organismic" simply means that the system is not constructed of components, as a machine, but that it is intrinsically one formation, such as a living body. It is the difference between parts and features. That is not only the concept informing all great art, but also the original idea of the corporation (*corpus*).

The modern word "essential" is commonly used in two ways; both are meaningful in organismic systems. First, it indicates absolute necessity; that is, the thing in question is indispensable. Second, and closer to the nominal definition, the word refers to the essence of the thing itself, its fundamental and thorough nature. The whole is contained in any feature; any feature contains the whole. In a somewhat similar fashion, poets often use a figure of speech, *synecdoche*, to ascribe this concept of oneness to artifactual constructs—for example, "sail" for ship. But, then, so do ordinary folk—"motor" for automobile, "hearth" for house. In these applications, typically the most significant part is used because it is that which most readily signifies the entire object to an observer, even mentally. But that does not mean that it is the most important part, or that the others are unnecessary. In essentiality, there is no consideration of comparative significance, no rank, and no priority.

Perhaps a more mundane analogy would illustrate the unique qualities of essentiality—say, a jigsaw puzzle, specifically a thousand-piece puzzle, with a thousand and seven pieces. Yes, even this recent perverse trick of extra pieces is illustrative of a principle of essentiality: anything that does not fit is discarded. But more to the point, there are two aspects of the puzzle that are pertinent to strategic organization. The first is the relationship among the pieces. The tenet, succinctly stated, is this: change one, change all—even though the picture, the intent, remains the same. That is, if the shape of only one piece is altered, all relationships are affected, not just those of the contiguous pieces.

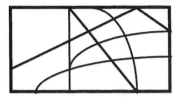 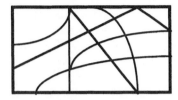

Obviously, if the image on the piece is changed, the whole picture is different. In artistic composition, this is known as *synectics*.

Source: Images®, copyright 1999 Photodisc Inc. Reprinted with permission.

Second, there is no rank order among the pieces. In essential systems, there is no such thing as priority. Certainly the corner pieces of a puzzle may be played first, but that does not mean that they are more valuable than the others. The phasing of action must never be confused with the importance of the actions. There is only one instance when relative importance is a consideration; that is, when a piece is broken or missing, and then only because it is critical to the whole.

MOTIVATION

All human systems are dynamic, admittedly. That assertion is more postulate than argument. Although it is the nature of systems to be active, there is often present, in human systems especially, an equal and opposite force of either inertia or friction. So perhaps it would be more accurate to declare that thriving human systems are dynamic—a dynamism, beyond the vital internal interactions, by which the system sustains and reinvigorates itself, a dynamism that activates the widely proclaimed whole system even from its inception. It is noteworthy, particularly in this, the second Age of Enlightenment, that Newton built an entire cosmology on the proposition that all particles in the universe have velocity and direction. He reduced his observations of the physical universe to three "laws": briefly stated, inertia, acceleration, and equal and opposite action. But these laws ultimately entailed much uncertainty, as Heisenberg finally acknowledged. Only in the twentieth century did scientists such as Erwin Schroedinger, who fretted over his famous cat-in-the-box illustration, advance the theory that observation (light) determines reality. Human systems have the same characteristics of motion, only here is not physical direction or velocity. In a practical world, the where and the how of the movement of organizations are usually plain enough. The real question—and the one Newton did not ask, because he assumed a divine creator—is, "What actually moves them?" That is the ultimate *why*.

In keeping with the idea of postulation, it is better to put this discussion in the form of inquiries. There are three issues that must be addressed if the answer is ever to be discovered.

The first is whether control and motivation are the same. That question was raised in the previous discussion of control; specifically, internal vs. external control. Just as a matter of note, Newton assumed an *a priori*, external force. It is possible, for example, that external control is met with little or no active response from the system itself, a kind of capitulation. It would be strictly an academic, although perhaps a logical, argument that the acquiescence is, in fact, commensurate action. In simple terms, it would be the same as the old adage, "Inaction is action." The only consideration that makes this a practical question is that in human systems there is some measure of responsibility implicit in any answer. Or is it possible that external control may be met with not merely equal and opposite, but greater resistance? If that were possible, then it seems that internal control and motivation are the same. For human enterprises the answer carries a wide range of implications; for example, reaction to market conditions, to regulatory authorities, to competition, and to enviornmental factors of all kinds. Moreover, the reaction establishes the organization's temperament, that is, acceptance or challenge.

The second issue is whether human systems are motivated by the same forces as individual human beings. That should be a rhetorical question, but it is not. Why would anyone expect that human beings in the plural would be different from human beings in the singular? But they may be; they often are. The problem is that in systemization, the system itself can get in the way. The result is serious variance, even conflict, between the interests of the individuals in a system and the interest of that system. There are many impinging factors here, from free moral agency to political and economic order, but in the final analysis, the answer is the degree of tolerance one has for the other. This issue has emerged during the twentieth century as the most serious affliction of Western organization.

Although labor unions were founded on the premise, Chris Argyris was the first to admit that there is an inevitable conflict between the interest of the traditional corporate organization and the people in it. Downsizing, mergers, outsourcing, and relocation are most emphatically always for the benefit of the corporation.

So far, no one has taken seriously the warning of the late Mr. Soichiro Honda: "If we do not find a way to make the interests of our employees and the interest of our company the same, then we will have neither."

The third issue is a rather theoretical one, but it is so only because the question has never been addressed, certainly not in modern times, and certainly not in a culture that has all but forsworn the spiritual dimension of the person, considering them only "resources" to be used in decreasing measure according to Newton's second law. They are never considred "sources" of intelligence, energy, and action beyond that of the existing system. Contrary to the principle laid down in Newton's third law, it is possible for human systems to generate energy rather than consuming it. This is obviously not a matter of production in which basic materials are subjected to a transforming agent or process (applied energy) and turned into something judged at the time and occasion to be of greater value than the energy and material it required to produce it, that is, wealth. The question here is far more fundamental: can human motivation create energy beyond itself? That question alone, so much more an affirmative answer, is critical to the basic assumption about human systems and promises to usher in a new era, not only of organization but of human enterprise.

Each of these three questions requires and deserves a fairly radical answer. "Radical" in the strict meaning of the word—a bold departure from current designs and expectations, from existing norms. Any one of the answers could potentially radically alter all existing human organization beyond recognition.

The answer to the first question is in the understanding and appropriation of Newton's first law, inertia: moving objects tend to continue to move. The current thinking is, "Yes, but the second law is also true—friction and drag." Such equivocating ignores the power in that phenomenon in which momentum creates momentum and energy creates energy. Anyone listening to a symphony is fully aware of that. Or, in a wild swing, does not the "slingshot" orbiting technique employed so beautifully in space travel provide at least some inkling of the virtually limitless energy within energy? Speaking of space, there is recently discovered evidence of this phenomenon throughout the entire cosmos. For centuries scientists had assumed, and, therefore, had built all their systems on the assumption that the universe was shrinking—that is, running down. Now what do they find? It seems that that was a slight misperception. The universe is actually expanding. The only reasonable theory is that mirco-tiny particles of matter, so small that they have not yet been seen, are generating energy upon energy, continuously creating the universe. The effect of this thus far is only a recalculation of the force of gravity, and even though that fact may completely alter the historical concept of physics, it pales when compared to the prospect of energy within human energy. For human systems, it means not only continuous vitalization but continuous expansive creation. For the person, it means not only continuous generation but unlimited capacity. That is ultimate energy.

The second issue can be settled only by the wholesale abandonment of all artifactual constructs, which are unnatural and, therefore, adverse to the human being, and in place thereof, the willing, abandoned embrace of natural formations. Contemporary organizational development experts—consultants and professors—have for years been much enamored of "synergy," a concept popularly preached but seldom understood. The idea was misconceived and misplaced; synergy was at best a placebo for systems intrinsically broken. Natural formations, quite in contrast, are by nature characterized by a concept as foreign to the modern mind as the word itself. *Sophrosyne* literally means "prudence," "sense," "moderation," but in reference to human beings and their social relationships it is often translated "harmony." "Synergy" was misconceived because it was interpreted as meaning that the sum of the parts is greater than the whole, not the original meaning of everyone achieving gain by virtue of his or her interaction with others. It was misplaced because the concept was completely at odds with the workings of the corporation-model organization. *Sophrosyne* is the ultimate system.

The third issue demands an understanding of the difference between purpose and quest. It is one thing to be motivated by the achievement of some goal but quite another to be dedicated completely to an ideal so far transcending self that the champion, the pilgrim, or the servant gives his or her life to it, only to discover life.

That is ultimate motivation.

Chapter 7

Arena V: The Dynamics of Human Organization

Human organization is instinctive; there is nothing either intellective or intuitive about it. Since 1675, the corporation-model has been the dominant organization of Western civilization. Sometimes it seems synonymous with that civilization. Intended strictly as an expedient for the collective effort of wealth accumulation—as in mercantilism—it was subsequently adopted by wealth-producing enterprises, such as manufacturing; and eventually by wealth-consuming activities, from clubs and cabals to government and the church. Every aspect of life, even the most personal, was dominated by it—schedules, family relationships, location of habitats, traffic patterns, educational opportunities, and neighborhoods. Amazingly, few people ever dared to question its omnipresence, and fewer still its omnipotence. It was a convenience that by sheer force of presence came to rule those it was designed to serve.

Two facts were persistently ignored: the corporation was exclusively Western, a unique and contradictory combination of ecclesiastical doctrine and rationalistic science; and, like any other artifact, it was subject to the principles of the life cycle. Disregard for the first led to unmitigated disaster when the West chauvinistically attempted, through economic and political coercion, to impose its order on the East. Japan was most susceptible to democracy and capitalism because it had been conquered militarily, governmentally occupied, and socially Westernized. But China, in its eternal tranquillity, refused to yield to the upstart arrogance of the neophyte Western culture. Russia, on the other hand, although Western by ethnicity, history, and tradition, opted rather to live at the end of the social, political, and economic continuum opposite the most prominent Western nations. Other Western countries, such as Mexico and most of those in South America, because of the domination of the Catholic Church and the minimal influence of rationalism, struggled unsuccessfully with the corporation model of *el norte,* and developing countries had neither knowledge of or need for artifactual organization, even though from time to time they tried to mimic it mostly to curry the favor of foreign patrons (i.e., the World Bank and the United States).

Disregard for the second fact about the corporation, its inevitable obsolescence, resulted in the quick rise of alternative natural systems throughout virtually all of Western society—systems that displaced the change-resistant, anti-human corporation model. Some observers have suggested that technology and the explosion of information precipitated the breakdown of the corporation structure; and, indeed, it is true that order decreases as information increases. But it is a more accurate assessment to say that technology and information expedited a natural process that had begun decades before, during the so-called "age of information."

By the end of the twentieth century, the corporation-model organization, despite a raging stock market, was in rapid decline, and it was irretrievably disappearing as the society's dominant order. Mergers, downsizing, and government pillaging were the overt manifestations of a terminal condition. The corporation model is being replaced not by a single prototype but by various patterns and designs that emerge from blends and mixes of the qualities of natural systems. There is no prescription, no template, and no permanence.

It is unnecessary here to expound on the past and future of the corporation model. That is comprehensively analyzed in a companion work. And the emerging organizational possibilities are discussed in the "strategic action" portion of this book. So it will be sufficient here (1) to summarize the philosophical variations in the corporation-model organization, (2) to briefly note the difference between artifactual and natural organization, and (3) to contrast the traditional corporation model with the emerging organization. Because this information will be familiar to most, in order to expedite the discussions, and in keeping with the structured, analytical style of the corporation, each will be advanced by the use of an organizational chart.

PHILOSOPHIES OF ORGANIZATION

There were four models of corporate organization during the twentieth century, each based on a basic theory of human behavior, and although each is usually assigned roughly its own historical period, it is inaccurate to say that any one, with the exception of the "scientific" version, ever existed alone in its pure form. Carryovers and mixing led to considerable confusion, even conflict, in actual organizations. The fourth, "circumstantial" or "contingency," was by definition a frustrated hodgepodge of the other three. In order to put in sharp relief the comparisons and contrast, each philosophy is analyzed here by the same organizational aspects (see Exhibits 8 and 9).

It is necessary also to understand the difference between artifactual and natural systems. While that which is natural is universal and consistent, the artifactual varies according to perspective. The basic question is whether it is a construct or a formation. For the purpose of this discussion, the features listed here are those of the corporation model.

PHILOSOPHIES OF MANAGEMENT

It would be helpful here also to recall the particulars of the science of management that were part and parcel of organizational theory and practice. First, there were six principles of management, articulated in the 1920's by Henri Fayol. For some reason beyond reason, business school curricula are still hinged on these precepts: planning, organizing, staffing, directing, controlling, and evaluating. Some low-bid schools teach three: planning, organizing, and implementing. A few teach inexplicable combinations, such as planning, organizing, staffing, coordinating, communication, and re-cycling.

Second, so-called management styles were supposed to be the manifestation of a certain attitude toward "getting work done through people," the standard definition of management. Typically, the five styles were depicted along a continuum (see Exhibit 10).

Although often explained with considerable variation, usually the styles were characterized by the following assumptions:

Authoritarian

1. Traditional organizational structure

2. All authority/knowledge at top

3. Authority delegated reluctantly

4. Responsibility delegated completely

5. Knowledge withheld

6. Primary means of communications is directives and orders (memos)

7. Failure not forgiven

8. Climate for "blockers"

9. Managers and employees are dependent

10. Decisions are made at top; others implement

Exhibit 8
Theories of Human Organization

	SCIENTIFIC
Theories of Human Behavior	• Frederick Taylor, an industrial engineer, established management as a science in the principles of scientific management (c. 1911). He advocated that there was only "one best way" to perform any task, including organizing. He believed in pay for performance or payment by units produced. He emphasized efficiency as derived from time-and-motion studies.
	• Max Weber (c. 1920) developed a set of principles about organizational structure that optimized efficiency and effectiveness-bureaucracy: (1) fixed and official job responsibilities, following an SOP; (2) a clear division of labor; (3) the hierarchy or rank-order; (4) job-related criteria for personnel decisions; (5) uniformity and impersonality without regard to person; (6) work as a full-time occupation. He was the first to tie the Protestant work ethic to capitalism in *The Protestant Ethic and the Rise of Capitalism*.
	• Luther Gulick and Lyndall Urwick (c. 1937) introduced a form of management into the public system; that is, new-profit systems. In *Paper Towards the Science of Administration* they delineated seven organizational activities: planning, organizing, staffing, directing, coordinating, reporting, and budgeting. These "functions" differed sharply from those proposed for management by Henre Fayol in 1926: planning, organizing, staffing, directing, controlling, and evaluation.
Assumption	The "one best way" is a formal structure that maximizes effectiveness and efficiency. Human beings are measured as machines.
Emphasis	The formal structure of the organization is by universal principles.
Motivation	All reward is economic. Human beings are "economic animals" that respond to punishment and reward, hope, and fear.
Management Style	The only way to "get work done through people" is by command and control. The style is termed "top-down" or "authoritarian."
Conflict	Conflict within the organization is inefficient, so must be eliminated. Policies and rules stipulate accepted behavior. Discipline is severe.
Environment	All external factors are irrelevant. The activity of the corporation is its own context.
Change	Change is non-productive. Stasis is best for maximum efficiency. Future depends on today's work.

Exhibit 8 (continued)

	SOCIAL
Theories of Human Behavior	• Originated with Robert Mayo in the early 1900's. He believed (1) humans are "vital machines" but (2) they are distinct from mechanical devices because (3) they are susceptible to motivation by external factors.
	• Mary P. Follett, an educator, was the bridge between the scientific (classical) and the humanistic philosophies. She advocated specialization and coordination, but she believed that organizations are evolving, not static. She was interested in the psychology of individual workers, and considered authority two-way, not just top-down.
	• Elton May conducted the now-famous Hawthorne experiments at Western Electric Lighting (1924–1932). He concluded that change always has a positive effect on production—at least temporarily. Beyond that, the studies highlighted the impact of seven anticipated social influences on workers.
	• Chester Barnard wrote *Functions of the Executive* (1930), a study of human relations in the organization. He believed that the interaction of individuals creates an informal organization that continues without purpose and is not governed by or affected by the formal structure. Unwritten rules emerge; social beings form informal groups; interaction produces group norms.
Assumption	The "one best way" is through groups; that is, any contact not in job descriptions or the organizational chart. Behavior is often irrational but is subject to group pressure.
Emphasis	The effects of individual behavior on organizational behavior must be recognized. There is a need to identify the processes and norms of the group and to be aware of the social and psychological influences on individuals and the group.
Motivation	The best motivator is job satisfaction.
Management Style	Management is a two-way process. Interested and concerned managers, through creating job satisfaction, increase performance.
Conflict	Conflict is prevented by organizational goals being accepted by all. The key is socialization and training.
Environment	The corporate society is self-identifying. External factors are minimal.
Change	Change can produce gains but only because of the effort it has on the social and psychological aspects of individuals and groups.

Source: Author.

Exhibit 9
Theories of Human Organization

<table>
<tr><td></td><td colspan="1" style="text-align:center">HUMAN RELATIONS</td></tr>
<tr><td>Theories
of Human
Behavior</td><td>

• Abraham Maslow published *Hierarchy of Needs*. The thesis was that motivation is based on five needs, and that the needs exist in an order of urgency: safety and security, economic, social (belonging), self-esteem, and self-actualization. Each must be fulfilled before progression to the next level; a satisfied need is not a motivator.

• Chris Argyris, a sociologist (1950–1960), explained that any organization based on the principles of the scientific model will inevitably have conflict between the interests of the individual and the interests of the organization.

• Douglas McGregor identified two "leadership" (management styles) that he termed Theory X and Theory Y. He suggested a matrix, from 1 to 10. The first held that people, if left to their own devices, are lazy, gullible, and self-centered and must be controlled. The second believed people to be inherently creative, self-motivated, innovative, and self-controlled. In 1981, William G. Ouchi took the X-Y matrix to a new dimension with Theory Z, a participatory management style practiced in Japan.

• Frederick Hertzberg, a sociologist, studied satisfaction as motivation on organizations; he identified two kinds of motivators—"satisfactors" and "dissatisfactors."

</td></tr>
<tr><td>Assumption</td><td>The "one best way" approach creates conflict between personal and organizational goals.</td></tr>
<tr><td>Emphasis</td><td>Attention must be given to the causes of conflict between personal and organizational goals.</td></tr>
<tr><td>Motivation</td><td>Maslow's hierarchy of needs said it all. In practice, the simultaneous existence of all the needs was overlooked; typically it was understood as ascending steps.</td></tr>
<tr><td>Management
Style</td><td>The Y-Theory was preferred, but not always practiced. "Participate management" became the approach for best decisions. It was never defined.</td></tr>
<tr><td>Conflict</td><td>The conflict is between personal and organizational goals and interests. It had to be overcome if the organization was to be healthy.</td></tr>
<tr><td>Environment</td><td>The organization must be responsible to external factors. Typically, behavioristic principles were followed; reaction, not pro-action.</td></tr>
<tr><td>Change</td><td>Social, economic, technological, and attitudinal change have a critical effect on organization.</td></tr>
</table>

Exhibit 9 (continued)

	CIRCUMSTANTIAL
Theories of Human Behavior	• Herbert Simon (1946) wrote *Proverbs of Administration*, a work that introduced the contingency model of organization. The other previous approaches mixed facts and values, but Simon advocated the separation of facts and values. Specifically, the idea is to distinguish between reality ("what is") and circumstance ("what ought to be"). This approach necessitated information and insights from all relevant disciplines—economics, sociology, psychology, and history. Peter Drucker was heavily influenced by this philosophy.
Assumption	There is no "one best way." All organizations are different and variable, so there is no pat answer.
Emphasis	The organization is a series of related parts (atomistic), all interacting in various ways and yet composing a system. Focus must be on the entire organization. Each organization is unique, so it must be understood on its own terms.
Motivation	Motivation is different from organization to organization, and from individual to individual.
Management Style	There is no set requirement for effective management. Rather, it is important to stress the process of decision making, not who the manager is.
Conflict	Conflict is inevitable. The response will be dictated by the circumstance.
Environment	External factors are important. They must be responded to in a manner that is consistent with the situation.
Change	Change is inevitable. There are two kinds: incremental and cataclysmic. The only explanation is that people change slowly, conditions suddenly.

Source: Author.

Consultative

1. Traditional organization
2. Most knowledge at top
3. All contextual knowledge at top
4. Some specialized knowledge at points throughout organization
5. It is all right to ask subordinates for advice (consultants)
6. Final decision made by manager

Democratic

1. Complicated, layered organizational structure (many dotted lines; gerrymandering)

Exhibit 10
Management Styles

AUTHORITARIAN   CONSULTATIVE   PARTICIPATORY   DEMOCRATIC   LAISSEZ-FAIRE

— — — — — — — — — — — — — — — — — — —

Source: Author.

2. Decision by majority rule
3. Characterized by special interests
4. No focus on common interests
5. Separation into winners and losers
6. Ideal conditions for autocrat

Laissez-Faire
1. Systems and people need to be left alone
2. Both will take care of themselves

The participatory management style was somewhat more complicated, probably because it was basically a contradiction of terms, so it was never actually settled, either in theory or in practice. However, a constructivist version includes the five assumptions that were common to most variations.

- The person doing the job knows more about it than anyone else.
- That which is strategic must be validated by the operational; that which is operational must have strategic context in order to be significant.
- Authority, accountability, and information are commensurate.
- Decisions are made at the point and time of action.
- Issues are decided by "consensus."

Unfortunately, none of these assumptions could be realized in the corporation-model organization. Management had promised something the organization could not deliver. First, the corporation-model organization could not assume that the person doing the job was the expert because it refused to invest in the ultimate development of capacity. Expertise was judged by how closely the person followed the prescribed duties of the job, thus was limited to what the prescriber(s) knew. There was virtually no opportunity for building capacity beyond the present requirements of the job.

Second, seldom did the corporation-model organization create an understanding of the relationship between the strategic plan and the actions of the various departments and individuals. It was not uncommon, even in the most progressive systems, to find that most individuals could not specifically relate their job to the strategic intent of the system. Many worked in a kind of benign isolation, unable to judge the effectiveness of their own performance because they had no idea of its impact on the system's goals.

Third, as long as authority was the first consideration, neither information nor accountability had much meaning. Information was invariably either too little or too much—both have the effect of confusion. And accountability was artificially forced by irrelevant standardized and centralized behavioristic evaluation methodologies. None of the three was consistent with the others.

Fourth, decisions at the point and time of action were high-risk ventures, simply because no one could be sure that the person doing the job really was competent to perform in this fashion. Second-guessing invariably followed any attempt at on-time, on-site decisions.

Fifth, "consensus," in practice, degenerated into majority rule. The strange term "majority consensus" became common terminology for decisions that were made by a majority vote supported, or at least acquiesced to, by the minority. The phase "I don't agree, but I will go along" became the indicator of consensus.

ARTIFACTUAL VS. NATURAL ORGANIZATION

During the last decade of the twentieth century, much was made of the distinction between the traditional organization and the patterns and designs that new-age philosophers thought they were observing in nature. The flocking of birds, the spiraling of galaxies, and the dancing of quanta held a special fascination. The more philosophical of them artifactured a "new science" that professed to reveal the hidden secrets of natural order, with the indefatigable assumption that artifactual systems could be energized by the emulation of these natural phenomena, often stated as natural laws. For the most part, corporation-model organizations ignored the prophet-scientists, although several companies and institutions did flirt with the ideas in seminars, workshops, and symposia.

Perhaps the simplest, as well as the most dramatic, way to contrast contemporary artifactual organization and natural organization is through a point-by-point contrast (see Exhibit 11).

So completely foreign to the artifactual was the natural that corporation-model systems acknowledged only three of the eight characteristics as valid, and even those were adapted to the corporation structure. *Co-opetition* was actually the title of a somewhat popular book that advocated cooperating with competitors in order to gain shared market advantage—a sort of poor man's merger, or a wise man's ploy to avoid an anti-trust suit. The *qualitative* aspect was quantified by tech-

Exhibit 11
Contrasting Philosophies of Organization

CORPORATION-MODEL ORGANIZATION	NATURAL ORGANIZATION
• Construction	• Formation
• Purpose: to produce wealth	• Purpose: to serve the greater good
• Materialistic	• Spiritual
• Scarcity	• Abundance
• Surviving	• Thriving
• Competition	• Co-opetition
• Quantitative	• Qualitative
• Interactive	• Relational

Source: Author.

niques derived from operational research, and *relationships* were in some cases personalized, but they were still based on rigid authority and rank order.

Yet that should not be surprising. The unnatural has a natural aversion to the natural.

TRADITIONAL ORGANIZATION VS. EMERGING ORGANIZATION

It also is instructive to consider the contrasts in the dynamics of the organizations. Here again the inherent difference lends itself to a point-by-point contrast. However, the distinction is often a matter of degrees, varying with each point. The "crosswalks" in Exhibit 12 indicate the continuous movement along each point of contrast. Yet, even so, each organization will have a dominant personality reflecting its disposition toward persons within the system and well known by those outside. The

Exhibit 12
Traditional Organization vs. Emerging Organization

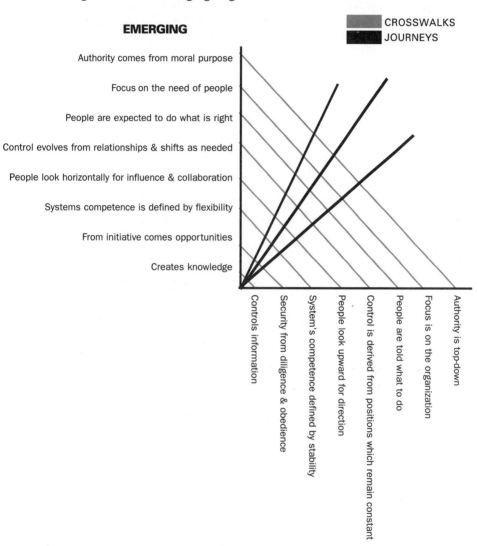

Source: Dr. Gerrita Postlewaite. Reprinted with permission.

"journeys" signify either actual practice or intent; all systems move along a specific azimuth.

The best way to dramatize the contrast between these two philosophies as well as to indicate the transitions necessary to move from one to the other is through a simple diagram (see Exhibit 12). No elaboration is necessary, since the language, as well as the experiences, is quite common.

Part II

Strategic Planning

Chapter 8

The Definition
of Strategic Planning

Typically, in modern organizations, commercial or non-profit, the larger concept of strategy is reduced to a strategic planning process. Often the attempt is without the benefit of strategic thinking and, even more frequently, there is little diligence given to realizing the plan. It is in that rather narrow, even stunted context that most systems ostensibly create their future. There is no end to the variety of approaches to strategic planning, because there are as many definitions of it as there are experts. So strategic planning currently takes many forms: from brief encounters with excessive data to prepackaged prototype plans delivered via the Internet to burdensome and tedious academic exercises conducted in official "planning centers" by fashionable gurus. In the most complex processes, especially those employed by institutions, there is an endless accumulation of information, overanalysis, little synthesis, and no action. Strategic plans occupy considerable shelf space.

Strategic planning, if it is true to the original concept, and if it is to have the power of the original idea, can have only one definition: *it is the method by which a community continuously creates artifactual systems to serve extraordinary purpose*. That definition is so important that it deserves some elaboration, word by word. The significance of each will be made clear in the discussions of the process and discipline, so here a brief note on each will suffice.

Method signifies that strategic planning is not an end within itself. It is to be judged only by the results it produces, therefore it cannot be so rigid that it must be served, instead of its serving the purpose.

Community is the place (metaphorically) in which one sees himself or herself reflected back. It is the reflection of a common core of values that transcends anything that would otherwise separate.

Continuously implies that strategic planning is not an event; it is, in fact, a way of life, the only way of life. It is not a project to be completed; it is not a series of plateaus and valleys. Rather, it is a process of continuous discovery.

Creates captures the power of strategy to actually bring about systems that are not just new in time, but especially new in kind. This word has no prefix (as in "re-creates"), indicating that strategic planning is not to be about re-doing a system, but imagining and effecting something completely different.

Artifactual systems simply admits that any construct arising from planning is merely an expedient; none is a permanent fixture. And it is expected that their life will be limited to their usefulness.

Extraordinary purpose states the only reason for strategy. That reason is the commitment to unprecedented possibilities. It is a tribute both to intuition and boldness. It compels the development of extraordinary capacities, and so it always calls forth the best in all persons involved in the pursuit.

Furthermore, the overriding assumption is the acknowledgment of the basic law of systems, that is, no external forces or factors can bring about positive change or improvement of any kind. They can do harm, but no good. Strategic planning must be impelled by the realization that the future of any system depends strictly on its own internal motivation, perspective, and commitment. Therefore, strategic planning is not really an option and certainly not a luxury. It will occur even by denial. Having no strategic plan is, in fact, a strategic plan.

It would be presumptuous to suggest that there is a single best methodology for strategic planning. True, there are some inviolable principles if credibility is to be maintained and desired results achieved. So the protocols discussed here allow for variations and latitude to accommodate the unique situation of every planning organization. And, consistent within industry types, the real determining factor is the maturity of the organization in question. For example, in North America today, organizations range from medieval feudal orders to new-age jazz.

But it does seem that all eventualities may be addressed through a basic protocol that can serve both *maturing* organizations—those that have a legacy of traditional corporation-model structures and management practices that have historically been context-driven but that are seriously contemplating the freedom of a completely new system, and *mature* organizations—those that already are operating with capacities exceeding current demand, that have long since abandoned corporation-model structures, and are strictly values-driven. This protocol is not for traditional organizations that only want to improve the existing system.

Strategic planning requires a willingness to give up anything and every-thing about the existing system to achieve the extraordinary purpose.

This approach, which is intended to be the *Omega* Protocol—the ulti-mate in strategy—will not be altogether unfamiliar to students and prac-titioners of strategic planning. Many of the components and much of the vocabulary are used in virtually all current methodologies. However, here the attempt is made to return those features to the original context of "strategy"—before it was watered down by modern interpretation, thus most are significantly redefined. Therein lies the power. It is useful to discuss this protocol in its two dimensions: the *discipline*—that is, the plan, and the *process*—that is, how the plan is developed. Of course, there is a process in the discipline and much discipline in the process; and, of course, neither can occur without the other. Yet, for understanding, it is best to discuss each separately.

Chapter 9

The Discipline of a Strategic Plan

Nothing creative happens until energy is forced into a discipline. That is the only purpose of discipline. The discipline recommended here is basically a rational, completely integrated construct, yet it is designed to generate innovation, creativity, and radicalism. In a larger context, when the discipline is combined with the process, there are actually three disciplines working together: the intellectual discipline of the ideas themselves; the discipline of time; and the discipline of subordination of special interest. The intellectual discipline is conceptual but eminently practical. It has twelve components.*

√*Beliefs*: A statement of the organization's fundamental convictions, values, and character. (This component differs from the others in two ways: it is a formation, not a construct; and it is more emotional than rational.)

√*Mission*: A broad statement of the organization's identity, the unique purpose to which the organization is committed, and the basic means of accomplishing that purpose.

√*Parameters*: Strict pronouncements that establish the boundaries, limits, and

---

*The terminology used here, while not cast in bronze, seems to communicate most effectively the idea behind and within each part of the plan. However, should local preference dictate alternative terms, the original ideas must remain intact, as described in the following text. And if changes in the words are to be made, they must be made at the outset of the planning process.
√The check marks indicate that these components (1) are developed by complete agreement and (2) constitute the published plan. If the other components are published, it is as an appendix to the plan.

rules within which the organization will accomplish its mission; self-imposed restrictions that position the organization among others similar to it.

Strengths: Internal assets or characteristics that contribute to the ability of the organization to achieve its mission.

Weaknesses: Internal liabilities or inadequacies that limit the ability of the organization to achieve its mission.

Organizational Design: The arrangement of actions and relationships within an enterprise.

Competition: Any entity that attempts to provide the same goods, products, and services to the same clientele as the planning organization.

External Analysis: An examination of those forces over which an organization has little or no control. External change usually impacts an organization by virtue of its existence in larger, sometimes more complex, circumstances.

Critical Issues: Those factors that compel the choice of either radical change or extinction.

√*Objectives*: An expression of the desired measurable, observable, or demonstrable results for the organization.

√*Strategies*: The broadly stated means of deploying resources to achieve the organization's mission and objectives.

√*Action Plans*: The explicit portion of a given strategy that outlines the tasks and actions required to realize the strategy, and an analysis of the benefit and costs for each specific action plan.

If strategic planning is to achieve its potential of creating new realities, each of these components must be understood in non-traditional ways, and that requires taking the ideas to their ultimate meaning and then discovering the significance of that meaning within the planning enterprise.

BELIEFS

It was pointed out in the section dealing with motivation that the driving force in all human systems is values. Further, a distinction was made between values based on need and those based on conviction. It was also suggested that in strategic systems the value system translates into that system's culture, and that from culture arises the legitimate leaders. So the statement of beliefs establishes the moral dimension of the plan, energizes the planning process, and provides ground zero for strategy. These beliefs *are the fundamental, deep, and abiding convictions* of those who make up the system, principles they will never compromise, matters of conscience. Obviously, no organization, *per se*, has convictions. So the beliefs are not intended to be an institutional creed or credo, nor a litmus test for membership; nor are they to be a fabricated, public relations, image-building pretense. The beliefs are merely the values held by the actual people who make up the organization. The beliefs are not a construct; they are the acknowledgment of a formation already present. In this way, the statement of beliefs is different from all of the other components of the discipline. The others are, by nature, constructs and inventions. The statement of beliefs is the formal expression of the organization's fundamental values: its ethical code, its overriding convictions, its inviolable moral commitments. Essentially, it describes the character of the system. That means that the statement of beliefs of an organization must represent a composite, a distillation, of the personal values of those who make up the organization. The fact is that every organization has a distinctive value system, even though it may not be formally articulated, perhaps not even admitted. However, the statement of beliefs should not be merely an acknowledgment of what the organization is in practice but an expression of what it is at its best. Beliefs are, in fact, moral imperatives.

In order to ensure that the beliefs are stated as an absolute imperative, they must be phrased with the use of a relative pronoun, that is, "We believe *that*"—never, "We believe *in*." The use of the preposition calls for an object that is, more or less, an abstraction or a general idea that can be intellectually accepted, but without any particular compulsion to act upon it. For example, "We believe in freedom" does not carry the necessary imperative of "We believe that freedom is worth defending at any price." Typically, although there is no numerical requirement, in a statement of beliefs, the phrase "We believe that" will be completed with twelve to fifteen clauses, stated as separate propositions.

The statement of beliefs serves a dual purpose: First, it will provide the value system upon which the subsequent portions of the plan will be developed and evaluated; second, it will, as part of the published plan, become a public declaration of the organization's heart and soul. With regard to the first, without a common core of values, all discussions become issue-driven. The disputants come forearmed and ready for combat, and settlement is reached only by force or compromise. But once mutual values are established, there is no issue that cannot be concluded at the highest common denominator. Settlement or compromise occurs at the lowest common denominator. Agreement is achieved only at the highest. With regard to the second, the statement of beliefs will provide clear and uncompromising tenets of the organization's character and, consequently, its conduct.

The phrase "common core of values" is significant. It is not the intent that those in the organization be conformed to some rigid ideology or dogma but that they realize a common bond that transcends anything that would otherwise separate them. Their allegiance, therefore, is not as much to principles as to each other. Graphically, it may be explained like this:

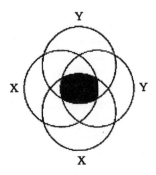

Source: Author.

The extremes of "X" and "Y" still exist, but in harmony. The common core of values is the center that holds the system together. If it does not hold, then no organization can survive, much less create a future.

Experience dictates that it is necessary to warn against a quick, superficial treatment of beliefs. Therefore, there must be adamant insistence that beliefs be stated as precise and absolute moral imperatives. Sometimes it helps to explain things by what they are not. So it is with beliefs. They are often confused with four other imposters. First, beliefs are not platitudes. Admittedly, this is a difficult matter because of the cultural weight attached to any declaration. What is a platitude in one context may be a serious, substantial conviction in another. Technically, the only determining factor is the passion with which the statement is imbued. In many cases, the only difference is passion. That is not to suggest, however, that any belief statement should be judged in any context other than its own. Nevertheless, some statements are suspect even in the context of their own organization. For example:

- We believe that employees are an asset.
- We believe that people are important.
- We believe that humanity prospers when people work together.
- We believe that excellence is necessary to compete.
- We believe that all people have talents.

None of these are specific enough, absolute enough, or compelling enough to qualify as anything but warm and fuzzy pronouncements. Phrases and words like "an asset," "important," "necessary," and "have talents" are much too vague to have substantial meaning and, so, could hardly be expected to rise to the level of conviction.

Second, beliefs are not mere observations or descriptions of the real world. They are not reports on the condition of the world, business, or human nature. Rather, they are expressions of the ideal character of those who make up the organization. Quite often, this distinction is difficult to understand. For example, suppose someone says, "I believe that everyone deserves to live in a peaceful environment." There is an immediate thought of challenge, because in the real world not all people live in a safe environment. Yet that fact does not negate the belief, which raises an interesting point: if an idea can be proved, then it is no longer a belief; it is not a matter of faith, but a matter of fact. For example, "We believe that broad, informed participation committed to a common good is critical to democracy." Experience has proved that allegation. This is where absolute statements are particularly necessary. For instance, "We believe that people are motivated by self-interest" is an observation, but, "We believe that each person is motivated *primarily* by self-interest" is a belief. Beliefs can have no qualification, no hedge.

Third, beliefs are not enterprise specific; that is, they are not about the business at hand, either specifically or generically. Rather, they are so profoundly personal and universal in application that they would easily transfer into any individual or collective endeavor anywhere. For example, "We believe that all people have equal worth" would be significant as a moral imperative in any setting, under any circumstance. While "We believe that customer service is the key to our success" is a business tactic, understood in a specific context, that statement does raise a point, however. Metaphors ("key") must not be used; they are too ambiguous and subject to many interpretations. Explicit language is the only assurance of accurate communication.

Finally, beliefs are not stated as prescriptions or even as advice. For example, "We believe that we should treat everyone with respect," or "We believe that diversity strengthens society and should be honored and protected." Those statements are merely an implication of a fundamental, bedrock conviction that can be discovered only by asking "Why?" The answer would probably constitute the belief. The word cue is "should," "must," or "ought"—all of which indicate some desired response, but without an understanding of the moral precept underlying the imperative. If the moral imperative can be identified, it will manifest itself in any situation, not just in the limited context of the statement. Beliefs are the ultimate why. By the way, the first example above demonstrates the problem inherent in compound clauses. Beliefs are terse, pithy postulates.

With the caveat that no belief can be judged outside of the context of those who hold it, these are examples of actual statements developed in corporate planning sessions.

- We believe that nothing worthwhile is achieved without risk.
- We believe that fairness is more important than justice.
- We believe that every individual has the right to be treated fairly.
- We believe that loyalty is earned and is reciprocal.
- We believe that personal well-being is based on commitment to God, family, and community.

MISSION

The idea of mission is certainly neither new nor uncommon. It is as old as strategic planning itself, as reflected by its long legacy of use in military operations, both ancient and contemporary. So it should not be surprising that when the word is applied in non-military contexts, distortion is likely. In both corporate and institutional application, several distracting myths have risen lately about mission statements. Each represents not only some basic misunderstanding of the idea but also a willingness to compromise the powerful strategic effect of a legitimate mission on the total system. For example, some planners mandate that mission statements must be short. But brevity is never a requirement; completeness is. Or they say, "Mission statements must be memorizable." Why? In practical application, mission statements may be used in a variety of forms. For example, it may be appropriate to feature only the purpose—almost as a motto. Finally, the experts declare, "Mission statements must be immediately understood." Nothing could be further from the truth. If a mission can be understood upon first reading, it obviously is not a transformational concept. If people recognize it, they are already there.

The truth is that the mission statement is simply a clear, concise expression of the organization's intended identity, purpose, and means. Always written in one sentence (one sentence—one concept), the statement should reflect both the clarity of thinking and the threefold sight characteristic of leaders (foresight, insight, and hindsight). While the mission statement must obviously acknowledge the real world, that must not limit the aspiration and commitment to the ideal. The mission statement should not be merely a description of the status quo, but rather a bold declaration of what the organization intends to be. In that sense, the mission creates and declares a new reality.

Above all else, the mission statement must represent the identification of and the commitment to the special distinctiveness, uniqueness, one-of-a-kindness, and originality that will set the enterprise apart from others in the same class. If an organization cannot identify its uniqueness, it probably cannot justify its existence. If another organization can use its mission, one of them is unnecessary. That means that all of the options available to the organization must be seriously deliberated and a single identity agreed upon. That is, in fact, the only way to metamorphosis.

The mission statement, like beliefs, serves two purposes—one in the planning process, the other in the application of the plan. In the first place, if the beliefs are the foundation, then the mission is the keystone upon which the entire plan depends. Everything else in the plan flows from it and must be judged by it, but everything else also judges it. Because, until all of the remaining portions of the plan come together to prove the efficacy of the mission statement, it is at best tentative. In short, the mission tests the plan. The plan tests the mission. The planning process also must incorporate this mutual validation.

The second purpose of the mission statement is obvious. In application, in practice, it serves to focus all of the organization's attention and to concentrate all of its energies on one common purpose. The mission is the one thing that should be known and eventually understood by every person in the organization, otherwise, how can anyone make any sense out of his or her job or other actions? There is simply no way to measure or describe the enormous positive impact that the knowledge of the strategic intent by all of those in the system can and will have on an enterprise. That will be realized only through strategic action.

Unfortunately, no one so far has been able to say for sure what the following actual mission statement means, much less what action it mandates; the only thing that could result from this sentence fragment is a quizzical warm glow. It was written by a professional educational association. The best analysis of it is: meaning everything, it means nothing. It is a sad example of words in search of meaning.

Mission Statement

A diverse, international community of educators, forging convenants in teaching and learning for the success of all learners.

Quite on the other hand, a meaningful mission statement for a school district might read as follows:

The Mission of X Public Schools, a pioneer in academic excellence passionately committed to lifelong learning, is to ensure that each student in our diverse population achieves his or her fullest potential in a safe and affirming learning center characterized by an extensive, student-focused collaboration of all segments of the community, with an emphasis on preparing students to live and excel in a global environment.

The mission statement of a corporation might be written as follows:

The mission of (name of organization) a land-based development and operating company, dedicated to its inherent vision of boldly shaping the future, is to create extraordinary value for shareholders, employees, and communities through the responsible stewardship of all resources and an array of synergistic family-oriented products and services, with emphasis on travel and tourism, commercial and residential real estate, while adhering to the highest standards of family values, ethics, professionalism, and quality.

Or, it might be as simple as:

The mission of the XYZ corporation, the nation's premier confederation of independent manufacturer-retailers of apparel, is to create optimal stockholder wealth through the manufacturing and distribution of high-fashion women's shoes through independently owned and operated retail outlets throughout the United States.

The three parts of the mission are obvious. The distinctive *identity* means that the enterprise has resisted the temptation to be all things to all people or to pursue random targets of opportunity; rather, it will limit its actions strictly to those that strengthen identity. This is not a matter of finding a "niche," as commonly supposed, for survival. It is a matter of creating an indispensable, unique identity toward which all energies can be concentrated. Only in that way is it possible to thrive. The *purpose* clearly states the reason the enterprise exists. In the education example, the purpose was (is) to guarantee student success, achievement, or performance. In the business examples, the only purpose, of course, is the creation of stockholder wealth. The *means*, in either case, becomes the critical attributes of the system of delivery or production. Quite often, the uniqueness of the enterprise is elucidated by these individual features themselves, or by combination.

Everything else in the plan will be predicated on the mission, and everything about the organization will be dedicated to it. The mission is the basis of all decisions, all allocations, all evaluations, and all measures of success.

PARAMETERS

Strategic parameters or policies are often overlooked in contemporary planning exercises, but they must be an essential part of the plan. In a sense, they have the effect of strategies—only in reverse. Rather than expanding, they focus; rather than prompting initiatives, they restrict action; rather than creating exposure, they limit possibilities. Parameters are strategic boundaries, limitations the organization places upon itself for good reason. They are the boundaries within which the organization will operate; they are the things the organization either will never do or will always do. Such parameters are strategic because they have the effect of positioning the organization against others in the same general classification.

Stated usually in the negative, parameters provide a kind of security alarm system to warn the organization when it is about to do something either unwise or dangerous. Stated sometimes in the positive, parameters are the imperatives that keep the organization true to itself. Parameters, as defined here, are not traditional board policies, nor routine, operational, administrative, or management rules and procedures. They are not laws or regulations handed down from the state or federal government. In short, they are not restrictions externally or internally imposed on an organization, and they are not a bilious recitation of the obvious. Rather, they are specific, rigid, self-imposed limitations. For example:

- We will not do business with communist countries.
- We will always promote from within the organization.
- We will never compromise safety.
- The debt-equity ratio will not exceed 1:3.
- We will not employ or retain persons who do not subscribe to and practice our beliefs.

There are certain requirements to be met in developing a parameter. First, the parameter must be enforceable and controllable; second, it must be absolutely definitive in its terms; third, it must represent practicality (in any matter, the organization's last practice—not what is written—constitutes its policy).

The notion of parameters is quite often difficult to grasp by planners, but if properly conceived, parameters are a critical part of the strategic plan. In fact, in their own way, they have the effect of strategy. They can establish "ground rules"; set in place protective mechanisms, ratios, standards, formulas, and the like; dictate codes of behavior; define or limit expectations; assert priorities; and define various modes of operation. Taken together, parameters have the effect both of focusing the mission statement and of preventing overzealous pursuit thereof.

INTERNAL ANALYSIS

Strictly speaking, both the internal analysis and the external analysis are as much a part of the planning process as of the planning discipline. While they are not normally included in the final published plan—except, perhaps, as an appendix—they must be considered here as a prerequisite to developing the objectives and strategies, which are the essence of the plan. In fact, it is not unusual for the strategies to be direct responses to these analyses.

That means that honesty is foremost. Complete objectivity, of course, is necessary throughout the entire planning process, but it is extremely critical in making these analyses. A failure at this point to deal with all of the issues openly and frankly will severely detract from the credibility, if not the validity, of the final plan. Forthright analyses produce not only valid objectives and strategies, they also demonstrate the organization's sincerity. The internal analysis consists of a thorough, unbiased, tripartite examination of the enterprise: specifically, its *strengths, weaknesses,* and the *organizational design* as it reflects decision making and information flow.

STRENGTHS

Strengths are defined as those internal qualities, assets, or conditions that contribute to the organization's ability to achieve its mission— those things that can be capitalized on, that reflect the best of the system. For that reason, not only should those strengths that directly relate to the existing mission be considered here but also any other particular attribute that the organization has accrued. That is to say, emphasis should not be on strengths that are comparable to other like organizations but primarily those strengths belonging only to the planning organization.

A recognition of strengths is important in planning because it signals to the organization the areas in which success may be most easily compounded. Real strengths represent achievement and, therefore, are testimony to the organization's ability to perform, as well as its potential for even greater achievement. In fact, excellence is nothing more than strength pursued to its ultimate. The strengths are listed as briefly as clarity and precision will allow. Examples from a corporate plan illustrate the wide range of possibilities for factors judged to be strengths.

- Borrowing potential
- Location of facilities
- Earnings stream
- Condition of physical properties
- Commitment and productivity of employees
- Diverse group of businesses
- Reputation of integrity

- Strong customer service program
- Postured to dominate marketplace

Examples from an actual educational system illustrate the subtle but very significant difference between non-profit and commercial enterprises.

- Excellent fiscal management
- High student achievement measured by test scores
- Exemplary special educational programs
- Affirmative Action Plan
- Rapport with State Department of Education
- Excellent employee benefits
- Numerous scholarships, awards, and recognitions for students
- Parent involvement and support
- Performance-based curriculum

The only restrictions are that the strengths be completely and honestly examined. Quite often, this analysis reveals what the organization does best. In fact, it is always instructive to identify the ten or so greatest strengths for future reference.

WEAKNESSES

The weaknesses of an organization are those internal characteristics, conditions, or circumstances that are impeding or even preventing the realization of the *current* mission. They are, obviously, not the opposite of strengths, although the same item may appear on both lists. Whereas strengths represent achievement, weaknesses usually indicate either a lack of performance or the inability to perform. However, weaknesses are quite often simply the result of benign neglect. Therefore, they are not necessarily a reflection of the current capacity or intent of the organization but either its present priorities or capability.

Actual examples of weaknesses from corporate planning teams illustrate the significance of this inquiry.

- Overdiversification of operations
- Competing with self
- No depth in senior management
- Volume of short-term debt

- High turnover of hourly employees
- Middle management gaps
- Information leaks on sensitive matters
- Weak MIS reporting systems
- Non-producing assets

Actual examples from educational planning teams demonstrate the frankness of the discussions.

- Unclear accountability and responsibility at all levels
- Important decisions made in isolation, without known criteria
- Inequity among buildings (facilities, supplies, books, etc.)
- Unqualified substitute teachers
- Weak communication between administration and local and state government agencies
- Too many special interest groups running their own agenda
- Some people involved in curriculum development not taking an active role or providing active leadership
- Too much dead weight; inconsistent treatment by administrators of inadequate employees
- Low-bid mentality

There is one very important thing to remember about weaknesses: all organizations have them and will continue to have them. The trick is to distinguish between those weaknesses that are tolerable and those that are critical. That is to say, some weaknesses can be, and sometimes must be, lived with; it is a waste of resources to attempt to overcome them. Organizations that attempt to do this are majoring in minors. However, critical weaknesses—those that negatively affect the realization of the mission—must, quite obviously, be identified for correction.

There are two provisos in the development of weaknesses. First, if an issue or a concern is not identified here as a weakness, then it should never be raised again. This should be taken as an opportunity to leave the past behind. Second, weaknesses should not be cast in the form of solutions; any suggestion that begins with "lack of" is a solution and is unacceptably premature.

Contrary to a popular romantic notion, there is no advantage in weakness; the only possible benefit is sympathy. All must be either solved or removed.

CRITICAL ANALYSIS OF ORGANIZATION

The third part of the internal analysis is the critical analysis of organization; that is, a close examination of the organization's internal dynamics, communication, and systems of accountability and authority as reflected in the current organizational design. This critique is not aimed at correcting, merely at determining what is working and what is not. In fact, at this point, "fixes" or solutions are totally inappropriate for this reason: the very last thing that will be done in the planning process is the creation of organization through strategic action.

One of the cardinal principles of strategic action is this: *always organize to the plan; do not plan to the organization.* Translated into practice, this means that organizing cannot properly take place until the final and complete plan is set. Ultimately, the organization will be the natural formation that arises from action, but even so, a thorough critique at this point in the planning process not only identifies the present difficulties that may need to be remedied but also establishes a somewhat philosophical context, if not the rationale, for future organizing. Quite often it leads to the complete abandonment of the traditional structure.

The traditional organizational design, that is, the line-and-staff arrangement, is still the structure of most commercial enterprises as well as all institutions. Even though it may soon be regarded as obsolete, there is much to be learned through a critical analysis—perhaps even why it can no longer work. The analysis must be approached along five avenues: (1) span of control; (2) layers, or verticality; (3) gaps; (4) redundancies; and (5) formality versus informality.

Span of control refers to the number of people or "functions" that report to any one person. The fact is that there is a limit to what a person can effectively manage; beyond that point there is a loss of control. While the old rule of thumb is five to seven subordinates in actual practice, effective span of control is determined by many variables other than numbers. For example, technological capability and applicability; the abilities of both the manager and subordinates; the type of work involved; the geographical spread or the physical layout of the work; and the organization's philosophy of decision making are all factors that influence, and sometimes dictate, span of control. A typical example of the kind of observations that might constitute the critique of span of control is: "The assistant vice president has 31 subordinates reporting directly," or "The director of personnel reports to both the president and the executive vice president."

Layers refers to the number of ranks in the organization, that is, the graduations of authority, from top to bottom. This aspect of an organization is critical because of its intrinsic relationship to decision making. Usually, the more layers the longer the decision-making process. In fact, it is possible through layering to substitute process for decision. When layering is further compounded by 'dotted lines running here and there throughout the organizational chart, there is clear evidence that the organization is not designed with specific authorities for decisions with the accompanying accountabilities, but rather to obscure accountability through deliberate vagueness in individual responsibility, thereby rendering decision making (as well as action) irrelevant. In fact, dotted lines in an organizational chart are a clear indication that the organization does not know what anyone is doing and has, in fact, deliberately confused accountability. Layering must be evaluated strictly in terms of its effect on the action of the organization. Too many layers results in activity, not action. An example of an observation dealing with verticality might be: "The department heads must go through three levels of management for the approval to purchase equipment," or "The maintenance director carries the only key to the supply room."

Gaps and *redundancies* are quite similar in the sense that they both represent the disproportionate application of resources to task. However, they are different in that one indicates too little, the other, too much. Specifically, "gaps" in the organization's arrangement occur when actions vital to the mission are not translated into actual responsibilities, authority, or relationships. That is to say, there is no position charged with the action; there is a person, but he or she lacks the authority to function; or there is a position or a person with appropriate authority, but it or he or she is relegated to ineffectiveness by short-circuited relationships with other parts of the organization. An example of a gap is, "We have no public relations office"; or "Everyone coordinates staff development, so there is no staff development"; or "There is no governmental liaison." Gaps usually are the major cause of "management by swarm"; that is, no one's responsibility is everyone's business.

Redundancies simply means that a job or task is being performed or supervised by more than one person or more than one organizational unit, without good reason. Not only does this result in expensive duplication of effort, it also obscures responsibility and accountability, because anybody's job is nobody's job; or, perhaps more to the point, if two people are equally responsible for the same thing, neither is. In practice, co-responsibility means no accountability. There is no such thing as shared responsibility. In short, redundancy means that a decision is being made more than once, and an activity is being performed more than once, without good reason. A typical actual example of a redundancy is "The affirmative action program is being administered by three offices," or "Each department provides its own training."

The final organizational analysis, *formality vs. informality*, is simply a comparison (or contrast) of the organizational chart and the actual functioning of the organization. The greater the difference, the greater the bureaucracy. There are two signs of dysfunctionality in any traditional organization: committees and "teams," especially "cross-functional" teams. Both are vain, almost ludicrous attempts to overcome the flaws in the formal structure with informal relationships, but neither can work—mostly because of the other.

If the organization follows non-traditional patterns—that is, anything other than a rank-ordered structure—then the critical analysis must be based on the terms implicit within the design. Specifically, that means ascertaining the original intent of the design and determining how well it is fulfilling its promise. In any case, the assessment of the design must be made based on how effectively it concentrates all energies on the mission and objectives of the enterprise. Efficiency will always be the last concern of a truly strategic plan or system.

EXTERNAL ANALYSIS

The external analysis is usually the most revealing part of the planning discipline because it is futuristic—looking into the future for five to ten years; prophetic—foreseeing events and conditions that will occur during that time; and challenging—identifying specific impacts on the organization as a result of those events and circumstances. This analysis is based on the realization that there are, and will be, many external factors over which the planning organization has no control; but that does not mean that these external influences control the organization. That, in fact, is what planning is all about—maintaining control, even in an environment that is out of control.

Stated quite simply, the purpose of the external analysis is to prevent surprises that may negatively affect the organization's ability or opportunity to accomplish its mission. But more than providing mere intelligence about the future, the external analysis may serve as the immediate rationale for the formulation of the strategic commitment of resources. That is to say, the external analysis is not for information only; it quite likely will be a call to action.

If the external analysis is not complete, it is not worthwhile. To be complete for any enterprise, it must deal with at least six categories of influence on the organization, namely: *social; demographic; economic; political; technological and scientific;* and *industry trends and influences.* Each category must be analyzed in terms of its several factors, assumptions made about each factor, and the impact of each assumption calculated. For example, in the social category, one company recently identified thirteen factors: language, music, diverse cultures, family structure, gender roles, communicable diseases, job or careers, leisure time, high technology, morals, religion, entertainment, and wellness.

This raises an interesting point. Most corporate planners have tradi-

Exhibit 13
Economic Factor Analysis: School District

CATEGORY: *Economic*		
Factor	**Prediction**	**Impact**

I. Public School Revenue	I. A. General fund revenue mandated by formula from state
	
	B. Board choice to hold budget/bond election
		I. A. 1. Limits programs
		  2. Limits staff
		  3. Limits supplies/ materials
		  4. Affects class size
		  5. Possible school closures, including busing
		  6. Reduced building maintenance
		
		B. 1. Revenues not guaranteed
		  2. Polarizes community

Source: Author.

tionally thought that the best information on subjects such as this comes only from big research firms or fancy think tanks. Some planners in the public service sector attempt to gather superfluous information from large groups in public hearings, but the fact is that the external analysis needed for practical planning usually is best performed by the professionals within the organization. Most of them know as much about the future as those paid to study it; and their perception of what the future means to the organization has a far more relevant orientation.

The examples provided in Exhibits 13 and 14 demonstrate not only the quality of the analyses typically achieved but also the best format for clarity and effect.

COMPETITION

Somewhat related to the external analysis but deserving its own special attention for planning purposes is the matter of competition. A competitor is defined as any other organization providing the same goods, products, and services to the same clientele in the free marketplace. The analysis of competition at this point in the planning discipline forces the

Exhibit 14
Social/Political Factor Analysis: Corporation

CATEGORY: *Social/Political*		
Factor	**Prediction**	**Impact**
I. Anti-development Sentiment	I. A. Increasing negative attitude toward continued development of XYZ company strand areas B. Forced development at faster pace C. Shareholder education	I. A. 1. New impact fees to be levied 2. Lower density, down-zoning and restrictions on land use 3. Increased regulation 4. More greenspace, more parking, more "space" requirements 5. Increase in property taxes B. 1. Accelerate geographic diversification C. 1. Decrease land values
II. Unskilled Workforce	II. A. Increased shortages of skilled labor; in long run, new training programs	II. A. 1. Shortages for up to five years 2. Higher wages to trained workers 3. Import employees and related costs for travel, housing, crime, and welfare
III. Race Relations	III. A. Will get worse before it gets better due to "flag issues"	III. A. 1. Our location becomes a lightning rod due to its financial impact/influence value to the state tax coffers 2. Tourism will "crash" 3. Industrial growth to be "standoffish"

Source: Author.

organization to acknowledge its relative advantages and disadvantages and, furthermore, to consider the points on which the competition is most vulnerable.

There are two ways to approach an analysis of competition: one rather complicated, the other simple. The more complicated approach first identifies all of the relevant points of comparison and contrast and then looks at each competitor using some sort of value scale. The purpose of this approach is (1) to assess thoroughly the planning organization in terms of its competition so plans can be made to strengthen it against competition and (2) to discover the specific weaknesses of each competitor in the event that the planning organization chooses to develop a marketing plan either to retain or gain market share against a specific competitor. Exhibits 15 and 16 illustrate how such an analysis is typically charted.

The second approach also is very effective, although not quite as thorough or detailed. It simply identifies the competitor by type (or by name) and then lists the advantages of both the competitor and the planning organization, side by side, but not necessarily point for point. Then the competitor's points of vulnerability are listed. This type of analysis is depicted in Exhibit 17.

The analysis of competition provides two specific benefits. First, as a straightforward comparison of the planning organization with others in the same business, it can be the source of real innovation. There is truth in the old adage that competition makes everyone better. Second, the planning organization is more informed about its own position in the marketplace, both current and prospective. However, it must always be remembered that ultimately the only way to overcome competition is through uniqueness. So any analysis that suggests imitation of competition or even the development of standardized industry "benchmarks" or "best practices" is in effect capitulation to dissipation of both effort and quality. Uniqueness cannot be standardized or normed, nor can excellence. Excellence, like uniqueness, is not a matter of comparison; both are matters of contrast.

CRITICAL ISSUES

At this juncture in the planning discipline, quite often it is helpful to identify critical issues, that is, areas in which the institution faces the prospect of getting either much worse or much better. As noted earlier, "crisis" is the point between life and death, success or failure. Critical issues, therefore, are those issues that must be dealt with if the organization is to create itself anew in the context of its own stated mission. Usually these critical issues can be identified only by a thorough recon-

Exhibit 15
Competition Analysis IA

COMPETITION (Education Organization)

Traits					
Size					
Image					
Funding					
Expenditure/Student					
Management					
Quality of staff					
Curriculum					
Co-curricular activities					
Teacher-pupil ratio					
Etc.					

Source: Author.

sideration of the beliefs, the parameters, the internal and external analyses, and the assessment of competition.

Critical issues are the juncture between the planning process and the planning discipline, so they will be examined at some length in the discussion of process, but suffice it here to simply point out that identifying the critical issues focuses attention on the paramount threats and opportunities, thereby providing a compelling rationale for the strategic deployment of resources. Threats are negative and inevitable; in the extreme, they disable or destroy. Opportunities are those blessings of time and circumstance that are uniquely those of the organization because of

Exhibit 16
Competition Analysis IB

COMPETITION (Commercial Corporation)

Traits (Rated 1–5)					
Size					
Image					
Market share					
Profitability					
Management					
Quality of staff					
Products and services					
Growth potential					
Intellectual capital					
Etc.					

Source: Author.

what it is, *where* it is, and *when* it is, and there is always just one best opportunity for truly recreating an organization.

OBJECTIVES

The statement of objectives is the planning organization's commitment to achieve specific end results. The objectives are tied very closely to the mission statement; in fact, they both spring from and define the mission. These are not administrative objectives, operational objectives, or department objectives: they are strategic objectives, and therefore they are

Exhibit 17
Competition Analysis II

COMPETITION: (by type or name)	
Their Advantage	**Our Advantage**
Points of vulnerability:	

Source: Author.

the overarching results that must be pursued by the total organization. Quite simply, the objectives are what the organization must achieve if it is to accomplish its mission and be true to its beliefs. Such objectives are the specification of the mission into results; therefore, they are derived only from the purpose portion of the mission statement.

Corporations or for-profit organizations usually will state the objectives quite simply in financial terms. In fact, in many cases, it may be as simple as specifying the expected or desired return on assets, or return on equity or investment. Others find it useful to calculate various financial equations over a period of time, say five years. That approach is particularly significant in public companies, enterprises that are heavily regulated, or in turn-around situations. And, of course, predicting performance in this way rather than analyzing it after the fact is an extremely prudent discipline. For example, any or all of the measures displayed in Exhibit 18 might be used.

Non-profit organizations have great difficulty writing suitable objectives because they are more process oriented than result oriented. In fact, many universities actually teach administrators to write objectives that are not only process but incremental as well. The reason seems to be a

Exhibit 18
Corporate Objectives Format

	Year 1	Year 2	Year 3	Year 4	Year 5
Return on assets					
Return on equity					
Return on investment					
Earnings per share					
After tax revenue					
Profit					

Source: Author.

genetic resistance to the one requirement of an actual result: that is, it must be measurable, demonstrable, or observable; otherwise it is not an objective but rather a dream or fond hope. The idea of "process objectives" is a figment of an inconsequential imagination. The matter is as simple as an "end-means" analysis; that is, what is the end? And what are the means of achieving it? The means will be stated later as strategies, but it is impossible to know the "how" until the "what" is known. Evidently bureaucratic systems and institutional mentalities that are so accustomed to activity believe that action is itself a result. Or it could be for another reason. Quite obviously, dreams and hopes are not as intimidating as objectives because they incur no risk and contain no built-in demand for responsibility. However, true objectives create risks and impose accountability.

Furthermore, while "process objectives" may be stated in incremental terms (such as an increase each year), real objectives are not. True objectives state the ultimate desired end, without being date specific. The fact is, all objectives are present tense. They cannot be allowed to postpone the future by being post-dated. All objectives have at least two of four possible dimensions (see Exhibit 19).

So the possibilities for objectives are also only four combinations:

Exhibit 19
The Dimensions of Objectives

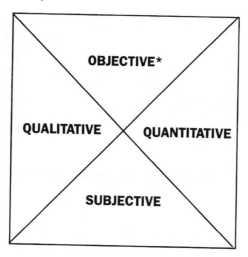

*The adjective *Objective* is used here in the sense of industrial, professional, or artistic criteria, often referred to as "standards," or, in the arts, as "mastery." "Objective" here relates to the object as opposed to subjective, as it relates to the person.
Source: Author.

(1) objective-quantitative, (2) quantitative-subjective, (3) subjective-qualitative, and (4) qualitative-objective. An example of each easily might be taken from the context of educational organization.

1. *Objective-Quantitative*: To have 100 percent of students in the top 10 percent of their peers as measured by any external system.
2. *Quantitative-Subjective*: To have all students achieve their own academic and personal goals.
3. *Subjective-Qualitative*: To have each student live without regret.
4. *Qualitative-Objective*: To have each student possess the highest moral character.

There is one other thing about objectives that is critically important. They must *not* be realistic. This is probably the most misunderstood thing about objectives, probably because of their confusion with "projections." Projections are realistic, proceeding from long-range or comprehensive planning that assumes first a baseline and then attempts to forecast incremental improvements or gains. However, objectives are derived from a strategic mission—a mission that creates a new reality. Therefore, when specified as results, it will be considered unrealistic by those who either do not see or cannot commit to the mission. The best analogy is this: it is the objective of every airline to have 100 percent safe landings. But

Exhibit 20
The Strategic Gap

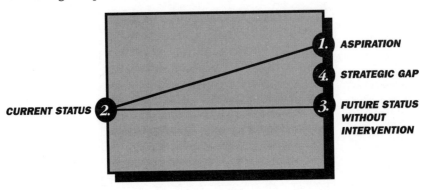

Source: Author.

their actuarial projections may not be so bold. The question is, which is the preferred reality?

STRATEGIES

It is far more than a turn of a phrase to say that strategies make the plan strategic. The strategies not only reveal the organization's commitment to a new reality but also identify the specific means by which that reality will be achieved. Earlier it was pointed out that all organizations have a strategy, even in the absence of a strategic plan; and it is, of course, not uncommon for aggressive, no-nonsense executives to make up strategies on the spur of the moment in response to some specific opportunity or threat, but strategies are much too significant to be addressed without the benefit of the context provided by mission, parameters, objectives, and internal and external analyses. If those components of the plan are properly developed, the strategies will naturally appear. The only question will be just how far the organization will go in displacing the old with the new.

Basically, strategies declare how the organization intends to acquire and deploy resources to accomplish its mission and objectives. Strategies are the significant initiatives that will be undertaken to close the gap between the aspiration and the current situation (see Exhibit 20).

That means that the strategies, taken together, will not deal with all aspects of the organization directly, nor will they address all of the external factors. Comprehensive planning would proceed in that manner, with the expectation that the system will survive intact. But strategies are concerned only with those things about the organization that must be conformed to the new mission and objectives—sometimes that means abandoned—and especially with those initiatives that will bring about a completely new order. In fact, there are two kinds of strategies: *maintenance* (i.e., those that furbish and develop existing actions) and *change* (i.e., those that are intended to create level II, or radical change—metamorphosis).

It is certainly true that the mission, objective, parameters, and strategies provide an entirely new context for every part of any existing organization; everything, even the most insignificant, is affected. However, strategies deal only with those issues that are indeed systemic; they become the context. It is for that reason that strategies are never categorized under each objective. To do so is to sacrifice the strategic to the operational. Further, to fragment the system into unrelated, competing particles, any semblance of a system is lost. It is very unfortunate that some business schools teach a methodology that assigns "strategies" to each objective, but to do so is to invite disaster. Strategies are the system. Each strategy must be significant enough to support and realize all objectives. Only to the degree that the strategies possess inherent power to move the entire organization along to its objectives will the organization enjoy control over its own destiny. No power means no control, and the power must reside in the strategies themselves.

ACTION PLANS

Action plans, as well as their development, are at once both simple and complicated: simple, in the sense that they are the several, assignable tasks that will be necessary to realize the strategy; complicated, because of the tendency to confuse activity with action and because there is more than one kind of action. In the simplest terms, an action plan is an initiative that can be accomplished by individuals or groups as part of their organizational responsibilities. That means every action plan must eventually be translated into personal responsibility. Ultimately, all job accountabilities will be affected by the action plans; and, in many cases, jobs will be radically altered, eliminated, or created. It is not incorrect, in a corporation context, to suggest that action plans are the operational applications of the strategies; and, as with all operational plans, eventually there will be active reciprocity with the strategies.

The complication begins with the necessity of differentiating action and activity. While it seems extremely clear in theory, it becomes confused in application. The guiding principle, however, is quite specific: action is a concentrated effort toward an intended result. Interestingly, that is also the definition of work. Activity is anything else—motion, movement, exercise, any energy consumed by process. The obvious indication of this debilitating condition is "process" objectives.

The second complication, however, is not as easily simplified. At least two kinds of action must be acknowledged. This distinction is ancient, but somehow it has been obscured by both modern scientific management practice and by rationalistic parables of administration. A critical flaw in most systems of strategic planning is that this difference is not taken into account at the outset, but two kinds of action require two kinds of plans. The first interpretation of action is more common. The best example is the instruction sheet contained in, say, a bicycle box. The intended result is specified—even pictured; the best way to achieve the result is explained in step-by-step detail. The action requires no thought beyond the instructions; in fact, the assembler could be completely detached from the outcome because it, like the objective, is purely mechanical.

Unfortunately, the development of even this kind of plan seems somehow contrary to the disposition of most managers. The overpowering urge and practice is to rush to activity without the benefit of planning (fire, ready, aim), and administrators have a proclivity merely to "plan" to plan, thus postponing even activity. But the most obvious action required by strategy deserves to be analyzed in advance. The up-front investment of time and energy will prevent false starts and unintended consequences. In action plans of the first kind, it should be clear that the requisite detailed planning has been done; all that remains is to get on with the implementation. In fact, that is the operative word; these plans are, in fact, *implemented* as prescribed.

While the format of an action plan may vary depending upon content and performance, to be practical it must include at least: (1) specific reference to the strategy it supports; (2) a statement about the result of the action plan itself; (3) a description of each step required to accomplish the plan; (4) an indication of assignments and responsibilities; (5) a time line for the plan; and (6) a cost-benefit analysis. Components 4 and 5 will be completed by management at the beginning of the implementation phase. There is one proviso: an action plan should always allow for on-time, on-site decisions by the implementors. An action plan must not be written so rigidly that it prevents creative thinking at the time of action; nor should it bind the organization to the past—the time the plan was written. Exhibit 21 provides a workable presentation of the ends and means of an action plan as well as a method of assignment and dating progress.

The cost-benefit analysis that accompanies each action plan is extremely important because such an analysis ultimately forces the question of best use of resources and the greatest return on investment. For that reason, the degree of accuracy in predicting costs and benefits is the major factor in validating the entire strategic plan in actual performance. The ultimate question will be, "Did the plan produce what it promised at the cost it projected?"

Exhibit 21
Action Plan Form

STRATEGY NUMBER : ____
PLAN NUMBER: ____
DATE: ____

STRATEGY: _____

SPECIFIC RESULT: _____

#	ACTION STEP (Number each one)	Assigned To:	Starting Date:	Due Date:	Completed Date:

Responsible: [ ]

(Shaded areas for administrative use in implementation phase)

Source: Author.

There is no single best way to format a cost-benefit analysis. Different undertakings require different methods of explanation; all that is required is that the analysis show what the action will require in both tangible and non-tangible investments, and what the tangible and non-tangible return on investment will be. The form displayed in Exhibit 22 is adequate.

Finally, it should be pointed out here that action plans are not to be considered, as some have thought, the actual implementation portion of the planning process. Action plans are plans, and only plans. Developing them does not constitute implementation; having them does not constitute implementation. Neither does talking about them in management meetings from time to time. But it is only by carrying out the plans that the strategies will be realized and the objectives achieved. It is significant that action plans are the *only* component of the strategic plan that will be implemented.

The second kind of action is that for which the specific outcome—therefore, the particular steps to achieve it—cannot be known until the course of the action itself reveals them. If the first kind of action is best described as a *project*, then this type is characterized as a *program*. Here, as in the first, it is expected that the plans will be developed as fully as possible before the action is begun. That is to say, these are not plans to plan. But sometimes the details cannot be determined in advance because of the scope of the program, or should not be because of the progression of variables. Action plans are developed in a relatively short period of time (three months), and therefore quite often information is simply not available to justify decisions about specific actions. So presuming to develop the specifics would be premature, probably superficial. Sometimes the details cannot be worked out in advance, simply because the variable, options, and possibilities are discovered only as one decision or action leads to another. Quite simply, each action provides the basis for the next. That is the reason these plans usually include "go/no-go" steps, or suggest more than one scenario with decision points specified.

Although plans for programs can be developed fully, the description of the action will be obviously less prescriptive than those in project plans. For example, these plans will state the general objective as it is conceptualized at present, establish the criteria of both the final action and the decision-making process leading to it, recommend the types of sources to be used in gathering information, and put into place a date-specific process for activating the program. There are many endeavors that lend themselves to this kind of planning: for example, employee benefits programs, public relations, and customer service. Education systems might use this kind of action planning in matters pertaining to curriculum, safety, and staff development. In short, any undertaking that

Exhibit 22
Cost-Benefit Analysis Form

STRATEGY NUMBER : ____
PLAN NUMBER: ____
DATE: ____

STRATEGY: _____
_____

SPECIFIC RESULT: _____
_____
_____

COSTS	BENEFITS
Tangible:	*Tangible:*
Intangible:	*Intangible:*

(Have you considered opportunity costs?
Does this action plan have sufficient return on investment?)

Source: Author.

Exhibit 23
The Planning Discipline

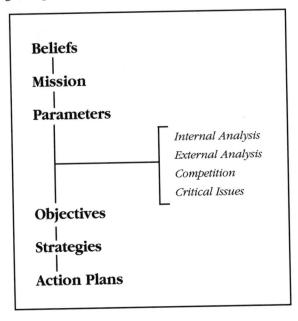

Source: Author.

is intended to create a continuing action—that is, it is not subject to completion—will naturally take the form of this kind of action plan.

With regard to the format of the action plans, the template used in project planning may be also employed here with two differences: the steps will be more expository than prescriptive, and there will be no cost-benefit analysis.

SUMMARY

With the action plans in place, the strategic planning discipline is complete, and the logical, progressive decision making forced by the discipline is obvious: Beliefs, Mission, Parameters (Internal and External Analyses, Competition), Objectives, Strategies, and Action Plans. Taken together, the components of the discipline tell *who, what,* and *how*—who the organization is (Beliefs, Mission, Parameters); what it is up to (Objectives); and how it is going to do it (Strategies and Action Plans). Formatted graphically, the discipline is displayed in Exhibit 23.

If this system appears to be a "model," then it is so only in the near-sighted eye of the beholder. It is, in fact, a fully integrated, dynamic, high-energy discipline by which the future can be created.

Chapter 10

The Strategic Planning Process

This is, no doubt, a somewhat discouraging word, but there are probably more variations of the process of planning currently being practiced than of the discipline. And, although there may be a legitimate philosophical and practical rationale for every approach, not every planning process is immediately transferable, certainly not universally applicable. The fact is that no single, rigid process is appropriate for all situations. However, it is possible to outline a basic design with enough specificity to be eminently productive, yet with enough flexibility to be generally usable. What is needed is a kind of scenario that best combines the immutable principles of planning with the time-proved critical attributes of decision making. Both the principles and the attributes are certain; together they will validate the process.

The principles must include:

(1) Reciprocity between the strategic and the operational. This does not mean that the plan is developed top-down, but that in any system that which is strategic must be justified by that which is operational; and the operational must have strategic context in order to be meaningful.

(2) Focus on results and outcomes. The object of strategic planning is always to reduce or eliminate the lag time between the idea and the action. A plan that does not instigate action is not a plan; it is a study, report, or review.

(3) The relationship between ends and means. This is perhaps the most difficult principle to grasp, yet simply states the old adage, "If you don't know where you are going, any direction will do." Institutions have a particular difficulty with this principle because activity usually is not directed toward any result. Ends are always measurable or observable;

they are the outcomes to be accomplished. Means always serve the ends.

(4) *Implementability is the final test of any plan.* If the plan cannot be taken immediately into action, without further planning, then it is not a plan but, at best, a recommendation. However, it is not enough just to develop plans that are implementable; the process itself must be enduring enough to ensure that the actions not only actually occur but also are evaluated for effect.

The attributes of decision making, while ultimately the reflection of the philosophy of the planning organization, must be based on ideals rather than rules. They become the assumptions undergirding the process. For example, it must be assumed that:

(5) *The person doing any job knows more about the job than anyone else.* If that is not the case, there is a likelihood that the misplacement or lack of expertise will erode the reliability of the plan. It also strongly suggests that the organization at the time may be too weak internally to create an authentic strategic plan. Planning must be based on knowledge, and knowledge comes only from actual experience.

(6) *Agreement by all involved is necessary for any plan to have staying power.* Acceptance is not enough. Certainly the current definition of consensus as majority will over minority acquiescence does not constitute agreement. In strategic decision making there must be no winners and no losers, but everyone must experience gain. Specifically, the six components of the plan—beliefs, mission, parameters, objectives, strategies, and action plans—must be matters of full agreement. If there is no agreement, there will be no commitment.

(7) *Methodologies for decision making must be understood by all of those involved.* For example, there is the traditional rational decision-making model: identify the problem; analyze the situation; set an objective; explore alternative courses of action; examine obstacles and adverse consequences; and reach a conclusion. Creative problem solving may involve any of a number of non-linear thought processes, such as divergent thinking, convergent thinking, lateral thinking, excursion, synthesis, and brainstorming.

It is always helpful if those involved in planning understand simple logic, inductive and deductive reasoning, analogy, and metaphor. The greater the intellectual grasp of those methodologies, the more genuine the plan.

(8) *Group dynamics in the planning process move quickly from the theoretical to the practical.* The facilitator(s) of the process obviously must be skilled in recognizing and fully appropriating the various roles that individuals play in a group. For example, this arrangement of roles shown in Exhibit 24 is probably as thorough as it is practical.*

---

*For an explanation of each role, see the Appendix.

Exhibit 24
Group Roles

BLOCKING ROLES	BUILDING ROLES	MAINTENANCE ROLES
• The Aggressor	• The Initiator	• The Tension Reliever
• The Blocker	• The Opinion Giver	• The Compromiser
• The Withdrawer	• The Elaborator	• The Harmonizer
• The Recognition Seeker	• The Clarifier	• The Encourager
• The Topic Jumper	• The Tester	• The Gate Keeper
• The Dominator	• The Summarizer	
• The Special Interest Pleader		
• The Playboy or Playgirl		
• The Self-Confessor		
• The Devil's Advocate		

Source: American Management Association, 1975.

(9) Credibility, without question, is the most important aspect of any planning process. If it is lost at any point in the process, as it indeed can be, then the entire plan is lost. The most important requirement of credibility is simply that everyone involved tell the truth. The second follows closely: one should never ask a question if the answer is not wanted.

The subject of decision making raises the larger issue of the planning organization's general philosophy of decision making; specifically, the question is about prerogative and responsibility. Typically derived from or constituting "management style," the answer, therefore, may range from authoritarian to laissez-faire. Although most "professionally managed" organizations now subscribe to "participatory" decision making, there is nowhere any uniform understanding of exactly what that means. And, as if to add injury to insult, it is usually force fitted into a rigid autocratic construct, which makes real participation impossible.

Even at best, a decision-making philosophy is a matter of degrees. So, because of this latitude, the strategic planning process must actually provide an example that will carry over into the day-to-day operation of the organization. In other words, the process of planning itself will be instructional, exemplary for decision making throughout the system. While the fullest involvement possible is the preferred course (better decisions and better support for the decisions), even that is not absolute and may be achieved in either an *open* process or a *closed* process. Those words are not intended as judgmental. They merely indicate the range and the method of involving individuals within (and outside) the organization in the planning process. Typically, commercial enterprises opt for a closed process; that is, the process of developing strategies is accomplished by the strategic officers—the board, senior executives, and managers; and the action planning is done by those in operational responsibilities (at one time long ago, that process was referred to as "top-down—bottom-up"). Non-commercial enterprises, in addition, to those participants, typically involve, through the entire process, parties from outside the organizations—customers, clients, funding sources, political allies, and the community at large; hence the process is described as "open."

The planning process is how the plan is developed—the means, the methods, and the sequence of planning activities. Typically, the process takes approximately nine months to complete and follows a rather rigid, linear course from beginning to end. But unlike the discipline, which is altered only at the peril of seriously weakening the plan, the process quite often must be adapted to local conditions and requirements in order to achieve optimal effect.

Yet, even so, the process must never sacrifice its necessary time-on-task, results-oriented character. Never can it be waylaid by convenience or comfort. And, most important, apparent inconsistency in the process can never be allowed to cast doubt on the credibility of the plan itself. Ideally, any modification in the process outlined here will be made and agreed upon before the actual planning is begun and set forth as a formatted schedule to which everyone will adhere rigorously. Mid-course changes usually run the risk of prolonging the process, diluting its substance, and compromising its credibility. The one cardinal rule of every facilitator and participant should be: "Trust the process." The discussion here will be based on the open process simply because it requires more detail; however, any differentiating features of the closed process will be juxtaposed and explained as applicable.*

THE CHIEF EXECUTIVE OFFICER

The most critical person throughout the process is the chief executive officer. Unless that person is a continuing positive force, the plan, even

---

*This basic process has been used successfully by over 700 organizations throughout the world.

though complete, will lack credibility, substance, and support. It will go nowhere. After all, planning is his or her first responsibility. It is not the responsibility of the board, nor can it be delegated. The chief executive of any organization has four obligations; if there are any more, that person is probably overpaid. They are: planning for the long-term future of the organization; developing people for organizational capacity and longevity; presenting and personifying the identity and image of the organization to the public; and, especially in smaller organizations, ensuring that operational systems are effective. Exactly how any of these take place is the prerogative of the chief executive—no one else. If, for example, a board attempts to dictate the decision-making philosophy of the organization, the role of the chief executive is seriously compromised; governance has been confused with management or administration. There is an old adage that states, "A person cannot be held responsible for that which he or she does not control." In the case of strategic planning, both belong to the chief executive officer.

That is not to say, however, that the chief executive should facilitate the planning process. The facilitator is a coach, not a player. The proper role for the chief executive is player—for two reasons: substance and credibility. Regarding the first, the success of the process depends on the material contribution of the chief executive; after all, he or she is responsible for the direction of the organization and has unique knowledge relative to the existing competition and future of the business. Second, the process, if it is to be credible, must be as objective as possible. And that means that, once the process is begun, the chief executive must also maintain an objective posture and allow the process to take its course. Too much subjective interference and, certainly, obvious manipulation, destroys not only the plan but also the morale of those involved in the process.

THE FACILITATOR

The first, and sometimes the most difficult, decision to be made in the planning process is who will be the facilitator. The necessity of a facilitator is a foregone conclusion; no planning process can be accomplished successfully without this functionary. In fact, the quality of any plan depends first and foremost on the personality, sincerity, group management skills, and technical knowledge of the facilitator. The facilitator does not necessarily have detailed knowledge of the enterprise for which the plan is being developed, but must, of course, be an experienced planner. In fact, sometimes expertise in the specific business at hand can be a disadvantage; it is possible that a facilitator can know too much. The best questions honestly seek answers, and sometimes seemingly foolish questions prompt the wisest responses.

The basic question is whether to use an external or an internal facilitator. That is not easily resolved because there is not a substantial body of evidence supporting either choice. In the private sector, most corporations find, all things being equal, that an external facilitator is more effective in challenging and moving the organization in new directions, as well as imposing the rigors of the planning process on those involved. Even so, many major corporations have designated a full-time "planner(s)" on their staff. There is one critical caveat, however. Accountants and other financial experts, whether internal or external, while extremely valuable throughout the process, must not be allowed to facilitate the plan. Strategic planning is about risking the future; it is not about compliance with generally accepted accounting procedures. Nor should the facilitator be someone who has retired from an institutionalized bureaucracy, such as an old-line traditional corporation or the military. Nor should it be a university professor whose only experience is in academia. Actually, the credibility of the facilitator determines the credibility of the process. So the choice of facilitator may well be the most important decision the chief executive makes in the entire strategic planning process.

The decision whether to use an internal or an external facilitator must be made carefully, without presupposition, in light of the advantages of either approach.

Briefly, the advantages an external facilitator provides are as follows:

(1) *The professional facilitator brings an objectivity to the planning process that no one inside of the organization can possibly enjoy.* This objectivity is necessary if the organization is to: concentrate its attention on the planning process as a serious project, not something someone is handling part time; face up to critical or sensitive issues in a manner that strengthens relationships and builds mutual self-confidence and *esprit de corps*; and subordinate personal wishes to the good of the organization.

(2) *The professional planner is more adept at translating the strategic plan into action plans; that is the point at which most internal planners falter.* That is true because no matter how strong the internal planner may be, he or she is still usually identified with his or her own operational responsibility, and usually bailiwicks do not mix.

(3) *The professional planner, while not a consultant necessarily, is generally a source of "cross-pollination," bringing with him or her to any organization substantive ideas and techniques that have worked in other instances.* His or her academic background, as well as actual line experience, makes the external facilitator a valuable resource, a provocative catalyst, and a thoroughly unbiased arbiter of ideas and information.

(4) *The planning process, by its nature, excites people and raises their expectations, so it is very important that the process chosen be the one that offers a guarantee of ultimate success.* Participants may tend to be disappointed, even a bit cynical, about planning if the first attempt does not meet their expectations.

(5) In most instances, the professional planner becomes somewhat of a confidant to the board or chief executive officer of the organization and is able to assist in identifying and developing organizational capacity.

(6) Professional planners do not get paid if they do not produce, and they are more easily fired.

The advantages of an internal facilitator are as follows:

(1) The internal facilitator is immediately available, so the process can be implemented at the convenience of the organization. This planner is always present to ensure the long-term commitment to the plan and compliance with the discipline and process of planning.

(2) The internal planner is already on the payroll, so additional funds for planning do not become a major obstacle to beginning the process.

(3) The internal facilitator is in tune with local issues, concerns, and politics, thus may be able to surface critical matters that may be effectively hidden from an external facilitator.

(4) The internal facilitator knows all of the players, and the players know the facilitator. Assuming a mutual respect and trust, rapport between facilitator and participants might be more quickly established.

(5) The internal facilitator may have planning skills equal to any external facilitator, but that will be true only if the internal planner has had the requisite training and experience, as well as the commitment to planning as a profession.

Perhaps the most important consideration, however, is the internal facilitator's own assessment of his or her role. To be effective, the internal facilitator must meet at least five basic criteria. He or she must:

1. Report directly to the administrative or executive head of the organization, that is, the person usually responsible for strategic planning.

2. Have been given the sole responsibility for strategic planning; that is, it must be his or her first job, not an additional duty, and not merely assisting someone else who is the "planner."

3. Have been granted the authority to impose upon the organization a rigid work process and to expect strict compliance.

4. Have good group skills, a forceful personality, and technical knowledge of planning.

5. Not value too highly job security. Planning is risky business.

Some organizations have found that the most effective facilitation is done by a combination of internal and external facilitators. The external facilitator typically directs the overall process and is directly involved at the beginning and end of the process (first and second planning sessions); the internal facilitator conducts the action planning phase.

TIMING AND TIME

In existing enterprises, there is only thing more important than strategic planning, and that is today's business. If that is not taken care of, then the whole idea of planning becomes moot. So the concern about both timing and time is very legitimate. The timing is not as important as the time. Strategic planning may be initiated virtually anytime during the calendar or fiscal year, and almost anytime during the life of an organization. There is only one caution: typically, the best time to plan is when the organization is at its strongest, because that is a sure sign of maturity—and imminent decline. The worst time to plan is when the organization is in a position of weakness or disarray. In rare instances, when the enterprise is in truly serious trouble, radical action must be taken before planning begins: for example, re-organization (this will be tentative, since the plan may require a completely new organization); re-staffing (this also may be tentative, because it will be necessary to staff to the plan); autocratic decision making (this, too, will be relaxed once the culture and capability of participatory decision making is established); and re-alignment of resources, financial and otherwise (this also will eventually follow the plan). The point is simply that planning cannot proceed when the urgency of today's business, perhaps rightfully so, is distracting.

In start-up ventures, of course, strategic planning, simply as a business necessity, must precede any commitment of resources. In fact, the strategic plan will provide the discipline required for new organizations to avoid the pitfalls that cause early failure—undercapitalization, loss of concentration of effort, lack of market identity, and the incapacity for constant emergence.

Sometimes in existing enterprises the tenure of the chief executive is a factor in the timing of strategic planning. For example, if a transition is imminent, should the planning take place before the present chief executive departs, during an interim period (perhaps with an acting chief executive), or after the new chief executive is on board? Interestingly, the answer may be "Yes." Quite often, it is highly desirable that a retiring chief executive leave, as it were, a legacy—a type of last will and testament. Sometimes planning in an interim period provides the basis for the selection of the succeeding chief executive. Most often, however, the planning process is delayed until the new chief executive has had the opportunity to become fully versed in the condition of the enterprise and the circumstances of the marketplace.

Another question regarding timing is the relationship of planning to budgeting. Initially, the timing of the planning process will not have an immediate impact on budgeting, so it may be started at any time during the fiscal year. There will, out of necessity, be a period of adjustment, usually twelve months, during which the budget is brought in line with the plan. But in subsequent years, the updates of the plan should be timed so that planning precedes budgeting by a comfortable interval and so that budgetary evaluation of the plan can be effected continuously during the fiscal year.

Regarding the time requirement for planning, typically the process itself (initial communication about planning through board approval) requires six to nine months, depending on the amount of time allocated to the action plan development phase, which depends on the velocity of the business and the urgency of the situation. Usually, three months is adequate for thorough action planning and short enough to be effective. In no case should it exceed six months. Obviously, time is of the essence, so care must be taken to expedite the process without compromising the quality and credibility of the plans. If the planning process is extended by more than one year, the plan becomes history rather than future.

Of particular concern is the time requirement of individuals involved in the process. Typically members of the planning team will give six to seven days to the process over the six-to-nine-month period. Members of the action teams will have to dedicate considerable time—both on the job and personal—over the three months or so for action planning, and perhaps several more days after the second strategic planning session for revisions or expansions of the plans.

Departmental plans and day-to-day operations should be addressed together, since both ultimately depend on the system's plan. The rule is simple common sense: both will continue apace until the strategic plan is approved and moved into action. There is always, during the planning process, a natural and growing influence on the thinking of the departments or units within the system, so transition into strategic action will actually occur gradually. By the time the strategic plan is approved, the actions should already be understood and accepted by all who will be instrumental in the plan's realization. Exhibit 25 illustrates the point.

The rapidity with which the strategic plan comprehends the total system depends on several variables, but they all can be reduced to one contingency—the capacity of the organization.

EXISTING PLANS AND OPERATIONS

Of special concern, of course, is the disposition of existing plans and current operations during the planning process. It is not only a matter of continuity but also of credibility. Abrupt and frequent shifts in planning methodology or in significant business direction are always counter-productive. A system can tolerate only so much shock or stress. Usually there are two kinds of existing plans: system plans (long-range, comprehensive, or strategic) and departmental or site plans (opera-

Exhibit 25
Transitioning to Strategic Action

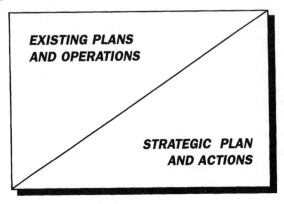

EXISTING PLANS
AND OPERATIONS

STRATEGIC PLAN
AND ACTIONS

Source: Author.

tional). Regarding the first, it is very important that existing plans be acknowledged, and, insofar as possible, honored. Usually, it is not a good idea to trash them; after all, there is a real possibility that those very plans have been the genesis of the current success of the enterprise. That is not to say, however, that strategic planning begins with a consideration of these plans. Strategy must be developed *de novo*. If, in fact, portions of existing plans are truly validated by the new process, both continuity and credibility are enhanced. However, if the new plans merely echo the old ones, strategic planning probably has not occurred.

SETTING A CLIMATE FOR PLANNING

At this juncture in this planning process, the differences between commercial and non-profit enterprises become significant enough to require attention to be given to each. It is the difference between the closed process and the open process. Although it would be impossible in a single book to deal specifically with all of the variations and shadings—even if they could be identified—at least a practical distinction can be made between the salient features. There is actually an auxiliary advantage in this approach to the discussion, because quite often concepts are best understood by contrasts. Furthermore, many organizations are, in fact, a kind of corporation-institutional hybrid; that is, either institutions that operate as corporations, or corporations that have been institutionalized. For example, there are public service enterprises, such as utility companies, which are stockholder owned, and commercial organizations that operate charter schools, using public funds for public good. In these cases, the planning process itself represents what the organization intends to be, because it establishes the way of doing business, if not a culture. An organization that does not intend to operate routinely in a participatory manner should not plan in that fashion. The long-term effect of the process on the organization simply cannot be overestimated.

The most expeditious approach to this discussion, therefore, is to consider the most unlike organizations and then to describe the process as it relates to each. The assumption is that all systems, to some degree, partake of those combined characteristics and, thus, would be able to appropriate the planning process accordingly. A closely held private company might be posited as one type of organization, a public school system, the other. Almost every working person has experienced at least the disposition of the first, and most have had some involvement in the second. In fact, public school districts are probably the most open organizations on earth, by law. But the real difference appears most strikingly in communication and involvement, especially information or decisions affecting the future of the organization. This approach is not an attempt to rigidly typecast those enterprises, because the philosophy and attitudes of either may range across a broad spectrum, from restrictive autocracy to full participation. Although it is inconceivable that a company operate in a laissez-faire mode, one school superintendent actually announced that he operated the district according to a "secret" plan. However, it is recommended, and assumed, that either type of organization subscribe to a process that invites participation because of the obvious dual advantage of quality and support; but the kind and degree of participation remains a matter of prerogative and judgment.

The creation of a receptive climate for planning is, of course, the responsibility of the chief executive. This may sometimes be accomplished through normal existing methods and instruments, depending on the culture of the organization, but the most effective way is the direct involvement of the chief executive in personal awareness sessions and conversations with those who will be actively involved in the process or affected by it. That cannot occur merely by the chief executive calling an important meeting and carrying on about some vision, nor can it be done by electronic messaging. The chief executive must personally communicate with all of those who will be involved in or affected by the planning process. It is important also that the board be informed of the intent and process and given some idea of the expectations and its involvement, if any. Most corporations, even those privately held, will benefit from informing all of the key players, including department heads, technicians and specialists, salespersons, and first-line supervisors. All should be considered a source of information, if not of actual participation. In short, every aspect of the company must be somehow directly drawn into the process. The only necessary criteria for participation are a special knowledge of the business and a commitment to tell the truth. In educational systems, in addition to those within the organization, all segments of the community must be informed and invited to participate. The facilitator or superintendent must wage an intensive effort to inform the community at large about the project. Information packages and interviews should be made available to all of the local news media and, if possible, presentations should be made to civic clubs and other appropriate community groups. Eventually, the strategic planning process will involve and affect the entire community, so general community awareness and support are invaluable. Special emphasis should be given to the fact that the process potentially will involve anyone and everyone and that the process inherently contains safeguards against special-interest dominance, political manipulation, and temporary stupidity.

In either type of organization, there is a critical need to address potential resistance to radical change, personal inconvenience, and new accountability. Resistance is probably a natural human reaction if planning is considered a threat; and the very phrase "strategic planning" often brings out the full-body armor, so the chief executive must take special care to address the issue of special and personal interests up front.

Unfortunately, there are two serious areas of concern that invariably impede open communication and involvement. The first is the so-called "second tier" of management, especially if it consists of the old guard—those who have, after a long tenure with the organization, risen to the near top. In most traditional organizations, this is the greatest point of resistance because these individuals seem to have the most to lose. The current system has been good to them, so they are inclined to return the favor. This is a universal affliction of all corporation-model organizations. The second difficulty, although more easily overcome, is certain union contracts or labor laws that explicitly forbid executives and managers from conversing directly with employees about issues pertaining to their jobs. That barrier to effective communication and participation, however, may be readily overcome—and with good results—through contractual representation. Yet the very possibility that this kind of engagement might be taken advantage of to focus attention on distracting special concerns not specifically related to strategic planning most often discourages any involvement at all. The situation is quite unfortunate because of the obvious loss of both good will and information.

There may be one other impediment as omnipresent as Newton's first law, that is, inertia. The status quo is an enticing trap. It is not that people fear change—they actually seek it—but they do fear loss. Only if they see some benefit accruing to them, something better, will they respond positively to strategic planning.

SYSTEM CAPACITY AND DESIGN

Perhaps the most important consideration in preparing for planning is the organization's capacity not only to develop a truly creative plan but also to actualize its plan. Surprisingly, many corporate as well as educational systems outplan their ability to manage their own creation. The result is worse than no planning at all. False promise always leads to frustration, disappointment, cynicism, and most of all, loss of credibility on the part of investors or clients. Often the immediate and extensive effect that the strategic plan, or a single strategic decision, will have on the total organization is drastically underestimated. Recently, one major bank developed a strategy that produced so much new business that the back-room operations could not keep up; and one on-line service provider almost swamped itself by a seemingly innocent decision to lower its rates. This is the only danger implicit in strategic planning; that is, the planners do not count the costs in advance. The nature of strategy demands a radical transformation of the system. *If an enterprise can implement its plan with the organization that developed the plan, then it does not have a strategic plan.*

The initial examination of system capacity should not be a detailed analysis of the various components of the system based on correct assessment methodologies or comparison and contrast with other exemplary organizations; that is, "benchmarks," "best practices," or "standards." That would only encourage imitation and would, in fact, mire the organization in the past. Rather, it should begin with an exploration of the current and emerging philosophies regarding human systems—from the traditional corporation-model to the emerging natural systems. Since the corporation-model organization is in serious decline, emphasis should be on understanding the characteristics of completely new, non-templated, natural systems that continuously create themselves as they aggressively appropriate technological, economic, and social possibilities. Thriving systems of the future will look nothing like those of the past. In fact, they will not look like anything at all, because they will not be susceptible to graphic representation; they will not be structures. Exactly how this exploration is conducted is, of course, the prerogative of the chief executive, but a wise planner will ensure that especially the most radical ideas are given serious consideration. There should be no attempt at this point to choose a specific philosophy, rather, merely to understand the various concepts and their implications for the existing organization and to begin serious thinking about future possibilities. While the examination of capacity and design cannot be prescribed, and while solutions at this early stage are premature, the conversation must deal at least with the two basic components of any organization, ironically the same issues that were argued at the advent of the industrial age: human nature and the ramifications of technology.

If this discussion is properly planned and prepared, it can be accomplished in an extended-day session (two days at most). Many organizations choose a retreat environment for what should be a casual but no-holds-barred examination of possibilities. All of those who are to be active in the development of strategy should be invited to participate. Throughout this extended discussion, one thing must be made clear: the strategic planning process, not to mention the plan, will leverage the entire organization into an entirely new way of doing business. It can never go back to what it is. And one final question—perhaps the most important question in the entire process—must be answered: "Is there anything about the existing system that we will not give up?" No new system can be created without displacing the old.

INFORMATION BASE

The first rule of gathering information regarding the organization and its circumstances is, "Don't overdo it." Typically, numbers people have an addiction to data, and if left to their own devices will overdose very quickly. Strategic planning is not research; it is not number crunching; and, certainly, it is not an exercise in analyzing historical institutional data and projecting the future based on trend lines. All data is history. They may have nothing to do with the future. The second rule of strategic planning, therefore, is, "Never let the numbers cabal run the business." Furthermore, a plethora of minutiae merely confounds. Research has become an end unto itself when it postpones or prevents decisions. The net effect of too much information is the same as no information at all—confusion and doubt. One of the more recent fiascos perpetrated by planners for public agencies is the convocation of a huge community forum for the ostensible purpose of gathering information to be included in the planning process. Invariably, this kind of schmoozing results in seriously prejudiced demands and raises expectations that cannot be fulfilled.

Truly strategic planning is based more on the collective intuition of the planning team than on so-called hard data. The most effective and efficient way to format organizational information is a collection of "vital" signs. Any human organization, like any human body, has certain health indicators that, when taken together, become a reasonably accurate profile of the organization's total condition and a predictor of its potential for better or for worse. Any professional executive could suggest impromptu a dozen or so such indicators, so there would be nothing either revelatory or inclusive in a suggested list.

The primary purpose of this package of information is to remind the participants in the process of the fundamentals of the business and, in the case of open processes, to provide reference points for those participants not entirely familiar with the critical attributes of the system. This information will be particularly helpful in the planning team's analysis of the organization's strengths, weaknesses, and basic design. It will also be used by the action teams as a basis for further discovery.

THE PLANNING TEAM

The planning team is the most important consideration in the strategic planning process. Since planning is the chief executive's responsibility and the decision-making philosophy is his or her prerogative, the strategic planning team serves at the pleasure of that officer. Usually, although some members of the team, by virtue of their responsibility, are logical, perhaps necessary, selections, the chief executive—especially in public sector organizations—must exercise particular discretion to guarantee that the team meets certain requirements. Here again, the fundamental difference between commercial and non-commercial organizations looms rather large. In both cases, the planning team should have three characteristics, but there will be significant variation even here, depending upon the range of involvement.

First, the team should be manageable in size. Most corporate systems, if they err, do so on the side of restriction. Quite often, these teams are very small, sometimes even a subcommitment of the board or a half-dozen or so "top-management" executives. However, for reasons already stated, and for reasons yet to be discussed, the team, and the plan, can benefit from judicious expansion. Educational systems and their kind, political entities, have a distinct proclivity to go to the other extreme, no matter what the size of the organization itself. Recently, the governor of a Western state convened a 500-person "team" for two days to develop what was touted as a "strategic" plan. Nothing has been heard from them since. For practical reasons, a corporate team should not exceed 25 people; a public systems team should be made up of no more than 30 members. These are absolute limits, no matter what the size of the organization.

Second, the team in both cases must comprise, insofar as possible, the complete organization; that is, there must be members from all aspects of the system. In the corporate process, this representation is achieved by placing division heads, along with specialists and technicians, on the team; the only question, an issue of decision-making philosophy, is the range of participation. The answer, obviously, may depend on the size of the organization. Smaller companies will involve all department heads. In educational systems, there must be not only members from every major division of the system but also teachers from the various disciplines and from the professionals in the non-academic support functions. It is also recommended that students and parents be included, because they are, in fact, directly involved in the organizational aspects of the system; for example, student government and parent-teacher associations. Both corporate and public teams must also include no more than two members of the board, not merely for their contribution to the plan but because they provide an informal conduit of information to the entire board—a critical comfort factor.

Third, and especially important, each participant in the process—specifically, the members of the planning team and action team—must be willing to subordinate his or her own special and personal interests to the goals of the systems, the reason it exists. In commercial organizations, that means a willingness to abandon political turf and departmental profitability for corporate profits. It is a misleading and dangerous myth that departments are made better through internal competition, and an even more deceptive adage that each department serves internal "customers." Nothing could be further from the truth. If either of those assumptions are the basis of internal relationships, the organization is in terminal trouble. The only customers are those *outside* of the organization who represent new revenue, not other departments that vie in the shuffling of resources. The fact is, every aspect of an organization has a vested interest in all of the others. Here again, it is extremely unfortunate that most union contracts do not lend themselves to this kind of venture in common interest; nor, for that matter, do the profit-sharing schemes of corporations.

Strategic planning will be successful only to the degree that barriers are ameliorated or eliminated. As Chris Argyris wisely observed a generation ago, the traditional corporation-model organization has created for itself a real dilemma: there is an inevitable conflict between the goals of the organization and the interests of the people in it. Strategic planning can provide at least the beginning of reconciliation and unity of effort. It is still true that a house divided against itself cannot stand.

In non-profit or public service organizations the commitment must be to the best interests of the client, assuming that is the purpose of the system's existence. For public education organizations, the question is simply whether those participating in the process will make all decisions based on the best interests of the student. It is significant that the singular form of the noun is used; "students" would weaken the commitment and would conveniently ignore the inherent problem of the individual vis-à-vis the group. All of the teams in the planning process, as pointed out earlier, will be obligated to make decisions by complete agreement. That cannot be achieved at the lowest common denominator, only at the highest; and, in education systems, that must be the student. In the public sector, agreement may be just as difficult as in the corporate world;

after all, there are many who feed at the trough of government largess. But unless all can agree on the paramount commitment to the student, the system is irredeemable, and the process will degenerate into petty squabbling.

There are three disciplines in the process under discussion here: the discipline of thought—the vocabulary and corresponding ideas; the discipline of time—for the planning components as well as the total project; and the discipline of subordination of self to common purpose. Of these, the discipline of honoring the common purpose is supreme.

There is a fourth characteristic of the planning team that is vital for public systems, most especially local education entities. They must be a microcosm of their community. That is to say, the members of the team must reflect all segments and all aspects of the community. No one is allowed to "represent" any group or ideology. The segments include business, governmental agencies, religious organizations, civic clubs, health care providers, law enforcement, and other related groups. In addition, every demographic aspect of the community must be mirrored— age, gender, race, ethnicity, political and religious philosophies. If anyone in the community can look at the team and not see themselves reflected back, the planning process has already lost credibility. Some facilitators worry about getting agreement within such variety, but without it the real diversity will be exacerbated and resolution either postponed indefinitely or rendered impossible.

There are two final criteria related to this characteristic of the planning team. First, in composition, it should be equally divided between those from the school system and those from the community. Second, the team will have no formal organizational structure and will operate typically on a first-name basis, without a chairperson.

Chapter 11

The Strategic Planning Process: Planning in Action

FIRST PLANNING SESSION

The most significant exercise during the entire planning process is the first planning session. During this two and one-half to three days, the planning team develops every component of the planning discipline except the action plans. Essentially, whatever results from this meeting becomes the draft plan. Even though everything about the plan is still subject to further development and testing by the action teams and to approval by the board, each part of the discipline must be approached and concluded with the assumption of finality.

In practice, the components that are developed here seldom change, at least until the first periodic update. That means that the components of the discipline (beliefs, mission, policies, internal analysis, external analysis, critical issues, objectives, and strategies) cannot be seen as independent or sequential pieces, nor can the process be approached as linear. Rather, these items must be considered as a logical, progressive relationship through which the plan eventually evolves. But the order in which the components are introduced for discussion is critical to the organic development of the strategic concept. So that order must be translated into the meeting agenda; to alter it is to compromise both the integrity and the effort of the plan. Simply stated, the process is not an exercise in connecting the dots, or painting by numbers, or applying some formula. The plan is a holistic creation, so the process must be holistically creative. While it is desirable, even necessary, to vary the working organizational arrangements of the team, the rational and creative processes, and the pace, it must be remembered that unjustified variations or mere hotdogging quickly results in distraction and confusion. It also should be noted that, while complexity may be a necessary precondition of simplification, simplicity is never the consequence of complexity.

FACILITATION OF THE PLANNING TEAM

The most important responsibility of the facilitator is keeping the team true to the planning discipline. Another sure sign of an amateur facilitator is trusting one's own genius rather than a discipline, tried and true. There is overwhelming evidence that the discipline outlined here does not fail; but facilitators do.

The second most important function of the facilitator is to keep the team's attention focused on the tasks at hand. The initial planning session must be an isolated, high-intensity, time-on-task concentration of intelligence, energy, and resolve. Experience has proved that far more can be accomplished through this immersion method than through any number of traditional committee meetings held conveniently over several months. It is impossible to establish a meaningful context when the concentration is dissipated by time and distractions, or to be truly creative through electronic conferencing. Distance communication may be effective in the sharing of information or in operational decision making, but strategic planning requires personal face-to-face, often heart-to-heart, deliberations—conversations that reveal possibilities seen only through mutual reflection. As a matter of fact, many issues are resolved in informal discussions outside of the scheduled agenda. For this reason it is highly recommended that the first session be held in a retreat environment—at least in a venue away from routine business facilities.

Forcing the proceedings into the strict time limitation of 30 to 36 hours over three days achieves several results critical to good strategic planning:

1. The total mental saturation with every aspect of the organization has a way of compelling coherence in thinking and, also, of sparking new thoughts, thus guaranteeing the discovery of new insights and mutual resolve.
2. The sense of urgency imposes a necessary judgment on the importance of issues and concerns and separates out those that are not critical to strategic planning, thus engendering boldness.
3. The ardent, prolonged group interaction, along with fatigue, raises the deliberations to a level generally void of pretense, intimidation, and self- or special interests, thus assuring sincerity.
4. Time for political manipulation is not available, thus ensuring credibility.
5. The return on effort is manifestly superior to expectations, thus compelling action.

The facilitator must be a stern, yet congenial—even charming—task-master, exacting compliance to both schedule and group processes, never arguing, never doubting. The facilitator, without becoming overbearing or suppressing participation, must establish from the start his or her control over the group and must maintain that control throughout the planning session. The best control is the facilitator's own example of disciplined behavior and thinking and commitment to the common purpose of the group. Facilitation is not a role for autocrats, bureaucrats, wimps, or pompous poseurs.

The facilitator is, in the highest sense of the word, a leader; the role is best served by those who by dint of their own character, commitment, and personality compel others to follow. Unfortunately, anyone who is or who is considered "The Boss" (the chief executive, for example) usually is not effective as a facilitator. Authority invariably gets in the way of both full expression and group agreement, and these two things are vital to the initial planning session.

Ideally, the facilitator will devote full time to the planning process for approximately six months. In all cases, at least, the action planning phase, about three months, will require full-time facilitation.

In addition, the facilitator will require clerical and administrative assistance throughout the process. Typically, this is a half-time assignment. However, the assistant will be involved in all of the sessions of the strategic planning team and will be instrumental in all aspects of the communication regarding the plan. The assistant should be thoroughly versed in both the discipline and process of planning and must be able to provide immediate information and service to the members of the planning team and action teams.

CHALLENGE AND ORIENTATION

The initial planning session is best begun with an evening session, perhaps after dinner, in which the facilitator presents briefly both the "why" and "how" of strategic planning. Typically, the discussion of the urgency for planning will address the various, somewhat global aspects of change, such as: the transition from the information age to the age of hyper-technology, the transformation of values, increasing competition in a free market, and evolving demographic trends. It is extremely beneficial here to briefly review the characteristics of systems, particularly the principle of metaphors, with all of their implications. The object is not as much to inform as it is to stimulate an appreciation for the scope and possible implications of strategic planning, not to frighten or discourage, but to excite with the discovery of opportunity. After all, the best strategic plans come out of aspiration, not desperation.

The discussion regarding the "how" of planning typically first establishes the basic philosophy of planning; that is, the planners are causes and not effects. The planning team members must feel that they are indeed "change agents." Then the discussion should provide a brief explanation of both the complete process and the discipline, with particular emphasis on the role of the planning team. The team should know that it is a recommending body, without official authority, beyond the strength of its own recommendations. Yet its members must realize the necessity of reaching definite conclusions and providing specific direction for the organization. The mere generation of options does not constitute planning. And, finally, the planning team should be made to understand the absolute necessity for an open, honest, participatory approach to its task.

DEVELOPING THE COMPONENTS OF THE PLAN

The actual success of the initial planning session depends primarily on the personality and skill of the facilitator, and secondarily on the personality and skill of the team. The facilitator must seek constantly to adapt each to the other, not merely as the dynamics of the process require but especially as the process offers opportunity for mutual growth. The best plans evolve correspondingly with the growth of the team toward unity of purpose and effort.

Even so, the entire process of the first session must have an overall rigid discipline to ensure both efficiency and effectiveness. The discipline has four dimensions: *group sets, group processes, decision-making processes,* and *timing.* "Group sets" refers to the suborganization of the planning team into at least two variations (or sets) of study groups. For this purpose, the group size should be no fewer than five persons, no more than seven. The ideal number is five. And the sets, insofar as possible, should include a diversity of group members.

"Group processes" refers to the progressive interaction of the members of the group toward its objective and the roles that individual members play in the movement of the group (group dynamics). It is extremely helpful if the facilitator can recognize and respond appropriately to the various roles that people play in a group: building, maintenance, and blocking. "Group processes" also refers to the decision-making style demonstrated by the group. It is assumed that all groups will naturally assume a participative style, however, if the group shows signs of succumbing to an autocratic personality or of deteriorating into laissez-faire confusion, the facilitator must provide immediate and pointed counseling. The facilitator must constantly, yet unobtrusively, monitor the working groups in order to guarantee their good progress. Usually a gentle reminder is enough to get wayward groups back into concert.

"Decision-making processes," of course, refers to those commonly accepted rational and creative approaches to either creating or discovering decisions. The traditional rational methods are induction, deduction, and analogy. Among the most popular creative methods are brainstorming, morphological analysis, force-fitting, brain-writing, visualization (excursion), lists (attributes), lateral thinking (challenge), and convergent and divergent thinking. The planning process, by its nature, demands the extensive use of the creative approaches. However, that which is that creative, if it is to be realized, constantly must be tested, supported, and ultimately proved by reason. When creativity outpaces reasonableness, the plan drifts away into fantasy. Of course, that is not to say that the decisions must be "realistic," in the usual sense of the word. After all, the whole purpose of planning is to create a new reality, which naturally will be seen by others as unrealistic. But it must be based on the principles of reason, otherwise the imagination will reject it.

"Timing," of course, refers to the order and time limit to which each group task must be held. Only one task is exempt, and that is the refining of the mission statement, if necessary, by an *ad hoc* group formed by one member from each of the subgroups. That particular group, or groups, works along with the other proceedings and continues until the total planning team is satisfied with the statement.

Exhibit 26 depicts the overall group processes recommended for developing the components of the planning discipline.

Beliefs

Facilitating the development of the statements of *beliefs* is the most difficult task in the entire process. Perhaps surprisingly it is usually not as difficult with corporate planning teams as with those of institutions, but that may be easily explained by the fact that in the latter a broader range of participants is involved. The process is one of discovering the value system already present; it is not an attempt to fabricate a creed. In most corporations, the culture is readily identifiable. However, if the planning teams of public service organizations, such as education, are indeed a microcosm of the community being served, then obviously the discussions will require more time, just for definitions alone. The more culturally diverse, the more difficult it is to discover the common core of values.

In both cases, the major difficulty is definitions. The first problem is the meaning of words themselves. Type A personalities get very nervous when a team deliberates for half an hour over a single word. But there is more value in the discussion than the definition. The many dimensions of the subject are explored and clarified. Even so, the last authority that should be invoked is a dictionary. Meaning will not be found there; it is found only in the hearts of the participants. The second greatest chal-

Exhibit 26
The First Session Process

COMPONENT	GROUP SET	GROUP PROCESS	EFFECTIVE DECISION-MAKING PROCESSES	TIME (HOURS)
Beliefs	5/5 (A)	Individual to group to team agreement	Brainstorming/Analysis/Synthesis	8–10
Mission	5/5 (A)	Individual to group to team agreement	Visualization/Divergent and lateral thinking/Lists	2–3
Mission Refinement		Synthesis to agreement	Assimilation	Variable
Internal Analysis (Mission)	5/5 (B)	Individual to group to team general agreement	Analysis	3–5
External Analysis (Mission)	5/5 (B)	Group to team awareness	Analysis/Induction-deduction/Divergent thinking	4–6
Critical Issues (Mission)	5/5 (B)	Team awareness to agreement	Visualization/Divergent thinking	2–3
Objectives	5/5 (A)	Group to team agreement	Force-fit/Lateral thinking/Visualization	2–4
Parameters	5/5 (A)	Team agreement	Brainstorming/Analysis	2–3
Strategies	5/5 (A)	Group to team agreement	Convergent thinking/Visualization	3–4

Source: Author.

lenge is disciplining the team to abide by the definitions of beliefs: they are not platitudes; not observations or facts; not business or enterprise specific; and not prescriptions. Most problematic is the confusion of matters of faith with matters of fact—descriptions of the real world. The third difficulty with definitions is the requirement that beliefs be absolute. Somehow Western society has devolved to a state in which a firm conviction is regarded negatively—either an indication of rigidity or exclusivity. But fact is that beliefs are both rigid and exclusive. To qualify them is to compromise them. And the purpose of this belief statement is not to be politically correct or endearing; it is, rather, to establish the moral basis on which the plan will be constructed and the principles on which the enterprise will operate. Essentially, it is the organization's culture.

There are two special process benefits derived from the development of the statement of beliefs. First, during the intense, sometimes emotional, discussion of convictions, the planning group actually bonds into a team. From that point onward, there is a mutual respect and trust among all of the participants. There are no barriers to an honest, open discussion. Second, with a specifically defined value system, there is no issue that can come before the team that cannot be concluded by agreement. The reason groups are reduced to adversity and have to settle by voting or negotiation is because they go directly to the issue, and everyone comes forearmed and ready for combat. But if the discussions are values-driven, decisions will be made at the *highest* common denominator.

There is one very significant aspect of this discussion that serves to gauge the real progress of the planning team: humor. To paraphrase a cliché, the team that laughs together plans together. Not only is truth often found in genuine humor, laughter also breaks down artificial barriers among the participants. Furthermore, humor provides necessary relief from persistent cerebral engagement.

Procedurally, these are the methods of surfacing the common beliefs. Assuming four or five planning groups (no more), and assuming that beliefs have been thoroughly explained, the facilitator may first ask each individual participant to develop his or her own list and then have each group come to agreement on the common beliefs held by the group. Each group's list is recorded, the duplicates combined or eliminated, and the discreet subjects divided among the groups for crafting into final versions. These, then, are presented to the whole team for discussion and agreement. Alternatively, the facilitator may proceed by having each group in turn proffer a belief, identifying similarities with those of the other groups and then engaging in a full planning team discussion until agreement is reached on each one. This approach requires a seasoned facilitator, one who is not only well read but also extremely capable of immediate logical reasoning and synthesis. When this discussion is taking place, there is not a moment in which the facilitator can be disengaged. For many facilitators and participants, this is the most exhilarating part of the process and, for all, it is the most revealing.

Mission

Earlier, in the discussion of the planning discipline, the many myths surrounding *mission* statements were noted with mild disdain. Thus it should not come as a surprise to find that there is a popular misunderstanding of the process by which they are developed. Although the mission is the first component of the discipline to be considered in constructing the plan, it is not fully developed immediately, left as a *fait accompli*, and assumed to be the basis or source of all the other components. These components are not derived from the mission; rather, the mission ultimately will be derived from them. However, it is necessary to introduce the mission first and then to use the examination of the other components to play over its various aspects in a process of concept development. The discussion of the mission should always be exploratory, not simply an exercise in blessing the status quo. The mission, the first component discussed, will also be the last thing decided at the first planning session.

Making that happen requires a special deftness on the part of the facilitator. On the one hand, the facilitation cannot become, or be perceived as, manipulative or tendentious. On the other hand, it must not allow a final statement to be agreed upon prematurely.

This can be accomplished quite readily if the development of the mission is allowed to proceed in four stages (or attempts), with four inquiries, somewhat progressive, but not necessarily corresponding to the stages. The four inquiries are in fact criteria of a legitimate mission statement: (1) Does the format include identity, purpose, and means? (2) Does it specifically delineate clients to be served and products and services to be offered? (3) Does the first infinitive in the purpose indicate process or results? (4) Do the identity and means, taken together, declare unequivocally the special uniqueness of the organization? Regarding the first, great care must be taken to ensure that the organization honestly articulates its reason for being. For corporations, that is profit or the creation of wealth; for schools, the achievement of success of students. The second question is dramatically posed as a choice of one of four relative possibilities (see Exhibit 27). Every human enterprise must choose only one quadrant. That is the beginning of concentration of effort, and of true excellence.

The third inquiry is especially difficult for non-profit organizations. Invariably, they are tempted to use process verbs rather than those that

Exhibit 27
The Quadrants of Identity

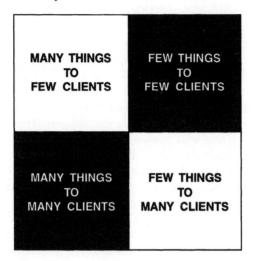

Source: Author.

imply results. This is an extremely critical distinction, because the issue involved is nothing less than accountability; that is, exactly for what will the organization hold itself responsible? Is it for doing or accomplishing? For trying or actually achieving? Everything else about the plan hinges on this decision.

Regarding the fourth, the means should specify the critical attributes—the salient features—of the stated identity. It must be remembered that if two organizations can operate with the same mission, one of them is unnecessary.

Each of these criteria must be raised, perhaps successively, as points for instruction and consideration at each stage of the developmental process. That is to say, unless the format is correct, there is little need to go on to the other inquiries. Of course, the last consideration will be the distinguishing characteristics of the organization, as detailed in the means.

The first attempt at writing the mission statement is by the planning team; all the others, by select groups within the team. The discussion and mission begins immediately following the development of beliefs. The best approach, after an explanation of the discipline of mission, is to have each member of the team roughly draft his or her version of a recommended mission. Then each group compiles from these individual interpretations a mission statement that they recommend for acceptance. The recommendation is accomplished simply by presentation and give-

and-take discussion. Obviously, since there will always be four or five versions, it is highly unlikely that any one of them will be immediately acceptable by the entire team. The facilitator's job is to make sure none is! No attempt should be made to craft a final statement through extended deliberation by the planning team. Rather, the facilitator should put together an *ad hoc* mission group, usually one person from each of the groups in the planning team, to prepare a statement derived from those presented and the accompanying discussion. Since the planning team's first consideration of the mission occurs late on the first day of the planning session, that means that the mission group has to do their work overnight. They will present their recommended mission as the first scheduled agenda item the following morning.

At that point, the facilitator, after hearing observations and assessments from the team, begins the series of inquiries into any or all of the substantial criteria of mission statements—clients, process versus result, and uniqueness. The result should be that the statement is not accepted. Another mission group is formed, with the same assignment as the first, to present another version after the analysis of strengths and weaknesses—typically just after noon on the second day of the session. That process will occur at least once and sometimes twice more, with mission presentations coming just after the external analysis and immediately before the analysis of critical issues. The discussion of critical issues will launch the final version of the mission statement. One small but important point: it is advisable that the two or three mission study groups during the day not converse separately from the planning team; they must remain full participants in the continuing main process. They will work during breaks and in other informal ways. Again, the idea each time is not to produce a final statement but to raise issues and possibilities.

Parameters

Parameters, or policies, may be developed in two ways. Both are effective, but one is eminently more efficient. In either case, the parameters are best discussed immediately before considering strategies. First, the facilitator may use a process very similar to the one employed in developing the beliefs. That is, each group recommends one or more strategic parameters and then the whole team agrees on the most appropriate. The drawbacks to this approach are that it requires considerable time, and most planning teams, especially those from the public sector, have real difficulty distinguishing strategic parameters from operational policies. The fact that typically there will be only four or five parameters is an indication of their overriding significance for the entire organization. Probably the best way to develop parameters is for the facilitator to take on the responsibility, without initially announcing it to the team. That means that from the opening discussions of beliefs and mission, and through all of the analyses, the facilitator is listening and probing for both the implied absolute rules the organization is willing to impose on itself and for the insinuated outer limits of its enterprise. Then, after the objectives are agreed upon, and just before the development of strategies, the facilitator suggests to the planning team the parameters that they have already agreed upon. Discussion follows, with agreement by the entire team.

Internal Analysis

Before beginning the discussion of the internal factors, perhaps even as the assignment is being explained, there is a simple and an entertaining exercise that both reveals the critical features of the organization's present status and establishes a mood of convivial frankness. The facilitator may simply ask the groups to draw a vehicle (transportation) that represents the current organization, present it with a full explanation, and answer questions pertaining to it. Obviously, this exercise is an open invitation to humor, but that is the most serious side of many discussions.

The *internal analysis* begins on the first evening of the planning session with a homework assignment. Each participant is asked to develop overnight two lists: one, no more than ten *strengths* of the organization; the other, no more than ten *weaknesses*. All are admonished not to bring solutions and to tell the unadulterated truth. The following morning, in group-set B, each group prepares a list of not more than fifteen strengths and fifteen weaknesses that they will present to the entire planning team. Even though solutions are not in order, reflections on the applicability of strategic thinking issues, such as the life and motivation of organizations, are extremely appropriate. Agreement is not necessary. Argument or defense is not allowed. The intent is merely to surface issues as they are perceived by at least some members of the team. They do not have to be facts, so no proof is required; no one can object. However, examples are permitted. Anecdotes are strongly discouraged because they waste time and are frequently off the subject. It is extremely important to maintain civility during the discussion of weaknesses, so the facilitator sometimes will have to assume the role of referee, making sure that the discussions are as objective as possible and that no one suffers a personal affront. However, it should be noted that, on occasion, upset participants have actually left during the discussion; but, so far, they have always come back. Even so, there may be some awkward moments, as when one young vice president rose to present his group's list of weaknesses, and began with, "No one trusts the president"—who was on the team. As it turned out, the statement was true. They had simply told it like it was. Typically, public systems have difficulty with this kind of frankness, so the facilitator must ask pointed questions in order to discover the real sentiment often masked in polite, oblique language. That is, in fact, a great technique because it diverts any pointed criticism away from members of the planning team, who really want to make the observation.

There is a process technicality that must be obsserved here. The internal analysis also consists of a *critical analysis of the organization design*, or "structure." Simply because of process expediency, that discussion should be delayed until the analysis of external factors. This is merely making the best use of the group's time.

External Analysis

The *external analysis* is at once both the easiest part of the process to facilitate and the most surprising. Predicated on the general and special awareness of the members of the planning team, this exercise often provides insights that radically change the assumptions that have been held until now. Sometimes it uncovers completely new possibilities. The task of the facilitator is to ensure that the discussions move briskly along and that each subject is thoroughly considered. In fact, this is the time to consider fully the implications of strategic thinking—especially the arena of cause and effect. Without steady provocation by the facilitator, the discussions can become mechanical and atavistic.

To achieve the best use of time, it is advisable to divide among the groups within the planning team the six categories of external factors for analysis and presentation. In addition, the analysis of competition and the critical analysis of organizational design (the third internal consideration) will be assigned to one of the groups. These analyses are conducted here simply as a matter of expedience. However, both analyses require similar understanding and expertise—usually from experience in commercial enterprises in the free market. With a team of five groups, the study assignments are best arranged as follows:

Group I: Social

Group II: Technological

Group III: Economic and Industry Trends

Group IV: Political and Demographic

Group V: Competition and Organization

With a team of four groups, the arrangement varies slightly:

Group I: Social and Political

Group II: Technological and Demographic

Group III: Economic and Industry Trends

Group IV: Competition and Organization

The idea obviously is not to have groups considering subjects that are inherently related. The analysis may be presented at the discretion of groups; the only recommendation is that the discussions of competition and organization be last.

Critical Issues

It was suggested earlier that the discussion of *critical issues* is the juncture between the discipline and the process. Whether the plan will be indeed strategic or merely a long-range or comprehensive plan is determined here. It is a matter of whether the plan is radically creative or only more of the status quo. This discussion can be accomplished in a short period of time because all of the previous analyses and inquiries have inexorably led to these conclusions—conclusions that would have been impossible to reach if they had been pursued directly. Presuppositions are devoid of insight, to say nothing of foresight.

In traditional planning, quite commonly there is an examination of what is referred to as "threats" and "opportunities," and that may well serve as the beginning of the explanation of critical issues. Only it must be remembered that true critical issues are those that occur at the point of crisis in the life evolution of an organization, so those factors are not ordinary adverse or beneficial circumstances or familiar strengths and weaknesses. They are, in fact, issues of life and death in the organization. How these matters are resolved will have a profound effect on the organization, often determining its entire future. So it should be expected that, as a result of this discussion, the organization will undergo radical change. That is precisely why no existing organization is ever able to realize its own plan. It is, in fact, the strategic gap.

However, beginning the discussion with reference to threats and opportunities can serve as a bridge to understanding strategic definitions. Threats actually have a strategic meaning, even though it is seldom appropriated. Specifically, threats in a strategic context mean those forces or factors, internal or external, that are contrary to the well-being or purpose of the organization. In the extreme, they will debilitate or destroy the organization. Those are not hypothetical possibilities, but present realities—either at the door or already across the threshold. Furthermore, they are not matters of volition; that is, they are not chosen by the planning organization—they have "chosen" the organization. They will not go away. To ignore them is to deal with them. Even worse, they must be approached on their own terms; any counteraction must be by their rules and on their turf. The organization never enjoys a home-field advantage.

The most effective way to approach this discussion is simply to have each group within the planning team identify the single greatest threat— and no more, otherwise the discussion becomes academic and prolonged beyond reason. The conclusion of each group is posted, without debate, but with appropriate discussion, for later reference.

The subject of opportunities opens completely new doors of understanding—first, about opportunities themselves. This must be made clear: *opportunities are not the opposites of threats.* That is, they are not the solutions to threats. It makes no sense to say, "Our greatest threat is a budget shortfall," and then to suggest as an opportunity, "To find some money." Opportunities, even in their fundamental, non-strategic meaning are freestanding conditions or circumstances that are completely neutral with regard to their effect in any organization. If, in fact, they are ignored, they go away. They never impose themselves. Interestingly, there is much wisdom in the hackneyed expressions "window of opportunity" and "seize opportunity by the forelock."

The word "opportunity" denotes happenstance—circumstances that exist through no decision or intent of the planning organization. That is why they are to be "taken advantage of." And, surely, that much is true. But there are possibilities here that only strategic thinking can fully realize. The idea of mere "opportunity" conveys neither the special advantage of the organization nor its unique, best way into the future. There is only *one* way to metamorphosis. Of course, it can be denied; but if the planning process is successful, the next identity of the organization will become evident to all those involved.

The most effective means of facilitation of this discovery is to have each group first seriously consider the *who, where,* and *when* of the organization. The answer to the first should be manifest in the statement of beliefs, since no other organization would hold exactly the same values. The answer to the second may be discovered in the external analysis and, here again, the planning organization's physical location will be uniquely its own. The third, derived primarily from the internal analysis, is actually a matter of both time and timing—time referring to the life stage of the system, and timing having to do with its present and future existence in a world context. Critical issues are the congruence of time and timing. Once the implications of the answers are understood by the planing team (or groups), the ultimate questions is posed: "*What* could we be that no other organization could be?"

In the discussion of internal analysis, it was suggested that the team might be asked to draw a vehicle symbolizing the current organization. Here it provides an interesting balance in the mental process, as well as a strategic contrast, to have the team (in groups) write a word-picture of what the organization *could* be. The description should be radical, unrealistic and, insofar as possible, rendered in a new vocabulary. Otherwise, it becomes a namby-pamby exercise in fantasy or "visioning." If any breakthrough is going to occur during the first session, it will be during this contemplative excursion. This is the amazing thing: when the various word-pictures are presented by the groups, there will be truly astounding congruence. They actually will constitute the many facets of the same ideal. However, that will happen only if the previous steps of the process have been faithfully executed. Taken together, these word-pictures become the substance of the final draft of the mission statement; that is why the resolution of the mission must be delayed until now.

Objectives

Here the distinction between commercial and non-profit organizations becomes immediately obvious; however, the process is basically the same for both. Actually, there are two approaches. First, *objectives* can be developed *de novo*; that is, each group suggests at least one objective, and then full team agreement is achieved using a process similar to that described in the section on beliefs. But the second approach is the most effective and invariably will be welcomed by the planning team. The facilitator, without being overly directive, may suggest categories for authentic objectives for corporations that may be as simple as return on assets or other measures of profitability; or the objectives may be cast in terms of comparison to the performance of other enterprises in the same business group. In many instances, it is advisable to have prepared, with the assistance of the chief financial officer, a chart similar to that depicted in the discussion of the discipline, and to simply distribute this to the groups for completion and discussion.

In non-profit organizations the objectives, drawn from the purpose in the mission statement, will be interpreted in three ways: the success rate of the organization in serving its clients; the immediate success of its clients as a result of the organization's service; and the continuing success of the client. For example, an educational system serving students has only three legitimate categories of objectives: the success rate of its students (that is, the number who graduate); the achievement of its students (however measured); and the success of the students after graduation (the proof of pudding, as it were).

The same decision-making process is used with either corporate teams or those from public service organizations—individual to group to team agreement.

Strategies

If the planning process has been faithfully followed, the *strategies* are obvious. They have been gradually realized by the intense and open discussions of all the other components of the plan. Some may come directly from the internal and external analyses, but most will arise out of the critical issues. There are, however, two technicalities that will have to be reinforced repeatedly: that is, *strategies are not programmatic or operational initiatives*. They are strategic, involving every aspect of the organization and establishing a context for everything within the organization. Second, *they are neither categorized under the specific objectives nor arranged in any kind of priority*.

The process for developing strategies is almost exactly the same as the first technique recommended in the development of beliefs. That is, from individual to group to team agreement, utilizing a connecting and sorting process to reduce the number to only the truly strategic initiatives—typically six to ten. The final wording must be approved by the entire team.

CONCLUDING THE FIRST PLANNING SESSION

The ending of the first planning session is as important as its beginning to the success of the planning process. Several items make for a strong finish. First, the facilitator should distribute to each of the participants a copy of the components of the plan that they have generated during the session. Care should be taken to emphasize that this is a draft; that it is the property of the planning team; and that it is a work in progress. Second, the planning team should be cautioned that the material is confidential and that it will be shared with others who are to be involved on a need-to-know basis by the chief executive officer, often through the facilitator. As will be pointed out later, it is extremely necessary for the entire plan to be explained to others as a complete concept, not randomly delivered in piecemeal fashion. Third, the remaining steps in the process must be clearly delineated, with special attention given to the second planning session of the planning team. If the dates of that meeting have been determined, of course they should be announced at this time.

The fourth item again marks the difference between corporate and public agency planning, that is, the role of the members of the planning team during the action planning phase. In corporate planning, members of the strategic planning team may actually lead action teams, although not in strategies that deal with their primary job responsibility. The quickest way to kill a strategy is to assign it to the person or the unit responsible. The idea is to gain complete objectivity. In public organizations, planning team members can serve on action teams, but not as the leaders—for credibility's sake.

Finally, it is always appropriate for the chief executive officer to end the meeting with expressions of appreciation to the participants and with a statement of personal commitment to the planning effort. Likewise, it is, also appropriate to allow the participants individually to comment on the session and informally appraise their efforts.

COMMUNICATING THE DRAFT PLAN

The depth and breadth of the communication of the draft plan depend on the range of intended involvement in the planning process. As a general rule, this phase of communication will follow the same routes as traveled in the awareness sessions at the outset of the process. For corporations, that will not be as extensive as in public service institutions, but usually it will be necessary to inform every segment of the organization.

The success of a strategic plan depends upon its credibility among the total organization. The best way to guarantee that credibility, assuming the efficacy of the plan itself, is immediate, full, and open presentation of every component of the plan, as it has been drafted by the planning team, to everyone involved. Quite likely, even prior to the selection of the planning team, the strategic planning project received considerable publicity, both inside and outside of the organization, and the initial planning session created a great deal of interest, curiosity, and perhaps even some anxiety. So the sooner the results of that session can be made public, the better.

In larger organizations, this is accomplished internally by a series of round-robin meetings at strategic locations. In smaller organizations, perhaps a single presentation at a general convocation is more appropriate. The chief executive officer, or the facilitator, or both, should make the presentation.

Every component of the plan, exactly as developed by the planning team, should be shown and discussed; usually it is not generally distributed. After all, this is a draft of the plan, and as such it should not be subjected to mass undisciplined scrutiny of its particulars. The ensuing process will allow for full examination and critique, but in appropriate ways and by responsible people. A general distribution at this point runs the risk of ideas and statements being taken out of context, thus distracting productive effort in inconsequential wrangling over details.

A special courtesy presentation of the plan should be made at this time to the board. However, this presentation is for the board's information only. It must not be taken as an occasion for the board to critique, approve, or disapprove. The board must willingly suspend its judgment until the plan is complete in every respect and is submitted in final draft for approval.

In public institutions, presentations must again be made to the various segments of the community being served. In a school district, that would mean formal reports to civic groups, chambers of commerce, and religious and political affiliations—in short, all of the groups visited during the initial awareness phase.

BUILDING ACTION TEAMS

The communication of the plan throughout the organization is necessary not only to guarantee the immediate and accurate flow of information but also to serve as an invitation for members of the action teams. At each presentation of the plan, the facilitator should discuss the formation of action teams (one for each strategy), the teams' critical role in the development of the plan, and the manner in which the teams will be selected. At the conclusion of each presentation, the opportunity may be provided for persons to volunteer to serve and to express a preference about strategy assignment. The facilitator, or the chief executive officer, may also find it desirable to actually conscript certain people to serve on the teams.

Sometime during the communication phase, the chief executive officer must select the action team leaders—only one for each strategy. Then, with the planning facilitator, an *ad hoc* group from the strategic planning team, and each action team leader, the chief executive officer ensures that each team is adequate and balanced in terms of expertise and representation of every kind. Of course, each should honor individual preferences as much as possible, but the main purpose of this exercise is to build strong, objective, committed teams who are a sort of "mini" version (typically, 10 to 25 members) of the planning team itself. Here again, the credibility of the planning process is of paramount concern. It is for this reason that members of the strategic planning team may serve on action teams but should not be action team leaders. Also, teams obviously dominated by special interests or riddled with perceived incompetence are automatically suspect and, consequently, will be disregarded by others in the organization. Again, one very critical proviso: *strategies should never be assigned to the operational unit responsible for the implementation.*

Action Team Work*

The action team phase of the planning process is critical to the strategic plan. In fact, this is probably the most important phase of the planning

*See Appendix: A Basic Guide for Action Team Leaders.

process. It is during this time that specific, operational plans of action are developed to achieve the strategies. In fact, this is the only part of the discipline that will be taken into action. A failure here means a failure of the strategy. The action teams will not implement the plans, but the plans they develop will contain such specific detail that they easily can be carried out when operationally assigned. That means that the plans cannot be just "plans to plan" but outlines of specific, detailed actions necessary to accomplish the strategy. Typically, each strategy will require about three dozen plans.

It is intended that, even though the action teams initially may have members who are not thoroughly familiar with the subject of the strategy, by the time they conclude their planning, collectively they will know more about the subject than anyone in the organization. They must become thoroughly immersed in the subject and must resist the tendency toward preconceptions. The learning curve is very steep. For that reason, the teams must be provided with the resources necessary to accomplish their task. It is well within discretion to have them submit early a proposed operating budget along with requests for any special assistance. This is one investment that always produces a bountiful return.

The action teams begin their work only after the facilitator has provided the team leaders, usually as a group, with comprehensive and detailed instruction regarding the action teams' responsibilities. Usually accomplished in a three-to-six-hour session, the instruction includes: (1) the role of the action team leader, (2) the relationship between the strategies and the action plans, (3) an explanation of the action plan form, (4) an explanation of cost-benefit analysis, (5) the relationship of the action teams to the planning team regarding final approval of the action plans, and (6) the time commitment usually required (typically 30 hours of meeting time—at convenient intervals of one-to three-hour sessions, plus an indeterminate amount of time outside of meetings). If specific training or instruction is required by any or all of the team leaders, the facilitator should see that it is provided as soon as possible. For example, quite often the facilitator will recognize a need for training the team leaders in group processes or decision making.

It is particularly critical that the action team leader understand that the action team must honor the strategy *exactly* as it is written. That is, the action team must accept the strategy with the full intention of making it work, not with the intent to change or eliminate it. However, if it turns out that, after demonstrated good faith effort, the strategy must be altered, then the action team is duty bound to make the appropriate recommendations to the planning team at the second planning session, but only after presenting the best-case scenario for the original strategy.

The first meeting of each action team should produce a general time line for the team's activities, an outline of possible action plans they will pursue, and any internal organization of the team according to tasks. Notes or minutes from this meeting and all subsequent meetings should be forwarded to the facilitator. The teams will be allowed to steer a rather independent course, adopt their own decision-making style, and conduct their activities at the convenience of the group. Each team should be encouraged by the facilitator to work in isolation from the other action teams. There should be no attempt to coordinate or merge activities or plans. Consolidation will be necessary, but it will be done by the planning team at its second session.

During the three or four months the action teams are at work, the facilitator must effectively monitor, discipline, stimulate, and support the teams' efforts. Some of the ways in which the facilitator functions during this time include: coordinating meeting times and places for all teams, providing various clerical and other support services, arranging for release time or additional compensation, and being available to answer specific questions or to provide personal assistance when necessary. Most important, the facilitator must meet formally with each team (or team leader) once each month to assess progress and to project upcoming requirements. Finally, the facilitator must ensure that the action plans and cost-benefit analyses submitted by each team are in the appropriate form for evaluation by the planning team.

THE SECOND PLANNING SESSION

At the conclusion of the action planning phase, the planning team conducts its second session (two days) to put into draft form the complete strategic plan. This session does not demand the physical isolation that was so crucial to the first session; nevertheless, the meeting should be held at some convenient, non-work site. Nor does the intensity of this meeting equal that of the first. The pace is slower and more deliberate but still subject to the discipline of a fairly strict schedule.

The first order of business is to review all of the action plans that have been submitted by the action teams. Ideally, the members of the planning team have each received a complete package of the action plans, at least one week before the session, so the review should proceed expeditiously. To facilitate the review, each action team leader, individually, makes a scheduled appearance (30 to 45 minutes) before the planning team to clarify, explain, or justify the team's recommendations. The team leaders do not attend any other portion of this session (unless, as in corporate planning, they are members of the strategic planning team).

Each action team leader should take approximately half the allotted time to present a summary of the plans and the remainder of the time to deal with questions from members of the planning team. It is very important that the only questions asked are those for clarification and explanation. This is not an occasion for argument and debate; and the action team leader must not be placed on the defensive. In fact, no member of the planning team should even be allowed to express any evaluative opinion of the plans. When the action team leader leaves the meeting, he or she should have no idea about how any member of the planning team feels about the plans. It is the facilitator's role to guarantee this detachment.

There are at least three reasons for this restraint. First, assuming that the action team has prudently accomplished its tasks, they will know more about the subject than anyone on the planning team; the members of the action team have become the resident experts. Second, nothing can be learned with a closed mind; snap judgments limit thinking to that already known. Third, common courtesy dictates a respectful, non-aggressive approach to inquiries. Arguments always contain more thunder than lightning. Reserving judgment saves time and ego and contributes mightily to the quality of the final product.

After all presentations have been made, the planning team then begins its assessment of each plan and through agreement makes a final disposition of every one. The most expeditious way to go about this endeavor is to organize the planning team in group set A and to assign one or more strategies to each group. An attempt should be made to equalize the tasks for each group. The equalization, of course, may not be as simple as a proportional share of the number of plans. Many individual plans can require as much discussion as those of an entire strategy. If at all possible, there should be no one in a study group with a vested interest in the subject, certainly no one who served on the respective action team. The study group's responsibility is to evaluate the plans and, at the appropriate time, to report its conclusions and bring the planning team to agreement on one of four dispositions regarding each plan:

- They can accept a plan *carte blanche*. (That does not constitute acceptance of the cost-benefit analysis. Costing will be accomplished later when the total plan is completed.)
- They can reject a plan. (The criteria for accepting and rejecting follows.)
- They can delete portions of the plan as long as the deletion does not amount to a substantive change, but they cannot add to or modify the plan (otherwise, credibility is lost with the action team).
- They can return the plan(s) for additional development or for further justification. (The planning team must not guess at the meaning or consequences and must not presume to expand the plan(s).)

There are two things the planning team *cannot* do. The first is to put any plan on hold; each and every one must be dealt with by some definitive action. The second is to change or add to an action plan; planning teams do not write action plans.

The criteria for judgment are in the form of three questions:

1. Is the plan relevant to the strategy? If it is not, even though it is a good idea, the plan must be rejected. Also, plans from one strategy should not be assigned to another just to make them fit. This is, in effect, the same as adding to a plan.
2. Does the plan provide an acceptable return on investment? Total cost must not be a consideration here, and it must not be assumed that the organization has limited resources. The only issue is whether the result of the plan would justify the required investment.
3. Does the plan pass the sanity test? It rarely happens, but it is possible that a plan meets the first two criteria and yet, for some reason—usually an external consideration—it would not be a wise or prudent thing to do. For example, an action team in a public agency presented a cluster of plans that was directly on target, actually revenue positive (savings), but had the potential of reviving the issues recently settled to avoid a federal court order. Acceptance of the plans could have easily been tantamount to winning a battle, but losing the war.

The study groups' recommendations are not presented to the planning team in numerical sequence or by topical arrangement. Rather, they are discussed, beginning with the easiest, or most simple, and moving to the most difficult, or most complicated. The plans of any given strategy may fall into all four categories of disposition—some accepted, some rejected, some with deletions, and some returned. In every case, the disposition must be by full agreement of the planning team.

There are two technical devices that greatly serve to expedite the planning process: *stipulations* and *cross-references*. The first should be employed to clarify any aspect of a particular plan that was explained by the action team leader's oral presentation but is not evident in the steps of the plan. Or, stipulations may be used by the planning team to limit or expand an action as long as the stipulations, always written directly on the plan, do not change the plan. The planning team in this way can avoid sending a plan back to the action team.

Cross-referencing is purely an administrative necessity. If it is not done during the acceptance of the plans, it will have to be accomplished later by the internal facilitator or those responsible for assigning the plans. It is simply a notation that two or more plans must be undertaken together, which raises a small but critical point. Many times, (almost) duplicate plans or plans that depend on each other will be presented under different strategies. They should not be combined, nor should they be eliminated. Both will be needed, in place, at the next update of the plan. So a brief note should be added to each, indicating the companion plan(s).

Immediately after the session, the facilitator will debrief each action team leader individually, explain the planning team's decisions and requests, and establish a date for any re-submissions. The final meeting of the strategic planning team occurs two weeks to 30 days later. At that time (usually one day), only the revisions of the action plans are considered. The only option the planning team does not have is returning the plans. The plans are either accepted (with deletions) or rejected.

In addition to reviewing and selecting action plans to support the strategies, the planning team usually finds this an appropriate time to review again every component of the plan, just to confirm its own satisfaction with the content and coherence of the total plan.

The final task of the planning team is to develop a recommended schedule of implementation for the strategies and plans, including a year-by-year cost projection. Usually this is put into a rough draft by the entire planning team, refined by a smaller *ad hoc* group working with the finance director, and approved by the entire team before submission to the board, via the chief executive, as a part of the plan. Typically, the implementaton schedule with resource projections is a simple chart listing each plan, under each strategy, with a recommended beginning date (see Exhibit 28).

It is very important that this schedule not be interpreted as assigning priorities to the plans. Rather, it is a matter of phasing. Whatever is done here is merely a draft indicating the feasibility of the plan, obviously based on several assumptions. It is adequate to simply categorize the plans in three phases.

Phase I: Plans to be begun in the first two years

Phase II: Plans to be begun in years three and four

Phase III: Plans to be begun in years four and five

The overlap in Phases II and III is explained by the cumulative effect of action that will be acknowledged in the periodic updates of the strategic plan. The criteria for phasing are:

1. How urgent is the plan? Some plans must be addressed immediately, no matter how difficult or inconvenient; for example, safety issues, compliance, or technological advances.

2. How manageable is the plan? Systems can withstand only so much stress until change becomes counterproductive, thus massive projects must be undertaken advisedly and with sufficient capacity development to ensure success.

Exhibit 28
Phasing of Action

Strategy # _____	Year 1	Year 2	Year 3	Year 4	Year 5
Action Plans					
1					
2					
3					
4					
5					
et cetera					

Source: Author.

3. What is the total cost? The absolute last consideration in strategic planing is the total amount of resources necessary to implement the strategic plan. Up until this point, all of the plans have been adjudicated by cost-benefit analyses, but now it is necessary to consider the best way to manage them into existence.

As with the first planning session, the planning facilitator is the person who is responsible (1) for moving this planning session to the necessary ends; (2) for the construction and validation of the implementation and resource schedules; and (3) for transforming everything into a final draft, ready for the board's consideration.

BOARD APPROVAL

One critical point: Prior to submission of the plan to the board, the facilitator must observe two serious matters of protocol, if not obligation. The first is the apprisal of all the action teams regarding the final disposition of their recommendations, and the dissolution of the teams. This can be accomplished most easily by a debriefing session with the action team leaders, who in turn can inform their respective teams and, at the same time, announce the dissolution of the action teams. The second responsibility of the facilitator is the submission of the total strategic plan to the chief executive officer for final review before presentation to the board. This should be a mere formality because of the chief executive's active involvement in every part of the planning process; but the plan should not be submitted to the board without the commitment of a formal endorsement by the chief executive officer.

Sometimes the presentation of the strategic plan to the board is made by the facilitator at the behest of the chief executive officer, usually in two study sessions. Of course, both the planning team and the action teams should be encouraged to attend these sessions, but only the planning team should be granted access to the board, and then only in response to board questions through the facilitator. There must not be any direct interaction between the board and individuals speaking as action team members. The plan under consideration is the property and the recommendation of the planning team, and it should be dealt with accordingly.

Very seldom does a board significantly alter any portion of the plan. That is not to say that it merely "rubber stamps" it, but its quick and full approval is merely evidence of both the quality of the plan and the effective communication that has existed throughout the entire process. It is the facilitator's job to make sure that the board is neither painted into a corner nor surprised.

Part III

Strategic Action

Chapter 12

Words and Meanings

Action is much more than one usually thinks. It may not be the end of thinking, but the beginning. Earlier, in the introduction to strategic planning, it was pointed out that the protocol under consideration here yields to the assumptions implicit within traditional organization; specifically, that planning precedes action, that plans are to be implemented, and that a strategic plan is updated periodically. So the process and discipline described in the foregoing chapters were designed to accommodate that kind of organization—at least at the outset of planning. But, all along, there has been another fundamental assumption; that is, the traditionally organized enterprises must become, through strategic planning, something entirely different. Therefore, both the process and the discipline were calculated to push the traditional system to its outer limits, not only in the creation of a new identity but also in the practice of a new kind of organization. That is precisely the reason it was announced at the beginning of the process that a truly strategic plan cannot be realized by the organization that develops it. However, it is only in action that the new organization can be discovered.

The maturity of any organization is measured by the degree to which this secret is understood and appropriated. It separates the Middle Ages from the new millennium; it separates organizations trapped in effectiveness and efficiency from those with the freedom to exercise their full powers—those with the faith and assurance that human systems are neither effective nor efficient.

The words "new" and "organization" have special significance in strategic action, each in its own way. "Organization" is the most difficult to settle, because, in the vernacular, it actually conveys two ideas. First, it is used as a substantive noun in reference to a human enterprise—a business, a company, a corporation, a local entity, an affiliation. "Organization" has become an apt synonym for any of these concepts. Second, it is used generically to refer to the relationships of parts within a whole—in other words, the way a relatively complex thing is put together and the way it operates. The latter meaning is truer to the original idea. Interestingly, the ideas in "corporation" and "organization" come very close to representing the same basic analogy, although "corporation" has a longer history. *Corpus* was used as early as 500 B.C. to refer to an assembled group of people, most notably the "body politic." "Corporation" was used similarly during the Anglo-Saxon period of the English language as the common designation of politically distinct villages and towns. During the Middle English period, it was applied to the trades, and, eventually, in modern English, to commercial enterprises. The first corporation in North America, the New York Fishing Company, was chartered in 1675.

"Organization" came into the language even before the word "corporation," so it entered without a tradition that limited its context. Certainly it was not restricted to the context of corporation. By the beginning of the first century A.D., *corpus*, with reference to a political or an ecclesiastical assemblage, was probably no longer even considered a metaphor. Whatever the referent, it actually became a body. Now, although all of this meandering around in etymology may seem rather academic, there is a very practical implication, so practical that it is manifest in every corporation. That is, "corporation" carries the weight of a substantive noun—a thing or an object. It may be subtle, but it is, nevertheless, quite significant that in modern English to achieve any verb quality at all, a prefix must be "incorporated." And even that is understood as a point-in-time action; that is, it happens, and it is over. There is no inference of a continuing dynamic.

"Organization," on the other hand, has maintained the quality of an active verb, that special class of nouns that, because of their formation, necessarily connotes action. They are easily recognized by the suffix "tion." Used first also during the Anglo-Saxon period, "organization" referred to the arrangements and relationships of the components of living, organismic things, from plants and animals to human beings, or to the organization of the body, actual or corporated. It is significant that "organize," the verb, is actually a derivative of "organization." That is not true of "corporation"; in fact, the parallel derivative produces an adjective—"corporate."

There is more at stake here than satisfying curiosity about words and meanings. It is quite telling that when people are asked whether "organization" is a noun or a verb, after they get over the initial shock of an absurd question, approximately 10 percent of them knowingly reply,

"A verb." If the question is rephrased as, "What do you *hear*, a noun or a verb?" the number choosing "verb" quickly escalates to 30 or 40 percent. Yet the implied dynamic, the inherent action, is seldom recognized in ordinary usage.

Heretofore, in this book, "organization" has been used in both its current meanings—as an entity and as the arrangement within an entity. Since consistency of thought is more important than constancy of language, from this point onward "organization" will be used strictly to refer to the *dynamic of the internal relationships* within living, organismic systems. All relationships are changed by changing one relationship—that between organizing and action. Traditional, corporation-model structures organize *for* action; organismic systems organize *by* action.

It is the action that makes the organization continuously new in kind. Here again, a brief word study reveals a meaning typically overlooked. "New" actually has two meanings—both denotations. Those widely differing meanings are most accurately delineated by the Greek *neon* and *ainois*. The first simply means new in time. Most assuredly, if strategic planning is properly executed, the results will always conclude in the invention of an identity "new in time"—as in successive models of automobiles ("new," as opposed to "used" or "old") and formulas for, say, detergent ("new and improved"). But if strategic planning is righteously appropriated, allowed to exert its full power, the result can be even more radical—the creation of an identity "new in kind." That is, in fact, the lesson of metamorphosis: the form emerges from the very energy of life. The creature does not grow into a *schema* already in place; that is what it escaped. Rather, it creates its own *morphe* as it grows. That is the only way constant emergence is possible for human systems; without constant emergence, constant newness of kind, they quickly die.

Admittedly, this transvolution is difficult, well-nigh impossible, for corporation systems and mentalities. Yet it can and does occur. The new creation always is implicit in action. But it is fully realized only in the action of holistic or whole-context organization®. There are six aspects of this kind of organization. Four are the *dimensions* of organization; two are the *relationships* (or dynamics) within organization. The degree to which any human system partakes of these aspects is the degree to which it will thrive and prosper. The four dimensions were addressed in the context of strategic planning. In actual practice, two are developed in the strategic planning process (common core of values and mutual purpose). The other dimensions and the two relationships can be dealt with only in the *strategic action* phase. This is one place where philosophy does not count for much. Action has come to thinking.

Chapter 13

Whole-Context Organization:
The Four Dimensions

The first dimension of whole-context organization is the *common core of values*. Those beliefs are the life of the system—its driving energy. As the expression of the moral convictions held by those persons in the system, they are not very susceptible to change; in fact, they will change only as the makeup of the community changes, and that is seldom drastic. While the beliefs are not intended to represent a creed, allegiance to which is required to join the community, the fact is that once articulated the beliefs naturally become attractive to persons of like persuasion. The most recent new-age philosophers and pseudo-scientists used to speak of a "strange attractor," but they were baffled as to what it really was. If there is any force that could be so described, surely it has to be the common core of values.

Beliefs, like all other powers, can be dangerous to organization; in the extreme, they can destroy it, simply through the blind, internally focused concentration of energy. The system actually self-destructs. That occurs when the beliefs are pursued as an end within themselves, when their defense, proof, and nurturing become the mission. The implicit power of the beliefs collides with the explicit power of passion. No system can survive the crash. Furthermore, when beliefs become a cause célèbre, there is no longer any consciousness of the distinction between that which is real and that which the enterprise sees as its reality. Its reality becomes "the truth," its mission a crusade. So, in effect, the entire moral basis of organization is invalidated by the single-minded denial of other possibilities. But if these convictions are constantly and deliberately tested within the system by the admission of other valid beliefs not held in common, the tension between the common values and other conflicting values is sufficient exercise to compound the strength of the common core values. It is this energy that not only sustains organization but also provides the impetus and the wherewithal for its constant emergence as a system.

The second dimension is *mutual purpose*. In the mission statement, developed during strategic planning, there are three parts: identity, purpose, and means. Taken together, within the context of the plan, they are the expression of the system's reason for existence. However, purpose is not only central to the statement of mission, it is central to the overarching intent of organization. Without pervasive *strategic intent* the structural and operational integrity of organization is impossible. Internal fragmentation precludes any possibility of an actual system.

There are two critical considerations in purpose, both eminently practical. First, mutual purpose is found only in common benefit. This is the point at which whole-context organization most radically departs from traditional organization. For decades now, the most astute critics of corporation-model organization have observed that in it there is a fundamental irreconcilable conflict between the goals of the corporation and the interests of the people in it. The problem is inherent in the construction of the corporated system. The only purpose of the corporation is economic, that is, to increase the financial wealth of stockholders. Yet the explicit assumption going in is that all people are also motivated primarily by financial gain; that is, they are all "economic animals." So the adversarial dichotomy of the corporation is, in effect, built into the system. Internal conflict is always counterproductive, and a conflict of this magnitude—one that is fundamental to the system itself—is ultimately destructive.

Whole-context organization is realized only when there is perfect harmony between the strategic intent of the system and the personal interests of those who make up the system. It is a simple matter: either the system will serve those who constitute it, or they will be forced to serve it. There is no purpose in servitude—only despair or dreams.

The second consideration regarding common purpose is predicated on the assumption that it is indeed mutual. Only then can it become strategic intent, the ultimate expression of the mission. Unless and until the mission statement is translated into strategic intent, it is just so many fancy words emblazoned on a plaque in the foyers of administration buildings.

No mission is ever realized by going after it directly. Missions are realized only to the degree that they provide the context for all action within the system. To ignore that fact is, again, to destroy the system. The reason planning, strategic or otherwise, so often fails in a corporation is that the mission statement is perceived as having little or no relevance to existing operations. Only those actions or activities that are directly affected by the action plans are deemed to be associated in any way with the strategic plan. So, for most operations, it is busyness, as usual. Now, it is certainly true that the strategies and action plans deal only with those initiatives that must be undertaken to close the strategic gap; however, that does not mean that the rest of the system is somehow exempted from the context of the mission. The mission does not veer off into some abstract realm dissociated from the practical necessities of the moment; and the strategic plan is not some sort of adjunct to the real business of the enterprise.

The mission changes everything within the system—*everything!* Even the most mundane, the most ordinary, the most mechanical. It makes the routine purposeful; it makes the ordinary extraordinary; and it renders the mechanical human—organismic. Anything about the existing system that cannot be thus transformed must be abandoned. And anything not existing that is needed to complete the system must be created—from within the system itself. For example, in a bank, one of the most basic, routine activities is tellering; the specifics of the transaction may change from time to time, because of technology or regulations, but it is still tellering. Suppose the bank develops a mission statement; and suppose there is a senior teller who has been performing this job for many years. The question is, does the mission have anything to do with that job? In the typical corporation, the answer is, of course, "No." The plan is too far removed from practical operations. And in actual practice that is the case; the strategic plan seldom reaches to the basic operational aspects of the enterprise. But in whole-context organization, the action is given a new meaning by being cast into a completely new context. The teller might have a generation of experience in the job; but the job has never existed in the context of the new mission. It is completely redefined. And that can happen only if the mission statement is translated personally by the teller into conscious strategic intent regarding everything about the job. That is to say, the strategic intent not only informs all action, it also immediately adjudicates it, thereby providing almost instantaneous responsive action—time and place specific. This is, in fact, the critical difference between activity and action. Action presupposes a purpose, an intent; action is continuous creative energy. But activity is energy used without specific intent; it is the continuous dissipation of energy.

If action is not the practical expression of purpose, then it is something else altogether. Activity, perhaps. Maybe motion. Or simply process. The lack of purpose results in either malaise or panic. One eschews doing anything; the other is given to frenzy. Lost does not mean not knowing where one is or where one is going. Lost means not knowing *why*. By strict definition, action is impossible. Recently, an outstanding collegiate football coach was asked by a reporter to explain how he won so many championships, conference and national. His reply was quite revealing about the importance of purpose. He simply said, "I have always made a distinction between activity and action." One dissipates energy; the other concentrates it on a goal. Activity displaces action.

It is only through the infusion of strategic intent into every action within the system that organization can realize the promise of its own name—that is, an organismic creation of one mind dedicated wholly to one purpose. Organizational charts become as obsolete as slide rules; any artifactual structure would only get in the way of action. But if the only organizing principle is strategic intent, there is virtually no limit to the energy that is generated in action.

There is, of course, inextricable connections between and among the four dimensions of organizations. In fact, it would require a relatively sophisticated hologram to visualize the inter and intra relationships. But it is not inaccurate to discern that there is a special connection between the common values and the mutual purpose. The spirit of the purpose, as well as its intent, arises from the moral imperatives of the common values; and the values are both an unswerving advocate and a trust-worthy judge of the purpose. While values and purpose are necessarily connected to each other, the two other dimensions—excess capacity and creative action—are inseparable. It is impossible to consider one without the other.

Excess capacity exists only in organization. That is precisely the reason most corporate model systems are incapacitated. They are not, in fact, organized—in the vital, organismic sense of the word. They have capa-bilities, surely; but capabilities are barely sufficient to cover present exigencies. Capacity, however, is the domain of the system's future. For that reason, capacity must be given special, extraordinary emphasis in the exercise of strategy. It is instructive to recall here that the issue of capacity was the first topic of substantial discussion in the strategic thinking component of the planning process. Furthermore, it was ex-plained at that time that a truly strategic plan cannot be realized by the organization that developed the plan. The idea from the beginning was that organization would arise out of action—a highly unusual idea in artifactual systems that habitually organize for activity. In fact, for many, constantly reorganizing is a substitute for action—their only action.

Corporation-model systems destroy or prevent capacity in two ways. First, they negate the very idea of organization by constructing trunca-ted, non-organization systems, many actually anti-organization. For ex-ample, for commercial as well as public service enterprises, the rage of the 1990's was downsizing, for the sake of immediate benefit—either in profitability, cost reduction, or both. Outsourcing and contract services became the fads *du jour*. There is a certain insanity that always accom-panies the direct pursuit of any result. It completely obliterates any notion of a larger purpose, thus invalidating even the immediate accomplishment. Every achievement is followed by the question, "So what?" In this kind of self-cannibalism, the ultimate answer is annihilation.

Invariably this tactic is strictly in reaction to adverse external factors, such as decline of markets or the increase of competition in the marketplace. And it is simply that—reactionary. So when the external conditions become more favorable and the enterprise tries to recapture momentum and restore itself, it is either too weak or cannot muster the necessary resources. Capacity inversion is the quickest way to extinction.

The second way corporation-model systems destroy capacity is by preferring capability over capacity. The old principles of management require it: *planning, organizing, staffing, directing, controlling,* and *evaluating.* Once the "organizational structure" was set, each component was staffed with persons qualified to perform specified tasks, each task aimed at achieving a predetermined end. Subsequently, all training was directed toward improving the performance of those specified jobs. Training off-site always had to be justified by its prospect of improving that performance. Effectiveness of training, if evaluated at all, was strictly in terms of its contribution to the dictated result. Furthermore, the principles of directing, controlling, and evaluating presupposed rigid adherence to formal and filed job descriptions and performance standards.

Job descriptions were invariably developed "top-down." They conformed all action and thinking to three stipulations: qualifications necessary to perform the task; detailed activity stated as process, with an empahsis on uniformity and precision, and reporting relationships (authority). Performance standards were typically impersonal, standardized observations of behavior, all rated on a scale of 1 to 5. Most assessments had nothing to do with the actual performance of the job; basically, they were activity reports.

While that approach may develop capability, it has nothing to do with the development of capacity. There are two levels of capacity development. The first is most easily appropriated by traditional systems attempting to create constantly emerging systems. The second is realized only by emerging systems. Both levels are subject to two universal truths: (1) the capacity of human systems is developed one person at a time; and (2) capacity is always developed out of the present context.

The first simply acknowledges the often overlooked truism that, in human systems, capacity does not consist of financial assets, technological capability, physical facilities, or even proprietary information; real capacity is created only within human beings. Without that source, all resources are just so much paraphernalia. Further, human capacity is neither developed nor appropriated *en masse.* True system capacity is as diverse as individuals; and so it must be approached solely on an individual basis.

The second truth regarding capacity development is not only ignored but is also rabidly disputed by corporated mentalities. Yet it will not go away: capacity is always developed out of context—specifically out of the context of the existing system. Without that understanding and, furthermore, without a serious commitment to it, no system can transform itself much less constantly emerge. It will simply continue to do the same things, better perhaps, but with little hope of different results. That was, in fact, the false promise of the management craze once known as "continuous improvement."

Capacity is developed only by the person's being removed from the context of a "job" with predetermined outcomes and a strict regimen to achieve them. Capacity succumbs to capability in job descriptions; individual capacity is stunted by slavish compliance. Why, for example, would an educational system invest in the training of a math teacher to teach math? All such instruction would be cast in the past and present contexts of both teaching and mathematics—a double blow to capacity. Rather, why not drop that same math teacher in the high Sierras with only a bottle of Evian and some beef jerky? Now, that's development of capacity.

Science always falters at the door of the metaphysical. Its only response is denial. Cause and effect is a very simple matter in an empirical world, and perhaps simpler still in a world of machines where next direct immediate result is the standard of production. Very likely the current prevalent view of the way things work is not drawn from theoretical disputation and argument but from the inescapable affiliation and consort with machines. Human beings make of themselves "vital machines," just as the scientists predicted at the advent of the twentieth century, living somewhere along the long chain of cause and effect.

But in the realm of metaphysics, things are not always as they appear. Take, for example, the old adage, "Within every challenge is the power to overcome." Easily dismissed as existential German philosophy gone soft in the head, this apparent platitude may offer entrance into a world in which cause and effect are transcended by action. It is a delicious irony indeed that the sheer practicality of the metaphysical triumphs over the fantasy of rationalistic science.

In practical terms, capacity does not exist apart from action. It is not something to be developed, contained, and then unleashed, at calculated rates, toward some desired end. Rather, capacity exists within the action. Or stated in a new idiom, potential is in doing. Possibility is found only in action.

The first level of development of excess capacity requires the system to expect and facilitate the development of the individual capacity of each person. Corporations will not usually do this because they are re-luctant to accommodate individuality and, even more detrimental, they usually will not invest in anything on which they cannot project an immediate return. There has been much talk about the billions of dollars corporations pour into the training of employees. But that is a grossly overstated, self-serving accolade. The fact is, the majority of corporate training is a desperate attempt to catch up to the advancements in technology, expanding global markets, and the frantic games of musical chairs played by the major players in the business or industry. As a percentage of revenues—especially as a percentage of expenses—the total amount of money invested in even that kind of training is minuscule. Five percent against revenues is considered extravagant. In educational systems, extravagance is much less expensive—usually no more than than 1 percent of the total budget.

But here are the cold, bare facts. Unless each person in the system is devoting 20 percent of his or her time "on the job" to the developing of personal capacity outside of "the job," then the entire system is already obsolete. That means that the system, just to stay in business, must be 20 percent *overstaffed* by traditional standards. If there is a congenital defect in the corporation-model system, it is the misperception of excess capacity as a non-producing asset, if indeed it is considered at all. But without excess capacity, a system is already in decline. Excess capacity is the essence of constant emergence.

The second level of capacity development is that which is within the action itself, and only within the action. The traditional idea is that capacity is only the prelude to action, just as preparation is the prerequisite of work. The problem with such thinking is that preparation is, by its nature and without exception, limiting. Capacity, like work, never exceeds the prescription. And, when stored capacity is expended, the action ceases—the battery runs down. Actually, stored capacity—if that were indeed possible—is not really capacity. The moment it is stored it becomes incapacity. Capacity is found only in action. The ultimate purpose of action is not the achievement of a predetermined end but the creation of capacity, of new possibilities unimaginable outside of the action—and that is the only purpose of organization: *creative action.*

In the previous explanation of action plans, it was suggested that there are two kinds of *action*: that which is involved in the production of stated results, and that which is involved in the search for some aspect of truth. While it would be expedient to reduce these concepts to simple, modern terms, none could be as effective or as efficient as the original. Aristotle knew these, respectively, as *poiēsis* and *theōria* (see Exhibit 29). If carried to their fullest declension, they would present a striking contrast.

However, Aristotle acknowledged a third kind of action. *Praxis* is action of discovery and creation. The concept, like the word, is untrans-

Exhibit 29
Typical Kinds of Action

	CONTEXT	KNOWLEDGE	PERFORMANCE	DEFINITION	EXAMPLES
THEŌRIA	Search for truth ("the really real")	• Contemplation • Reason/Revelation • Empiricism • The truth	• Proof of hypotheses • Validation • Demonstration • Energy appropriated	• Decisions as action (words as action)	• Experimentation • Research • Evidentiary proceedings • Program planning
POIĒSIS	Production of results	• Pragmatism • Rationalism • Techne	• Object-determined facturing • Artifactual systems • Energy transference	• Achievement as action (reaction as action) • Effectiveness/ Efficiency	• Goals/objectives • Job descriptions • Traditional performance evaluation • MBO, TQM etc. • Standards • Project planning

Source: Author.

latable. Most attempts barbarize both by rendering the word "practice." Or some, such as a national teacher evaluation/training program, simply use "praxis" and assume the interpretation of "practice." Such is the strange power of anonymic attraction. But "practice" completely misses the meaning. "Praxis" literally means "passing," as through action. The passing is the experience; and in that experience there is uniquely each time a world of awareness and knowledge imperceptible to those outside of the experience. The experience becomes a panoramic vista of uncharted territory; it is the complete immersion of all of the senses. All that is required for this experience is that the subject—the person—be fully attuned to the experience and receptive to revelation. Moving to expected ends, as in implementation, is paradoxically distracting and, consequently, leads to disappointment; but moving into discovery creates possibilities never before imagined, and so it always is accompanied by exhilaration. In a completely illogical fashion, praxis thus becomes its own context and, therefore, its own meaning. That is why the answer is found always in the question, and why danger itself fosters the rescuing power. The declension of *praxis* presents an even greater contrast (see Exhibit 30).

The only reason for control of any kind is the creation of capacity. Controls that constrict or suppress are perverse; that is, they produce the effect exactly opposite the intent. Invariably, energy is dissipated, as in activity. That was the fatal flaw of corporation-model organization. Authoritarian controls, assumed to be necessary for the production of desired results, stifled any immediate insight or ability arising out of actually doing the task, performing the work. It denied any prerogative or opportunity of creation. So, in effect, the capacity of the individual, as well as the whole system, was forever locked into the past of preconceived ends. While that concept may be understandable, perhaps even necessary, in manufacturing a product for which uniformity, precision, and gradation are prized attributes—even the measures of quality—it is inconceivable that mechanization was adopted as the universal promise of organization.

In business and in industry, even in information enterprises, the fixation on end results was tempered only by the obsession with continuously improving, through quantitative measures, the process of production. But action driven by process is even more sterile than action driven by results. Philosophies and practices such as the once-popular Total Quality Management (TQM), by focusing full attention on the efficiency and effectiveness of the process, completely eliminated the possibility of divergent spontaneity and experimentation; "best practices," "benchmarks," and "standards" only suffocated true Level II creativity along the way. It was the most autocratic, the most restrictive and, ultimately, the most self-destructive of all the management philosophies

Exhibit 30
Action as Discovery

	CONTEXT	KNOWLEDGE	PERFORMANCE	DEFINITION	EXAMPLES
PRAXIS	Immediacy of complete intelligence	• Practical wisdom • Intuition • Spiritual • Emotional	• Discovery • Capability • Energy generation • Insight	• Freedom (continuous creation)	• An artistic creation • An attempt at exporation • An original work

Source: Author.

of the twentieth century. It encouraged, in many instances, doing the wrong thing right. The truth of the matter is this:

- All standards are minimum.
- All benchmarks are bulwarks.
- All best practices are history.
- "Continuous improvement" is a systemized retreat into the past.
- "Progress" is a headlong rush into the present.

Public service enterprises, slavishly following the example of their corporate progenitor, not only transmuted these atavistic shackles into "measures" of behavior but also, because of their natural affinity for activity, established the strange practice of beginning every endeavor with rigid stipulations about how the outcomes would be assessed. All evaluation of performance was predicated on criteria stipulated before the activity started. Such inverted thinking ensured only one thing: the system would never have the capacity to continuously create itself. If there is no surprise in action, there can obviously be no real growth. Only in this manner can control create capacity. Action is the ultimate discipline in creating capacity.

Whole-context organization is a developmental concept. It would be foolhardy to expectantly thrust an individual or a system to praxis without having beforehand progressively and thoroughly identified the common core values, affirmed the commitment to mutual purpose, and guaranteed excess capacity throughout the system. Only then can action be truly creative.

It seems quite odd to suggest that there is a secondary benefit to praxis, yet that is precisely the case. There are at least four practical time-present advantages in organization. Taken alone, they have the power to radically transform any existing corporation-model system. Taken together, they are both the origin and the impetus of the constant rejuvenation of any system.

The first is *immediate action*. In traditional organization, there is inevitable lag time, often debilitating, between the idea and the action, not only because of the links in the chain of command or braids in the rope of accountability but because the idea always precedes the action. The first necessitates explicit direction; the second requires approval. Often both idea and action are diluted; sometimes the action is abandoned because the idea is lost or becomes irrelevant. The ideas indigenous to corporated cultures have a very short life span. But in whole-context organization, because the idea springs from the action, the agents of action are also the discoverers of the ideas and, therefore, are best situated to make immediate decisions or to explore ensuing action.

An ephemeral glimmer of this possibility was seen in the old oxy-moronic philosophy of participatory management. One of its so-called principles was that the person doing the job knows more about the job than anyone else. But in corporation-model organization, that could never become reality. The system was contrary by decision and dispo-sition. Not only was the person performing a task too far from the idea to affect it, he or she was deliberately unable and unauthorized to make anything of the action other than that already prescribed. The much-touted attempts at decentralization and "site-based" management were all failures for two universal reasons other than the intrinsic structural barriers. Even if the structures were ostensibly dismantled, there re-mained two insurmountable obstacles—both in action. First, the person was unprepared for that kind of personal involvement; second, everyone labored in a climate of fear—the fear that mistakes would be punished. Decentralization did not work because it could not work. Almost meta-phorically, the realization of the idea was not to be found in turning the system upside down (as some superficial thinkers suggested), but in turning action inside out.

The second, *concerted independence*, is actually a dual dimension: con-cert and independence. That simply means that it is possible for every person in the system to act independently of, yet in harmony with, the action of everyone else. Admittedly, and with all due respect to tradi-tional organization, this dynamic was not possible before the age of in-stantaneous communication. Whole-context organization requires whole-context awareness. This recent capability alone antiquates the cor-poration model, along with any other authoritarian construct, organi-zational or intellectual. Information, by its nature, destroys order; the more rigid the order and the more abundant the information, the more cataclysmic the collapse. In concerted independence, organization be-comes a natural formation rather than an artifactual construct.

This concept, of course, was completely foreign to traditional organi-zation, yet all of its energy was spent futilely trying to compensate for the inveterate lack of harmony. The attempts ranged from the direct and simple to the oblique and complicated. For example, the ancient organ-izational chart (a.k.a. "flow chart") was supposed to delineate the rela-tionships—always in terms of authority, and reputedly also of "function"—between and among positions, if not people. It was an exercise in connecting the boxes. And, as if to acknowledge the ghost in the machine, dotted lines became quite famous, although the reality was never manifested in corporeal action. A second operational device aimed at "coordination"—concert and harmony were for symphonies—was the committee. Committees are an overt admission that traditional organi-zation is fundamentally and irreparably flawed. Any mode of organi-zation vitality that depends on an adjunct life-support system has already administered its own last rites. Those with standing committees are zombies.

In the 1980's, committees were taken to their ultimate unnatural state of suspended animation by the sustained ritual of "teaming." It was as if some kind of stimulant had been injected into the vitals of organization in the hope of bringing it to life, but rather than reviving the late departed, it only embalmed the remains. The supposed fix of teaming—"cross-functional" teams, "project" teams, even "vertical" teams—all were the elixir of homeostasis. To their eternal credit, even the most traditional systems by the mid-1990's had given up on teaming. The reason was simple: they did not work. Collectives are not organismic; they are artificial.

Yet if all the other dimensions of whole-context organization are present, it is eminently possible that organization be so organismic that it can achieve concerted independent action. Perhaps the best way to understand this is through analogy. One that illustrates the point is that of a number of persons in an inflatable raft in rough seas. All are bound by common (need) values, by mutual purpose, and by capacity that increases as they translate their simultaneous awareness of wind and wave into individual acts of balance and motion. Verbal communication is unnecessary; no one barks commands. It is purely an instinctive act. If that same principle is transferred from a circumstance of extreme physical necessity, the response can likewise be transformed into knowledge—even intuition. Corporation-model organization made much of knowledge, apotheosizing it first as "profound," then "proprietary," and eventually "intellectual capital," even though usually it was little more than information, sometimes only clusters of random data. But knowledge, however defined, was the bread of life. Professional development curricula swelled with it; training directors carried it around, selectively casting it here and there, hoping for a quick return, whether or not it was perceptible. After all, it was promised that knowledge "empowers."

But knowledge, if the truth be known, is a trap, condemning those who are sustained by it to a minimal existence. The problem with knowledge is that if it is allowed to set for very long it becomes stale, impalpable. Even worse, it has a distinct tendency, like nothing else, to be completely unfit for human consumption.

Human beings have three potentialities: the physical, or instinctive; the mental, or intellective; and the spiritual, or intuitive. The corporation-model capitalized on the first, minimized the second, and ignored the third. Yet the life source of organization is intuition. It is both the creation and the energy of constant rejuvenation. When traditional organizations detect trouble in their activity, they look for knowledge to serve the problem. When they lack the knowledge, they turn to research. But all research is based on the troubled activity. (Perhaps cycles do exist after all—at least once.) Intuition is the only domain of creativity, and creativity is found only in action. But, amazingly, intuition is also at home in the physical or intellectual, if it is invited. Had Michelangelo actually seen David? Or did he meet him through the chisel? Did Michael Jordan design and execute his flights? Or did he discover them in mid-air? And when it comes to intuitively perceiving truth, there is in the awareness the instant compassion and easy trust that only old friends share.

The fourth unique benefit of praxis is *unlimited motivation*. It has already been pointed out that all systems ultimately are internally motivated. In fact, the case could be made that external force, even though it might have the effect of moving a person or a system, is not motivation at all, because any response to it is strictly that—a reaction. Direction and velocity are determined strictly by the application and degree of the force. In authoritarian organization, the force is always downward. The equal and opposite force is either resistance or dissipation. Authority may force activity, but it cannot force action. Action, even by its most "real" definition, requires conscious intent to accomplish, whether by prescription or exploration. If action does not emanate from the consciousness—yes, even the heart—of the person(s), then it is at best only a superficial charade of going through the motions. So any attempt to compel compliance by reward or punishment, or even a change of conditions, will result in movement, but only temporarily. Constant reinforcement leads inexorably to greater and greater reinforcement until at last a bulwark is erected between the force and the activity. Only an opposing authoritarian system, such as a labor union, can provide continuing negotiation of the obstacle.

It seems incredible that traditional organization overlooked the most basic principle of both individual and system action: the greater the freedom to act, the greater the action. Authority is but a perverse substitute for both. Obviously, freedom here does not refer to either license or prerogative; those are derivatives of authoritarian power. It is the freedom that comes only from continuously discovering one's full powers in meaningful action, whether it is in context or is itself the context. True motivation is self-generating; true motivation has no limits. Organization is nothing other than the natural form of motivation in action.

Chapter 14

Whole-Context Organization: The First Dynamic

Whole-context organization is characterized by two dynamics that exist concurrently among the four internal dimensions. It was suggested earlier that there is a special relationship between values and purpose and also between capacity and action, but that in no way diminishes the effective dynamic between any one of the dimensions and the others. Change one, change all. Obviously, it is impossible to depict in a two-dimensional graphic the constantly changing relationships between and among these dimensions. Any attempt would involve not a chart but a demonstration and would have to be, not surprisingly, somehow four-dimensional. Only an interactive hologram could approximate their continuous morphing in infinite variety.

That raises an interesting aside about dimensions of organization. The traditional organization chart, although it provided the original metaphor, manifested a completely other concept of dimension. It was "vertical" and "horizontal," with emphasis on the vertical. Neither was intrinsically related to the other, and both were static. But, at the risk of being abstract, the idea of dimensions is indeed an apt metaphor of whole-context organization, only here there are four. The most meaningful interpretation suggests the following correlation: *depth*—beliefs; *height*—purpose; *length* and *width*—capacity and action. That rendering would mean the depth-height relationship is like an axis with an equator, at which one becomes the other—defined by the other, like north and south. That is the special relationship between beliefs and purpose. But in the other relationship, while each dimension (direction) may be reckoned separately, each actually defines the other. That is to say, capacity is action and action is capacity.

In a further aside, completely off of any map, there is little doubt that a natural proportion rules the life of any system. This is not an excursion into numerology; it is merely an extension of the mathematical factors that customarily have been used to ascertain or predict the health of any manifestation of the corporation-model organization. Commercial enterprises recognize "vital signs" such as return on investment, return on assets, return on equity, debt to equity ratios, *et cetera*. All of these indications are mathematical calculations that must be kept within tight variances if the system is to thrive. Non-commercial enterprises use similar indices, typically some proportional relationship between "input" and "output."

It is curious indeed that no one has ever sought to examine the possibility that the ratio that occurs in all living things might be relevant to human organization. There is a great body of work, done by respectable scientists and scholars, that relates this phenomenon to everything from flowers to music to atoms, yet no one has attempted to find significance in organization, even though it seems critical to life itself. Not only does the proportion occur throughout nature, including the human body, it is, in fact, naturally imitated in all human artifacts, from playing cards to the Parthenon. For centuries it has been called the "golden mean," but no one seems to know what it means, only that it is always there. It is not a vain hypothesis to suggest that to know the meaning is to know the secret of continuous juvenation. In the previous chapter dealing with the life of systems, it was noted that there is a magic ratio that is found throughout the universe—specifically, .618034. Since the very essence of nature is vitality and dynamism, it is reasonable to conclude that there is some connection between this ratio and life itself. It is, in fact, approximated in the helix design of human DNA. Yet precisely how it works or what it means remains a mystery, even after centuries of speculation. But all indications point to its association with energy—the fundamental resource of any system. Could it be, for the sake of pure speculation, that the optimal health of a system is realized by its maintaining force of capacity .236067 more capable than the immediate practical action requires? Or could it mean that the natural *crisis* point of any system is irrecoverably passed at .618034 "input" versus .381966 "output"? Or, similarly, could it be that systems, in order to thrive, must be .618034 generative against .381966 degenerative?

The first question might gain some credibility by comparison to other informal, although mathematical, measures of viability, such as return on assets (20 percent) and the ubiquitous, yet unscientific, Pareto's law (20 percent of the business produces 80 percent of the profit). The second possibility may be borne out in the traditionally acceptable debt-equity ratios. The third suggests that any creative action is not a zero-sum game.

But there may be a more fundamental secret at work here; that is, the hallmark of a thriving system is a proportional reciprocity between capacity and action. While attempting to reduce this dynamic to an exact formula would be futile (after all, *pi* is only an approximation, probably because of malperception, and the force of gravity recently has been recalculated to reflect an expanding universe), the least fantastic interpretation is that in continuously emerging systems .381966 of true capacity is action, and .618034 of action is capacity. And while exactly what it means in actual systems may never be known, it is, nevertheless, safe to declare the substantial reciprocity of these two forces, capacity and action, as fact.

But back to the mainstream thought. The four dimensions of whole-context organization interact between and among themselves along two dynamics, which produces an infinite variety in the forms of organization. "Commensuration" and "essentiality" may be "put-offish" as terms but as ideas they are simple indeed. So simple, in fact, that only the characteristic complexity of rationalism could have obfuscated them, lo, these many centuries. They are, not surprisingly, eminently closer to the natural order of things than the traditional organizational design allows. As a matter of fact, it is this dual dynamic that informs whole-context organization.

COMMENSURATION

The truth is, corporation-model systems violated every principle of commensuration, and therefore were doomed to a perpetual struggle of irreconcilable self-contradiction. For example, and directly to the point, it was genetically authoritarian, yet it ostensibly elicited democratic participation, at least in its later stages. It expected, or demanded, a community-like loyalty, but it demonstrated no regard for community-type values, by artificially fabricating collectives. It demanded obedience, but it did not feel obligated to justify its own demands. It held rank-order sacred, but it habitually violated subordinates. It fostered isolation, yet it attempted to construct systems.

These fundamental contradictions made commensuration impossible in the four matters of management. Unlike the *principles* of management, which were, in effect, the process for exercising traditional organization, *matters* of management were the actual substance of management—the subject and object of action—and the basic ingredients of organization. They were, namely, *authority, information, accountability,* and *power.* All management considerations involved all matters. The first three were always considered in that order and always proceeded from the "top" of the system downward, but power cannot be placed specifically in the order for two reasons: it was part of all the others; and it was never overtly acknowledged with the others, as though it rose above, or fell below, rational or deliberate considerations. Yet power was as much a matter of management as the others. Often, especially in incapacitated systems, only power, or force, could ensure that the work of an enterprise was accomplished.

However, there was an inherent disparity among the matters of management in traditional organization. For example, authority always flowed downward, and accountability flowed upward. Middle managers were caught in a crunch that was not only confusing but often debilitating. It was this kind of disparity that accounted for the various so-called "management styles." The quickest and most lucid way to explain this rather complicated situation is through an illustration (see Exhibit 31). The styles were either contradictory within themselves or they conflicted with the others.

Through commensuration, these systemic contradictions are not simply eliminated, they are re-ordered and transformed into their natural states—probably the original form of organization.

- *Accountability* becomes *mutual commitments and expectations*
- *Authority* becomes *the freedom to act*
- *Information becomes knowledge*
- *Position power* becomes *person power*

In traditional organization, had the original concept been followed, the first consideration should have been accountability; in a real sense, that was precisely the intent of job descriptions. Authority, then, would have been derived, exactly in kind and degree, from accountability—not conversely, as was the practice. Information should have always been available strictly on a need-to-know basis. Most information in the modern corporation is extraneous and confusing; it is not even nice to know. And personal power should have taken the form of leading. Whole-context organization, on the other hand, instills commensuration throughout the system by carefully examining and relating all of the actions, individual and in concert, of all of those who constitute the system. In Chapter 7, "The Dynamics of Human Organization," it was suggested that the five basic assumptions of participatory management, although valid ideas, could not be realized in the confines of traditional organization. More to the point, none could be achieved through the practice of management. Commensuration moves those assumptions outside of the structures of traditional organization, translates them into

Exhibit 31
Matters of Management

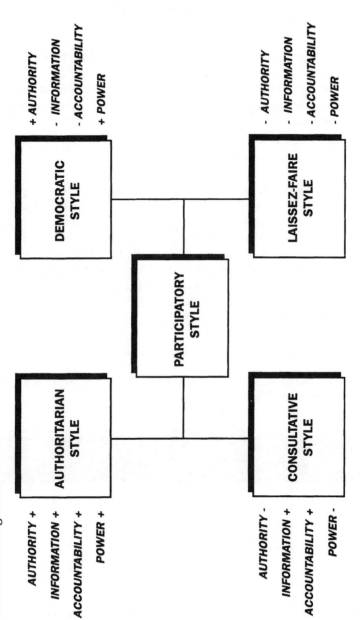

Source: Author.

principles, and allows each its full expression in a very practical dynamic. These principles, taken together, not only create new natural patterns of organization, they also constitute a completely new culture. And they themselves are significantly transformed.

- The person performing any job or task knows more about it than anyone else—even those who performed it yesterday.
- Everything about the system is given meaning by the context of strategic intent.
- Commitments and expectations, the freedom to act, knowledge, and power are proportionate.
- Decisions and action are immediate.
- All action is independent, yet in concert.

All organizational issues can be resolved only by the adoption of the practice and culture of mutual commitments and expectations. As in strategic planning, the explanation of mutual commitments and expectations is best presented as discipline and process, although here neither is quite as complex. Actually, both are quite basic, but they accomplish at once what job descriptions could never do. They give form; they establish the criteria for performance; and they provide system evaluation. Only in this way can the strategic plan be realized. All action is brought into the context of the mission and objectives.

THE DISCIPLINE

The discipline includes five components, arranged as a logical, progressive exposition of the job under consideration.

I Will Do This:	So That:	Specific Commitments: (Objectives)	Strategic Plan:	System Support Required:

Source: Author.

Interpreted, it would read:

What:	Why:	How Much:	Strategic Intent:	Resources/Assistance Necessary:

Source: Author.

A detailed analysis reveals the practical benefits of this approach.

Column 1: I (Will) Do This

This concept is a radical departure from the practice of corporation-model organization in several aspects. First, it begins with the person who is actually performing the job.* That is to say, the person who knows more about it than anyone else, not with upper-echelon prescriptions by those who may have only hearsay knowledge of the action. This is a critical point. Even if the "higher-ups" have previously held the job in question, they no longer really know it because they are not doing it, especially because the strategic plan changed its context and meaning.

Second, this approach comprehends the entire job, not just a few selected "goals," as in Management by Objectives (MBO). In MBO, as much as 90 percent of a job was never called into question after it was initially established.

Third, the specific responsibilities are presented not as they are or have been but as they *should be*, otherwise system change is impossible, and the special insights and preferences of the person doing the job are never realized.

Fourth, each job is localized and personalized. In traditional organization, a single, rigid job description, on file in the personnel office, applies to all individuals performing the same specified tasks. No allowance is made for differences in physical factors or in personal strengths and weaknesses. But in this approach, each person has his or

*This discussion will use the familiar word "job," even though there is a real possibility that the term may be disappearing from the vernacular of non-traditional organization. What will replace it is uncertain.

her own unique set of responsibilities. If two persons have exactly the same job, one of them is unnecessary.

Fifth, mutual commitments and expectations encourage the abandonment of tasks that are no longer consistent with the strategic intent. In traditional organization, every new plan was merely added on to existing responsibility. So it was the plan itself that was quickly abandoned, resulting in even more status quo. Or, if the new plans were not ignored, and actually attempted, the overload led to a system breakdown.

Sixth, the traditional organization forced individual performance evaluation to be based on job descriptions. Since that was a logical impossibility, adjunct methods of evaluation, which typically had nothing to do with the actual job, were invented as an artificial substitute. But the approach recommended here makes individual and system evaluation an integral part of continuing organization.

Seventh, in the traditional organization, typically the person doing the job was never told why—only what and how. But this approach begins with the reason for all action and assumes that the person doing the job knows what and how. In fact, nowhere in the discussion of the job is the "how" to be considered.

With regard to the details of the form, it is important that the specific responsibilities of the job be considered first as simple *nouns* (sometimes with modifiers). For discussion purposes, the phrase "I will be responsible for" may provide the introduction to the specific items of responsibility, within specific job *domains*, that each person intends to assume for the immediate future—say, one year. This is not to be a permanent obligation that is positional and attached to rank order, nor is it to be enshrined in the temple of the human resources office. The idea is to use only nouns that inherently imply necessary results, not mere activity or process. For example, "traveling," while technically a noun, implies no result of the activity. The entry must be the actual *purpose* of the travel— sales, inspection, customer service, research, *et cetera*—that from which results might be expected.

Only when the list of nouns is complete should the verbs be added. The verbs distinguish the relationships between and among those involved in the same domains. Again, this is fundamental. First, there is no such thing as "shared" responsibility. If two persons are responsible for exactly the same thing, neither is responsible for anything. It is especially important in systems that maintain supervisor-subordinate relationships that the verbs distinguish between the responsibilities, otherwise one becomes merely an echo of the other, and all decisions are made at least twice. Second, since the verbs express the degree of accountability, they should be as strong as possible. Wimpy words like "coordinate," "monitor," and "promote" are impossible to define in terms of results. (Real action coordinates, monitors, and promotes itself;

only activity requires life support.) If, in fact, such weak verbs are a part of the individuals "title," as in "coordinator," then the entire job needs to be re-thought in terms of results, not activity.

There is one special consideration about job responsibilities. Quite often, individuals in an enterprise take on special projects that are either related or not related to their primary responsibilities, such as developmental projects, research, construction, technologizing, or civic involvement. All of these duties must be considered just as any other part of the job, validated by results and objectified in the same fashion. However, it is advisable to make sure that some kind of graphic distinction be made between those and other items so that all persons involved or affected will know that those responsibilities are in a special, temporary class and not an essential part of the basic responsibility. For instance, the use of asterisks on a different style print or visual separation will immediately signal that these items are distinct.

Column 2: So That

The second column, "So that," calls for a specific statement of why each job action is to be taken. Stated as results that are measurable, observable, or demonstrable, the phraseology of the statement completes the verbs and nouns of the initial "I do this." However, the exact objective measures are not specified here. The idea is to test each action's contribution to the strategic mission and objectives of the enterprise. Actually, this is the litmus test of all individual action. Each job responsibility probably will have more than one intended outcome, and it is possible that more than one specific responsibility will bring about the same result. For sake of clarity, the standard outline form is recommended.

There are two major benefits of this exercise. First, it ensures that individual action is aligned with the strategic plan. Some jobs will be radically changed, or even eliminated. Second, it will impress the strategic intent into all actions, thus bringing strategic context to the whole system.

There is an especially critical consideration in identifying the results to be listed in Column 2. That is, each must be the next, direct, immediate consequence of the corresponding action in Column 1. True commensuration dictates that one cannot be responsible for that which he or she cannot control. And it must be remembered that there are two aspects of control—authority (or freedom to act) and immediacy (or absence of intervening factors). The first is settled only by the assumption that authority is implicit in responsibility and always carries the resources necessary to accomplish the action. The second, immediacy, is a simple matter of understanding cause and effect. For example, suppose someone, with the responsibility of training and developing staff, in Column 1 states that he or she will "direct staff development." There are three hypothetical results that could follow "So that:" (1) profitability is achieved; (2) staff performance improves; or (3) staff *can* improve their performance to some specified level. The first is untenable as a result because there are too many variables between the training and the system's profits over which the staff developer has no control. The second is most likely the domain of someone who is responsible for production. Only the third is reasonably the next, direct, immediate result of training.

This approach not only fairly and clearly appropriates outcomes to individual action, it also reconciles all related action within the system. No one is unjustifiably burdened, and no one can hide. And, in a larger sense, it builds system capacity. For that reason, rather detailed analyses are appropriate here.

At this juncture, it is necessary to raise again the concept of the different kinds of action, because there is a real possibility that individual responsibilities will contain all three. The discussion so far of mutual commitments and expectations quite easily accommodates *poiēsis*. And the entries in Column 1 also will be similar for *theōria* and *praxis*. However, Column 2 will be substantially different for both of these actions.

Action as *theōria* cannot be bound in advance to precisely specified results, because programs and explorations by their nature are directed toward outcomes not discernible at the outset of the action. The specific result is evolved through the action, so the results proposed here must meet three general requirements: (1) they must provide a favorable return on investment, (2) they must include evaluative criteria, and (3) they must be consistent with reason.

Action as *praxis*, however, is unique. In fact, ultimately it may not be reducible to this kind of analysis. Yet in order to guarantee that the system's creativity and constant emergence does not depend solely on serendipity, commitments and expectations must include the responsibility for discovery and the exploration of ideas and possibilities, even though they cannot be imagined in advance. Even here though there are certain criteria for expected results: (1) they must be out of the existing context; (2) they must have breakthrough potential; (3) they must provoke Level II change; and (4) they must be new in kind. At least one company refers to these as "grand slam" results.

Column 3: Specific Commitments or Objectives

The "specific commitments or objectives" column must accommodate, in both style and substance, the variations in results by corresponding variations in specific measures or indicators. For example, the first kind of action, *poiēsis*, will produce results that are measurable quantitatively or that are observable by established criteria. However, the results arising from *theōria*, although just as certain, will be less specific and will be determined by the action. Suppose a job responsibility is worded as "I will ensure effective advertising," the result stated "So that our goods, products, or services become a household word." The specific objectives would necessarily have to contain measures of efficacy, criteria for success, cost-benefit factors, and marks of internal systemization and market impact.

Praxis presents yet another scenario. Because this kind of action is about exploration, attempting to project any objectives up front would be premature and restrictive. In fact, strange as it seems, the only outcome that can be logically imposed is the outer limit of the action. Again, suppose that a job responsibility is stated as "I will develop replenishing point-of-sale merchandise." In this instance, the actual results cannot be known and, therefore, neither can the indicators of viability, until the action reveals opportunities otherwise inconceivable. It is possible that the action might discover merchandising possibilities that would render point-of-sale old-fashioned. In this kind of action, "objective" takes on a converse meaning. In *poiēsis* and *theōria*, the intent was to stimulate action toward the achievement of a very high objective; in *praxis*, which assumes impetus implicit in creativity, the idea is to identify any limits that are not to be exceeded, much like parameters in strategic planing. For example, "My specific commitment is always to affect positively the existing lines of goods, products, and services," or "to not engage in self-competition." But it also would be appropriate to include any of the indicators from *theōria* that would be applicable, such as return on investment.

Column 4: Strategic Plan Reference

The fourth column is more than a simple reference; it represents the only practical way to infuse the strategic plan into the day-to-day action of all individuals. Column 1 aligned the jobs with the mission and objectives; Column 4 ensures that all applicable action plans are translated into individual action. That is not to say, however, that each result and specific commitment will be referenced, because the strategic plan did not deal directly with all aspects of the system nor with all aspects of individual jobs. Typically, only 20 percent to 30 percent of the items will be referenced as action plans. A designation of II 3 (4) indicates strategy II, plan 3, step 4. However, it is appropriate to reference other components of the strategic plan, such as mission and objectives.

There is another process benefit of this column. Each strategic plan update (typically, each year) includes a report on the current status of each action plan. Referencing them in this way facilitates the tracking and retrieval of that information. The significance of this will be apparent in the later discussion of periodic updates.

Column 5: System Support

The last column expresses the special support that will be required to achieve the specific commitments (see Exhibits 32, 33, and 34). This support may be from other individuals or from the entire system. Usually, those conditions are identified only for those results and commitments that are extraordinary, that is, they have a direct connection to the strategies or action plans. There is a dual advantage in agreeing on the necessary support in advance: it prevents both surprise and disappointment.

THE PROCESS

The method of developing the mutual commitments and expectations may vary with the physical situation, decision-making philosophy, and technological maturity of the enterprise. What one system would accomplish in a relatively low-tech, but perhaps more human fashion, another might be more comfortable conducting via electronic means, such as an e-system. The only limits are the imagination and the acceptance of the medium. It is also true that the adoption of this process may be a matter of degrees, that is, it may be taken only as far as the enterprise can and will go. But, taken in any measure, it is superior to traditional organization. In every case, though, the basic process would be the same. To simplify, the process is described here in steps.

Step 1

This concept represents a radical departure from traditional job descriptions and evaluation methodologies, so it is critical that no attempt be made to develop the mutual commitments and expectations until all who are to be involved have been thoroughly familiarized with the discipline and process. Care must be taken to relate, by comparison and contrast, the aspects of the new approach with those of the previous method. Obviously there is a wide variety of ways in which to accomplish this, but, no matter what the manner, ultimately there will have to be considerable face-to-face conversation just to ensure understanding and acceptance of all of the many subtleties of this approach. And it is rather difficult, even then, to initially establish this approach as the routine way of doing business. Usually it is necessary for the chief executive officer to take the lead in instigating the new procedure.

Exhibit 32
Action as Poiēsis

I WILL DO THIS:	SO THAT:	SPECIFIC COMMITMENTS: (OBJECTIVES)	STRATEGIC PLAN:	SYSTEM SUPPORT REQUIRED:
• Direct/Immediate responsibilities	Results must be: • Consistent with Beliefs, Mission, Parameters, Objectives, and Strategies • Measurable, demonstrable, or observable • Direct immediate consequence(s) • Commensurate with: • decision-making prerogative • resources	• Specific measures in terms of time, money, quality, and/or quantity for each result • Observable indicators of specific results	• References to applicable strategies and action plans	• Expression of the whole system's commitment of energy and resources to expectations

Verb (2)	Noun (1)
	Domain
	Relationships

Source: Author.

Exhibit 33
Action as Theória

I WILL DO THIS:	SO THAT:	SPECIFIC COMMITMENTS: (OBJECTIVES)	STRATEGIC PLAN:	SYSTEM SUPPORT REQUIRED:
• Direct/Immediate responsibilities	Activity must be • Consistent with the context of the strategic plan	• Specific demonstration(s) of efficacy • Criteria of success		• Expression of the whole system's commitment of energy and resources to expectations
Verb (2) Noun (1)	• Dedicated to a general result	• Identification of benefits re: investment		
	• Inclusive of evaluative criteria	• Systemization of results		
Domain	• Commensurate with return on investment		• References to applicable strategies and action plans	
Relationships	• Consistent with logic * resources			

Source: Author.

Exhibit 34
Action as Praxis

I WILL DO THIS:	SO THAT:	SPECIFIC COMMITMENTS: (OBJECTIVES)	STRATEGIC PLAN:	SYSTEM SUPPORT REQUIRED:
• Direct/Immediate responsibilities	• Out of current context	• Limits not to be exceeded		• Expression of the whole system's commitment of energy and resources to expectations
Verb (2) Noun (1)	• Breakthrough potential		• References to applicable strategies and action plans	
Domain	• Level II change			
Relationships				

Source: Author.

223

Step 2

Each individual next completes a draft of his or her mutual commitments and expectations. This is quite effectively accomplished in groups of persons with like responsibilities. The intent is not to develop a single consistent outline of responsibilities for every one in the group—a template, as it were—but to localize and personalize individual duties. No two should be exactly alike.

The process should begin with the simple nouns, then verbs, results, references, and support. Once the like groups have completed their individualized form, the conversations must be extended to the broader context of the total system, especially those parts that are naturally related. For example, this stage of the discussion might include research and development, marketing, sales, manufacturing and distribution—or any combination thereof. The idea is to harmonize all action, to eliminate duplication, to close gaps, and to delineate specific compatible responsibilities across a broad spectrum of action. It must be emphasized that "shared" responsibility inevitably increases activity but amounts to little action.

It is important here to note that this approach does not compromise mutual support. It actually strengthens the supportive relationships through the understanding of individual roles and the vested interest that each has in all of the others.

Step 3

The next step in the development of mutual commitments and expectations is the systemization of individual responsibilities. The coordination of this exercise is more important than the procedure by which it is accomplished. Again, the method may vary widely from one enterprise to another. For example, it may be accomplished in ever-expanding clusters of individuals until the entire system is encompassed, or it may be more quickly handled by posting the complete mutual commitments and expectations on the organization's intranet and having each individual articulate his or her responsibilities with all of those related, directly or indirectly.

Acceptance or approval is also mutual, but ultimate approval is the responsibility of those who are charged with the overall performance of the system, such as the chief executive officer. Very likely, those individuals would have been involved in the discussions of responsibilities from the outset, providing whatever direction was appropriate, participating in setting expectations, and pledging support for extraordinary action.

The hidden advantage of this approach is that the person doing the job almost always sets higher expectations for his or her performance than the old-line supervisor or manager dared to do. Traditional job descriptions, "performance standards," and "goals" leave much capability and energy unused.

Step 4

In traditional organization, job descriptions were cast in stone; they became monuments to stasis and benign neglect. Evaluation was always top-down and, typically, more or less critical, sometimes punitive, and totally unrelated to the actual job. In stark contrast, mutual commitments and expectations are works in progress, constantly reviewed and updated, with a view toward reconceptualizing results and objectives and especially toward adjusting the resources and energies of the entire system to the tasks. It is, thus, not as much the evaluation of the performance of individuals as the evaluation of the system's performance and a constant check on the allocation of resources and energies. The updates and revisions are conducted simply by continually engaging in Steps 2 and 3.

With all due respect to traditional systems of organization, this continuous, immediate awareness of responsibilities and action throughout the system was not possible until the advent of modern technology. Information, like authority and accountability, had to flow through "channels" or "chains," but no longer. It now forms its own web of mutual commitments and interrelationships (even if the formal organizational structure does not recognize it). In this way, organization is translated from rigid constructs of line and staff positions, held together by command and control, into relationships that are continuously morphing into new forms. There is no template, no chart, no prescribed design with boxes to fill. There is, rather, the natural form of action.

One final word about mutual commitments and expectations. It may be that existing enterprises will have great difficulty adopting what must surely seem to be a laborious, time-consuming process without any appreciable benefit. Admittedly, it takes time to make the complete transformation—usually at least a year. But, during that time, attention is not directed away from responsibilities and strategic intent. Rather, concentration is focused like never before on meaningful action toward the achievement of mutual purpose.

Chapter 15

Whole-Context Organization: The Second Dynamic

Although commensuration ensures the optimal capacity of each individual in the system, there is another factor required to guarantee the excess capacity of the whole system. It was suggested in the previous discussion of the four dimensions—beliefs, purpose, capacity, and action—that the ideal consequence of harmony among these factors was "concerted independent action," that is, each individual performing his or her duties without direction, without correction, yet in perfect synchronism with everyone else. Even if that were possible, as indeed it surely is—especially in smaller systems—larger, more complex systems magnify another dynamic implicit in any demonstration of whole-context organization.

This dynamic is just as present and critical in smaller systems, only it is not as perceptible. This it true because the larger systems necessarily arrange themselves into clusters of related action, evidently in order to create an immediate context for action as well as to provide control. This kind of clustering is seen in the physical arrangement of all natural systems, including bodies, and is imitated, for efficiency sake, in most human artifacts, such as machines. Clustering of action reveals a dynamic of organization that is, in effect, the basic requirement of system identity. As for artifactual systems, the more complex the system—as in ultra-high technology—the more integral the principle, until they actually become organismic.

In the previous chapter on the nature of organization, it was pointed out that one of the characteristics of thriving systems is *essentiality* (along with control, life, and motivation). It also was suggested that this meant more than just the common figure of speech in which a part and a whole stand for each other (*synecdoche*), but that the system was thoroughly and completely of the same stuff—an organic oneness beyond collective unity.

Commensuration is critical because it energizes a constant balance between and among the vital actions of the system. Without it, the system would lose control and become an unwieldy monstrosity. So it is accurate to say that commensuration is a kind of quantitative regulator, obviously not in a perverse sense but as the discipline of creativity and expanding energy. *Essentiality*, in contradistinction, is the quality of the system—its life and its motivation. With it, everything about the system is qualitatively the same; without it, there is no system—only bits and pieces.

Essentiality is most readily detectable in the attitude toward and of the clusters of action within the system. It is here that the centuries-old question about whether systems are atomistic or organismic is answered. Not only is the realization of the strategic plan contingent on the answer, but the vitality of the system depends on it; that is, whether it actually moves, and, if so, does it move as one organism.

ESSENTIALITY

If there is any one flaw in the structure of traditional organization that attests to its abject unnaturalness and, at the same time, guarantees its ineffectiveness and inefficiency, it is the absence of essentiality. The gracious assessment of this glaring omission would be that this factor was simply overlooked in the mad rush to rationalize systems of production, all characterized by interchangeable parts, during the frenetic industrial revolution, and deferentially ignored since by organization experts and gurus who were too kind or too politic to expose the error. That is, in fact, the sad legacy of academic and professional commentary or organization during the nineteenth and twentieth centuries.

Organization theory, like history, is always screened through the perspective of those who write it and focused on the perspective of those who will read it. Neither may see, or want to see, the truth. As incredible as it is, there is considerable evidence that the omission of any concern for essentiality was deliberate—an intentional effort to assert authoritarian control over the system, even though it meant inherent conflict and disparity within organization. Actually, it was anti-organization; perverse control is always contrary to organization. It would be a case of double naiveté to suggest that the architects of the mechanistic, traditional organization did not know what they were doing, but even they could not have imagined the dire effect their construct ultimately would have on Western organization.

Earlier, in the section on the definition of systems, it was noted that human systems are either organismic or atomistic. Later in the discussion, in the chapter on organization, it was suggested that there was, at least in the minds of some, a real distinction between formations and constructs. It was also recalled that the question was a subject of popular debate during the nineteenth century, and that the issue was resolved, for the time, in 1908, in favor of the atomistic argument. It was a very practical decision at the end of a long intellectual debate. After all, any process of production takes on the form of its product (mechanical processes are required to produce machines), and organization takes the form of the production process. So, as the work was parceled out on the factory floor and neatly arranged into a systemized order, with the precision and uniformity of the product, the system was "organized" similarly into parts or departments. Quite logically, this systemization became the only real meaning of "organize." It was a one-word oxymoron. There was nothing organismic about it. The traditional organization chart, a misapplication of a design first used by the Lydians in 546 B.C., was cast into a permanent structure with no apparent moving parts, although all were replaceable by others built to the same specifications.

There were two devastating consequences of this inanimate construction. First, the parts within the system were irreconcilably isolated, and in most cases arrayed against one another, not just because of human tendencies, such as competition or jealously, but because the system itself encouraged fragmentation. As the effect began to be realized, management theorists attempted to make the best of a bad situation. First, they began extolling the rife divisions within the system by encouraging internal competition as a means, they alleged, of strengthening the whole system. Competition, as the notion was, always makes everyone better. But the result only proved to further exacerbate the problem. The fragments took on their own identity and pursued their own interests.

A quick example illustrates the adverse effect on organization. At a recent meeting of the senior executives of a bank, each department head—of course, all vice presidents—was presented with the monthly operating statements. The consolidated statement appeared first, followed by the statements for each department's performance. No one looked at the consolidated statement. Everyone turned to his or her own department. But here is the amazing thing: each department showed a net profit (each was able to charge another department for services), but the company showed a serious net loss. The chairman was so enraged that he changed the accounting procedure, as well as the organization, on the spot.

No doubt this fiasco arose from the management experts' advice about this time that not only were the departments considered competitors but that each should actually operate as its own company. It was an idea whose time had passed. The foolish notion evidently originated, or at least was popularized, in the 1920's, when General Motors tried unsuccessfully to gain efficiency by organizing into formal operating divisions, each with its own corporate structure. The idea waxed and waned alternatively over the next half-century until desperate times and conditions made it *de rigueur* in the 1980's. In an effort to stave off system collapse, control was instituted over and in the system by elevating the departments to "the primary decision-making unit" and the department heads to "unit presidents," although neither were given the authority or information necessary to fulfill the promise. This aberration was officially diagnosed as "decentralization," but it was actually nothing other than a cynical or desperate attempt to more firmly establish central control.

Without question, this movement was the most serious blunder in all the annals of organization. It caused more confusion, created more animosity, consumed more negative energy, and produced more foolish commentary than any other idea in the history of Western civilization. Decentralization, or "site-based management," created two unsolvable problems: it pitted the various departments against other; and it caused a great schism between the whole system and its components. Ultimately, it did not work because it would not work.

The effect of this misbegotten notion was different, depending on whether the system was a commercial corporation or a public-sector, non-profit enterprise. In most corporations, the idea, as well as the jargon, died before it could do any more harm. The final brief *delirium tremens* was something described as "teaming." But when that subsided, most department heads quietly went back to being rulers of their own empires, which had naturally followed the original departmentalism of organization. And why not? They were, after all, separated by the design from meaningful contact with others, out of reach and out of touch, usually forgotten until there was trouble. Each was an island; the only connection to the mainland was a thin vertical or horizontal line, often dotted.

However, that was not the case in the public sector. Administration theory and practice unfortunately is wont to gobble up the scraps that fall from the table of management; and, this time, they were so starved for any kind of sustenance to restore life to failing bureaucracies that they, especially education systems, went into a feeding frenzy, gorging themselves with stuff they could not even identify. They actually believed that credibility and efficacy could be achieved by imitating commercial corporations.

This idea, whose time had long since passed and had already proved unworkable in the corporation, quickly became the darling of the great "reform" movement in public education and other governmental agencies between 1985 and 2000. Permanent damage was inflicted when every state mandated through legislation "site-based (school-based) management" as the primary means of reformation. Reorganization is always a handy substitute for substantial change, an alibi for perpetuating obsolete systems, a happy distraction from the real issue of displacement of old concepts with the creation of new ones.

The lasting result was the terminal fragmentation of systems. Kingdoms were turned into so many fiefdoms—each with simulated authority, too much information that was actually data, and no real accountability. In public education, "school councils," a cheap imitation of district boards, were, by law, able to do as they pleased, thus establishing a *de facto* system of schools rather than an educational system. It was a farce, played out on a grand scale. At a national conference, a feature presentation was given the unlikely title of *"Sight*-Based Management"; sadly, no one knew whether it was an intentional pun or a serious treatment of the subject. Could that have been the defining moment of the whole reform movement?

The second adverse consequence was an inevitable dichotomizing of the system that allied the decentralized parts of the erstwhile system against anything that resembled centralization. Of course, in traditional organization, there was always an ironic, unnatural tension between centralized authority and decentralized (or even personal) ambition. How many military company commanders never cursed the incompetence of the officious charlatans in the S-1 (personnel) or S-3 (operations) offices? And how many civilian department heads never complained or whined about the basic stupidity of decisions made by central authorities? In those cases, the negative reaction was just as likely to have a somewhat positive effect. It relieved the tension and created a sense of victim camaraderie among those in the department. "We are in this together" and "this too shall pass" were common refrains sung by the choir of the mistreated and bent-out-of-shape. The dirge was an anthem of *esprit de corps*.

It was not until management/administrative theories began actually advocating this inherent conflict as a desirable, healthy way to organize that it became totally destructive. Their advocacy was both implicit and explicit. Some, such as the big-number accounting firms that ventured into management consulting, simply assumed that this duality was natural and audited organizational design accordingly. So-called "management audits" were based on this fundamental acceptance of the whole versus the parts. Their conclusions reinforced the dichotomy. Some independent consultants, such as Deming and Covey, actually proclaimed the schism as healthy and recommended a "loose-tight" relationship between the two. Evidently, this means that the relationship was continuously negotiable but that the freedom of the various parts of the organization would at some point be checked, even withdrawn. The perception was that the whole and the parts were two separate entities in constant play against each other, and from that tension good things would arise. Unfortunately, this advice overlooks the aphorism about a house divided against itself.

The test of essentiality, as well as its demonstration, is the way in which the clusters within the system go about planning, because planning implicitly carries the system's philosophy of organization into practice and explicitly manifests in the practice the inherent philosophy, whether intentional or situational.

Here words get in the way of clarity. The challenge is to shape the ideas in understandable language without allowing those terms to compromise the intended meaning. In this case, to use the traditional management/administrative terms such as "site," "unit," or "department" would cast the discourse in the very concepts that are being abandoned. That is precisely the reason actual systems have such difficulty in realizing new (in kind) ideas—they are shackled to old language. For example, "web site" makes no sense as either, and certainly not as one. But any new vocabulary runs the risk of seeming—at least initially—awkward, affected, and artificial.

Nevertheless, to acquiesce to traditional language is often to lose the idea. So in an effort to escape the stifling effect of traditional organization and its trappings, this discussion will venture into new language, suitable for new ways of thinking, to describe the liberal essentiality of the clusters of action within thriving systems. It will sparingly use terms such as "site-based planing," "unit planning," or "operational planning," because that terminology necessary connotes archaic, fragmented, dichotomized constructs. The operative new term that will be suggested is "action-cluster planning."

ACTION-CLUSTER PLANNING

In order to maintain congruence in the system and true *sophrosyne** in organization, the planning conducted by the clusters of action must be not only consistent with, but also facilitative of, both the strategic plan of the system and the mutual commitments and expectations of the individual within the systems. So it would logically hold that the simplest way to approach action-cluster planning is to replicate the process and discipline of strategic planning, and, indeed, that is correct. In fact, it is desirable that the same concepts and terminology be employed insofar

---

*This word has been given various meanings by those who have offered critiques and observations of modern organization. Usually intended as a recommendation, it often is defined as "discipline," "moderation," or "self-control." But in this study, within this context, it is to be interpreted as "harmony," as in music. That is actually closer to its nominal definition.

Exhibit 35
Ends vs. Means

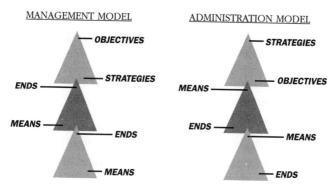

MANAGEMENT MODEL

- OBJECTIVES
- STRATEGIES
ENDS
MEANS
- ENDS
- MEANS

ADMINISTRATION MODEL

- STRATEGIES
- OBJECTIVES
MEANS
ENDS
- MEANS
- ENDS

Source: Author.

as possible. However, there are certain unique nuances in both the process and discipline that derive from the rationale for cluster planning.

In traditional organization, all departmental planning, at least until the chaos precipitated by site-based management, presupposed an interlocking pattern of delegation in which the strategies of any unit became the objectives of the "sub"-unit. That is, the *means* of one were inversely translated into the *ends* of the other, right through job descriptions. At least that was true in the corporate model. In public enterprises, the means and ends were inexplicably reversed, so the objectives of the unit became the strategies of the sub-unit; therefore, all of the objectives of the sub-unit were actually means, processes (see Exhibit 35). The results were unmitigated fragmentation and confusion.

But that approach, in either interpretation, although it gives the illusion of harmony, only institutionalizes fragmentation by setting in place interlocked but nevertheless distinct systems with variable relationships across a wide spectrum of possibilities, from aversion to mating. And that is the greatest danger in cluster planning—that it succumb to that mechanical design and become a "loose-tight" collection of parts.

However, in whole-context organization, action-clusters are, first, an *expedient* for facilitating the accomplishment of individual responsibilities within the context of the system's strategic plan, and, second, a continuous stimulus for individual creativity as well as the development of individual and system capacity. In the first instance, cluster planning, just as the process of identifying mutual commitments and expectations by clusters of action, provides an immediate and practical means of harmonizing and directing all individual effort toward the system's strategic intent. In the second, instant contextual referencing provides the impetus and validation for the creation of both individual and system capacity.

Exhibit 36
Action-Cluster Plan Discipline

STRATEGIC PLAN	ACTION-CLUSTER PLAN
1. Beliefs	1. Mission Statement
2. Mission Statement	
3. Strategic Parameters	
4. Internal Analysis	2. Internal Analysis
5. External Analysis	3. External Analysis
6. Competition	
7. Objectives	4. Objectives
8. Critical Issues	5. Critical Issues
9. Strategies	6. Tactics
10. Action Plans	7. Action Plans

Source: Author.

Existing somewhere between the system's strategic plan and the individual mutual commitments and expectations, cluster planning demonstrates essentiality. As a very practical example, all of the specific initiatives developed here (tactics) will be equivalent in the nature and scope of action to the specific job responsibilities of individual mutual commitments and expectations.

For all of the forgoing reasons, the discussion of action-cluster planning will proceed by examining the differences between its protocols and those of strategic planning. It must be noted in advance that the degree of similarity, especially in the planning disciplines, may well be an indication of the disposition of the organization to traditional rationalistic structures. That is, it would be expected that all sub-systems exactly duplicate the supra-system. It will expedite the discussion simply to use the aspects of the discipline and process of strategic planning as points of contrast.

THE DISCIPLINE OF THE PLAN

While a quick comparison (see Exhibit 36) indicates the compatibility of both the terminology and substance of the plans, the contrast lies in definitions.

Beliefs

There is no need for cluster plans to develop a statement of beliefs, since the strategic plan articulates the values of the system. However, more as process than discipline, the belief statement of the system should be thoroughly considered with emphasis on its implications for the cluster of actions that is engaged in planning. Three questions are appropriate for this discussion: (1) What is the real meaning of each belief? (2) How does the cluster of action currently manifest these values? (3) Do the individuals in the cluster actually hold these ideals? While the answers are not formally recorded, or even agreed upon, the effect will be an understanding of the moral discipline that undergirds the plan of the cluster and informs each aspect of it.

Mission

There are only two conditions that justify the development of action-cluster plans: the segmentation or compartmentalization of the strategic system's processes, and the physical or cyberspace location of the cluster of actions. Either or both provide the context for the identity, purpose, and means of the cluster of action. In fact, the mission is the expression of the commonality of action that determines whether there is indeed a cluster, as opposed to loosely connected fragments. Unless there is deliberate redundancy or duplication in the strategic system, the identity of each cluster will be unique. The purpose will be the mutual action of all within the cluster, and the means will describe the orchestration of concerted action.

Parameters

As with beliefs, the strategic parameters apply also to the action of clusters, so it is not necessary to reiterate them here, although it would be prudent to include them as a part of the cluster's plan. However, depending on the circumstances, it might be appropriate for the cluster to articulate its own policies, especially if it operates in an environment particular to itself—such as a distant location or a specific professional specialty—or operates in a larger sphere of political or social influence. However, any cluster parameters must be consistent with those of the strategic system.

Internal Analysis

The internal factors considered here are, as in strategic planning, the strengths, weaknesses, and critical analysis of organization, only here "internal" must be as interpreted as pertaining to the actions and relationships within the cluster itself, not within the strategic system. The critical analysis of organization should be a serious, open assessment of the interaction among the individuals in the action-cluster.

External Analysis

This analysis will not be as sweeping or as comprehensive as that of strategic planning. External factors here are the other aspects of the strategic system that have a potential impact on the actions of the cluster. Difficult to categorize completely, those factors may be the policies and procedures of the strategic system or projected events, conditions, and circumstances facing the system, or even the strategic plan. In some instances, the cluster also may be directly affected by factors external to the system, but consideration should be limited only to those that are cluster action specific and, consequently, may affect the entire strategic system. For example, a cluster of action involving personnel would surely want to calculate the effect of an increase in the minimum wage rate. A manufacturing cluster would have to consider the implications of recently legislated safety standards. Obviously this kind of analysis also can provide the system with intelligence to support strategic decisions.

Competition would be considered an external factor only if the action-cluster were directly pitted against some entity outside of the system. That can occur in two ways. First, in commercial systems, sometimes a cluster of action (say, a department), for the dubious reason of achieving high quality at a low cost, is compelled to operate in a free market in providing services for other parts of the system. In effect, it, as a profit center, becomes a vendor; the rest of the system constitutes its "customers." Sometimes the cluster may actually have customers outside of the system. Second, in public enterprises, any action-cluster in the system may have to deal with direct competition from the private sector. For example, an individual school in a school district may be forced to compete with a neighboring private or parochial school. In the first instance, the system, in effect, is competing with itself; in the second, the competition of the school is the competition also of the school district.

Objectives

The technical definitions here are the same as with strategic objectives. The only difference is the scope. Strategic objectives pertained to the entire system; cluster objectives specify the measurable, observable, or demonstrable results of the action of the cluster on the entire strategic system.

Critical Issues

Because the matter of life cycle is always a strategic consideration, critical issues for action-clusters take on a less ominous perspective. True, the life cycle of the strategic system is a relevant concern for the cluster since it is, in fact, included in it; but that would be addressed as an external factor. Here the critical issues are the threats and opportunities revealed to the cluster through the analysis of internal and external circumstances. Again, the threats are not matters of volition, but the opportunities are strictly optional.

Tactics

This may seem an out-of-place term, but the idea is to maintain consistency in the terminology of the protocols. Only a strategic system can legitimately create and undertake "strategy." So the initiatives of action-clusters are logically tactics, subordinate actions, yet wholly consistent with the strategies. In scope and influence, tactics are equivalent to the action plans of the strategic system. The steps in the tactics correspond to the job responsibilities in mutual commitments and expectations. Again, the essentiality of the system is demonstrated by this convergence of actions.

THE PROCESS OF PLANNING

The process of cluster planning will vary significantly, depending on many variables, including size and the philosophical disposition of those involved. But, most notably, it depends on whether and to what degree the cluster is formally organized and recognized by the strategic system. If in fact the action-cluster has the official status of what in traditional systems was referred to as an "operational unit," then the process will be a virtual mirror image of that used in strategic planning, adjusted to size and complexity. Comparison to the strategic planning process easily reflects the characteristics of cluster planning (see Exhibit 37).

Because most strategic systems still adhere to the traditional organizational structure with departments operating as "units" within a single structure, each with its own imitative organization, the process that best optimizes that arrangement is detailed here. It can be followed in the full faith and assurance that something unexpected will most certainly happen to benefit the entire system, so, the purpose of the strategic system will be more than served.

(1) The first step in the process, create a *receptive climate*, includes receiving authorization to proceed. Authorization typically comes from the chief executive officer, with the knowledge and consent of the board.

Exhibit 37
Process of Strategic and Cluster Plans

Strategic Planning	Action-Cluster Planning
1. Confirm commitment and readiness • Conduct basic awareness session(s) • Explore system capacity and design 2. Prepare for planning • Communicate about planning • Collect vital signs data 3. Build strategic planning team 4. Conduct first planning session • Prepare draft plan • Discipline components 1-9 5. Communicate draft plan 6. Build action teams 7. Develop action plans 8. Conduct second planning session • Achieve agreement action plans • Affirm agreement on strategic plan 9. Prepare implementation schedule (with supporting resource plan) 10. Obtain approval 11. Develop capacity for action • Develop strategic intent • Develop mutual expectations and system design • Systemize involvement/relationships 12. Validate plans and process continually • Regular reviews • Periodic updates	1. Create a receptive climate 2. Collect relevant information 3. Select planning team 4. Conduct first planning session • Discipline components 5. Communicate draft plan 6. Develop action plans 7. Conduct second planning session • Achieve agreement action plans • Affirm agreement on cluster mission, objectives, tactics 8. Approve plan 9. Design organization through action 10. Review progress 11. Update annually

Source: Author.

Developing unit plans without proper authorization can be risky. When plans are developed without authorization, they can be scuttled on a moment's notice by the chief executive officer or the board. Promises are made but not kept. Credibility and enthusiasm are seriously damaged.

Creating a receptive climate also involves clearly communicating to everyone involved why a plan is being created, what the plan is designed to do, who will be on the planning team, and when the planning will take place. It provides an opportunity to expand understanding of the strategic intent of the system and the role each part of the system plays in realizing that intent. This communication keeps everyone informed and reduces the suspicion and doubt that often arise when something "new" is being initiated.

(2) The second step in the process is to collect *relevant information* for the planning team. This information should provide a "snapshot" of the unit. It should include such items as performance data, personnel, budget data, staff evaluation, and staff development. Perhaps the most important information included is the district's strategic plan, since the entire unit plan must be developed within the context of the strategic plan. The intent here is to provide members of the planning team with the information needed to make decisions without overwhelming them. It is important to avoid "analysis paralysis."

This background information is crucial to the success of the planning process. It provides the context necessary to make informed decisions. If this step is done well, the planners will have the common factual base necessary to make reasonable decisions. They also will understand the strategic plan that provides the context necessary to develop appropriate unit plans. The background information should be assembled in a notebook and sent to the planning team seven to ten days before the first planning session.

(3) The third step in the process is to select the *planning team*. The planning team is the primary work group for developing the plan. Although it should be created in a manner similar to the strategic planning team, it should be a microcosm of the cluster rather than the system. The "director" of the unit should be on the team, as should other managers/administrators. Balance is very important. The desired outcome is to have a team that represents all of the perspectives in the unit.

There is one major qualification for planning team membership. Every team member must be a person of honest goodwill who cares about the success of the entire system. Planning team members should be concerned about the "common good" rather than "special interests." Although it is the director's responsibility to select the team, woe to the one who stacks a team with "his or her people." If this is done, the entire process will lack credibility and be flawed from the onset. In many cases, the director seeks the assistance of a small advisory group to build the planning team.

Conducting the first planning session is the most critical step in the process. At the first planning session, the planning team will develop a draft of everything in the plan except the action plans. This session is a highly structured experience. Under the direction of a trained facilitator, the team will accomplish the following agenda:

First Planning Session

1. Review the strategic plan
2. Understand the beliefs
3. Develop the unit's mission statement
4. Conduct an internal analysis
5. Conduct an external analysis
6. Identify objectives
7. Identify critical issues
8. Tactics

As in strategic planning, the planning team should make all decisions by agreement. There should be no voting.

Because there is much less time spent on beliefs, and because parameters often are not included, unit planning sessions do not take as long as the first planning session for the strategic plan. Typically, 18 to 22 hours will be sufficient to complete the agenda.

(4) Next it is necessary to *communicate the draft plan* throughout the entire system. This step has two purposes: to provide information regarding progress to date, and to invite involvement in the action plan development. This provides another opportunity to expand understanding of the strategic intent and to emphasize the importance of aligning the unit's change initiatives with the system's.

(5) The next step is *to develop action plans* for each of the tactics. An action planning team will be created for each tactic. In commercial enterprises, action team members may be assigned. In public service systems, some members may be assigned, but usually it is advisable to solicit volunteers also, both inside and outside of the unit. The charge of these teams is to develop the action plans necessary to fully implement the tactic. Members of the action teams should understand operational realities. They should know how to get things done. The action teams must honor the tactic as it is written. They do not have the right to amend or to reject the tactic. As with the strategic plan, the action planning phase is the most time consuming. Typically, two to three months are necessary.

(6) Once action plans are completed, the second planning session is held. The purpose of this session is for the planning team to review the action plans and to ensure that the action plans accepted are consistent with the intent of the tactics. The same criteria that were used in strategic planning also apply here.

There are two other purposes of the *second planning session*. First, the planning team should discuss an implementation schedule. Since it will be impossible to implement every action plan in the first year, some action plans will have to be held in abeyance for at least one year. The planning team can advise the director about which plans are to be implemented during the first year. This is critically important in preventing overextension in pursuit of too many initiatives at one time.

Second, the planning team should review the unit's mission, objectives, and tactics to see if any modifications are necessary. This is a check against inappropriate work at the first planning session. The action planning phase provides an opportunity to assess feedback concerning the components of the plan. If changes are necessary, they can be made at this session.

(7) Next is *approval*. This is done differently from the strategic plan. Usually a unit plan is approved by the chief executive officer. Formal board approval is rare.

There is a tendency to end the process here; however, this is extremely dangerous. A planner's chief responsibility is not to get a plan approved; it is to ensure that a plan can be realized; therefore, the next step in the process is to carefully organize for implementation. This involves two steps. First, the plan should be written and distributed to the unit and throughout the entire system. This step will inform everyone of the unit's direction. Effective implementation will require everyone to understand the intent of the unit and to contribute to its realization, whether or not they participated in creating the plan. This step alerts everyone to that responsibility.

Second, individual responsibility should be clarified for every action. If action plans are not part of normal responsibilities, they are often overlooked. The pressure of daily events in the normal busy schedule frequently squeezes out new initiatives. Consequently, *mutual expectations* and *commitments* are needed to align the work of each individual with the work embedded within the action plans scheduled to be undertaken during the first year.

(8) The last step in the process is to regularly *assess the progress* in implementing the plan. Quarterly reviews of the plans should be conducted. These reviews help identify implementation problems early, as well as allow for justifiable mid-course corrections.

(9) Finally, *periodic updates* of the unit plan should follow each update of the strategic plan.

THE CLUSTER PLANNING PROCESS

Because the action-cluster approach to organization has or needs no formal structure except the action itself, a set process for collaborative planning must not be prescribed. Any artificially imposed structuring of the process would compromise the personality and the creativity of the cluster of action. The cluster must be allowed the freedom to design or discover its own process, just as it is free to design its own work and discover new possibilities in it.

However, as with any creative act, there must be a certain discipline invoked to guarantee concentration of effect, credibility, and practicality. In cluster planning, that discipline consists simply of the fundamental principles of planning:

1. The strategic plan of the system must be honored, both in substance and in protocol.
2. The process must be inclusive, involving all within the action-cluster and those outside who are directly affected by the action.
3. All decisions regarding mission, parameters, objectives, and tactics must be by agreement.
4. The process must be dedicated to achieving a results-driven plan that can be put into effect immediately.
5. Once the process is agreed upon, it should not be changed mid-course.
6. The process should be one that stretches the cluster beyond its present capability.
7. Finally, the process must not be an event but a continuing experience in constant emergence.

Chapter 16

Continuous Creation

All systems, whether natural or artifactual, are either constantly emerging or dying. Whole-context organization—with its four dimensions and two dynamics—unlike traditional organization, is inherently generative and self-sustaining. The only thing that can slow or stop the process of juvenation is the inaction of those persons affected by it. But if its inherent energy is continuously released, there is virtually no limit to the potential of the system. While that occurs primarily within the practical action of the system, from time to time it is necessary intellectually and emotionally to recommit the system to the process of planning, to discover new possibilities, and to align the organization with the strategic intent. For most systems, that means a formal review and an update of the plan, along with a comprehensive assessment of accomplishment. The plan is an agent of radical change, so it should not be surprising that it also changes radically.

Substantial changes may be necessary in the plan for three reasons. First, societal changes obviously continue after the approval of a strategic plan. Some of those changes may make realization of the strategic plan more difficult than anticipated. Others may provide opportunities to accelerate actions that were not possible the previous year. These societal changes must be addressed to better help the enterprise achieve its mission and objectives. Second, the system's own efforts to realize the action plans may make it necessary to adjust the strategic plan. Some action plans will be implemented precisely as they were designed. Others may seem irrelevant four or five months into the action phase. Sometimes action plans lead to discovering completely new possibilities that were not apparent when the plan was originally developed.

Third, and most important, after a certain interval—say, one year—the system is no longer the organization that developed the plan. It has become something else, because of the plan. But unless the plan is recast in the new context, there is the distinct possibility that the plan itself will become an impediment. That is precisely why the absolute worst mistake made in planning is to develop a long-term plan (five years or so) and then attempt to accomplish all of the plans exactly as written. This kind of action is past tense. Periodic updates keep the plan in future tense.

There are several intended benefits of the periodic update. First, any difficulties in action can be addressed appropriately. Second, the system will reaffirm its commitment to strategic thinking. Third, the timing of the update should allow the enterprise to allocate budgeted resources to those action plans scheduled for implementation during the next fiscal year. Consequently, the periodic update should be timed so that the second planning session takes place about six weeks prior to serious budget allocation decisions for the next fiscal term. This is a key point for developing capacity through system design. If the budget development process is not driven by the strategic intent, a system will always be dissatisfied with its efforts to implement its strategic plan.

Although the entire strategic planning process must be repeated during the periodic update, everything happens in a more streamlined manner. Described next are some key items to remember about each stage of the process during an update.

COMMUNICATE ABOUT THE UPDATE

First, it is necessary to inform the various internal (and external) publics about the update. The communication related to the periodic update provides yet another opportunity to expand the number of people who understand strategic intent. Answers should be provided to such questions as: Why is the update necessary? Who will be involved? When will the update take place? It should be emphasized that the update provides both the opportunity for serious discussion of any difficulties in realizing the current plan and the opportunity to factor in new creative ideas that were discovered in the action.

COLLECT DATA PRIOR TO THE UPDATE

In this step, the background information distributed the previous year should be revised and made current. The strategic plan should also be included. This reminds the planning team that it is working from an existing plan rather than starting from the beginning. It will greatly expedite the planning session if this information also includes a short summary of progress on the objectives, strategies, and action plans.

Baseline data on the objectives should be included. But it should be pointed out that they have a multiple-year time horizon, and it is rare that a system has seen much progress within a year after approval. Yet the objectives are the chief factor in determining whether strategic planning has been successful. Since they are specific manifestations of the mission, the enterprise will know it is succeeding when the objectives are achieved. In fact, achieving strategic objectives provides the explicit proof that strategic planning was worth the investment. Therefore, at least baseline data should be shared with the planning team at the first update.

The information also should include a progress report on each action plan currently being implemented. These progress reports usually are organized by strategy, with no more than one page for each action plan. They should be honest, value-free assessments of progress. There must be no defense of shoddy implementation efforts, if there are any. Frequently, new opportunities are discovered and pursued during the earliest attempts to realize an action plan. This often includes taking action that was not explicitly written into an action plan, even though it made imminent sense to those responsible for the action of the plan. These efforts represent new opportunities that were created by initiating action. They need to be reported to the planning team as well. This progress report will help the planning team make decisions about any needed changes in strategies or action plans.

The information should be sent to the planning team about seven to ten days before the first planning session of the periodic update. Members should read the information prior to the planning session and prepare relevant questions.

SELECT THE TEAM

For the first periodic update, the original planning team is reconstituted, if possible. If attrition has occurred, members should be replaced in like kind. In subsequent updates, at least one-third of the team should be rotated. The reason for retaining the original team through the first update is that this update will require more continuity than any of those that follow for the purpose of the initial validation of the strategic plan and planning process.

CONDUCT THE FIRST PLANNING SESSION

The process of the first session of the update differs significantly from the initial planning session. The planning team, under the direction of a trained facilitator, follows a modified version of the original session. The same components of the plan are addressed, but they are addressed in a different order and in a different way. The agenda for the recommended periodic update follows:

DAY ONE

First Planning Session: Update of the Strategic Plan

1. Introductions
2. Orientation
3. A look back over the last twelve months: Factors and Impacts
   A. Internal
   B. External
4. A look ahead to the next eighteen months: Factors and Impacts
   A. Internal
   B. External
5. Critical issues
6. Review and revise mission
7. Review and revise parameters
8. Review beliefs
9. Progress reports: Objectives, Strategies, and Action Plans

DAY TWO

10. Reconsider mission
11. Objectives
    A. Revisit and modify existing objectives
    B. Formulate new objectives (if necessary)
12. Strategies
    A. Evaluate existing strategies
    B. Formulate new strategies (if necessary)
13. Review next steps in the process

There are several critical alterations in the process of the session that need to be apprised here. First, the review of past and present internal and external factors should be formatted, simply as a chart with two columns (see Exhibit 38).

The planning team should be divided into four study groups and each should be assigned a different category. It is important, as in the initial planning, that each group not offer solutions, only the impacts or implications of the factors for the enterprise.

Second, if the mission must be revised, it should be thoroughly discussed and assigned to a select group for revision overnight.

Third, the progress reports on the strategies should be a brief summary

Exhibit 38
Internal Analysis Format

FACTOR	IMPACT (OR IMPLICATIONS)

Source: Author.

of the information already in the hands of the planning team. Before the reports begin, the facilitator should rehearse with the team the classifications of strategies that will be employed the next day.

Fourth, the strategies will be classified in four categories:

1. The strategy and its plans are operational and/or routine. No further strategic attention is required. These are removed from the plan.
2. The strategy is relevant and the plans are adequate, but more time is needed to make them operational.
3. The strategy must be revisited. Sometimes it is necessary to revise or recast the strategy.
4. The strategy should be abandoned.

There is also a category of new strategies that will be developed based on the internal and external analyses and any change in the mission or objectives.

It is important that the first day end with a brief verbal progress report on the objectives, strategies, and action plans. This should supplement the written report included in the background information distributed before the meeting. A short assessment of progress on each action plan scheduled for implementation the first year should be given. Progress on those action plans provides a tangible way to assess the first year's progress on the strategic plan. Also, any new opportunities that emerged as a result of the first year's implementation effort should be identified. Sometimes these new opportunities, which were not even apparent when the implementation effort began, hold the most promise for accelerating the realization of a strategy or for creating new ones. After the progress reports, the planning team is ready to revisit the objectives and strategies.

The second day should be devoted strictly to the objectives and strategies (and first to the revision of the mission, if necessary). If additional strategies are written, an action team will be created to develop action plans for each strategy. It is also possible that existing strategies will be rewritten or that there will be the need to revise action plans within an existing strategy. In these cases, an action team must be recommissioned to revise, delete, or add action plans to that strategy. It is the decisions about the strategies that have the greatest impact on what follows in the updating process. Typically, about one-third to one-half of the strategies will be revisited by new action teams.

The remainder of the process is identical to the original strategic planning process.

Chapter 17

The Emergence of New Systems

The only reason for any strategic planning process and discipline is to reduce the lag time between the idea and the action. If that is not a valid reason, then the remainder of this discussion is moot. The Omega protocol described in the previous sections is the best process and discipline available for making the most radical transformation in the shortest time, yet it still requires considerable time, at least initially. Somehow the old analogy of "big ship, small rudder" seems appropriate.

It was pointed out at the very beginning of the discussion of this protocol for strategic planning that, although the process is linear and the discipline rational, the methodology was designed to push the planning enterprise to its outer limits, by using both the process and discipline to urge and provoke radical transformation. But it is also true that most contemporary enterprises, public or private, will not have the foresight, insight, and hindsight necessary for that transformation, at least not before the first planning session. That is especially the case with public entities that interact daily with various constituencies that are woefully uninformed, focused on special interests, and adamant about narrow opinions. It is expected that the force of that first session itself will radically alter perspectives and, consequently, dramatically affect both the substance and style of the enterprise. So the process and discipline, together, actually become a schoolmaster—guiding, provoking, and pushing the participants as far as they will go.

That metaphor is especially borne out by the continuous instruction, especially in the discipline, that occurs throughout the process. For example, there is a great need to explain the relationship between objectives and strategies, since this concept has been so misunderstood by academic institutions. Moreover, significant, extraordinary thinking about ordinary issues must be relentlessly raised to the highest level, beyond the issues themselves.

It is worth recalling that the only part of the strategic plan to be actually realized, or implemented, is the action plans supporting each strategy; these are developed over a period of months, with considerable research and deliberation focused on the necessary results and the best means to achieve them. In other words, while the planning enterprise may have the commitment and readiness to engage in planning, it does not have the capacity for action at that time—otherwise, why would planning be required? So it is necessary to virtually carry the system through the development of that capacity, and more, by a strong dose of strategic thinking initially and by emphasis on strategic intent, mutual commitments and expectations, and continuous creation subsequent to the planning exercise. It is as though strategic planning were the artificial stimulation required to restore the vision and vitality of the system. In a way, strategic planning, much like the proverbial committee, is intended to do for the system what the system cannot do for itself.

It is little wonder that many chief executive officers, when faced with their primary responsibility of planning, refuse to engage in the extensive process described in the previous sections. And, there are three good reasons, at least in their minds, for not doing so. First, the process takes a relatively long time. In businesses that move at warp speed, that obviously is unacceptable. The whole world changes several times during a nine-month period. Second, there is a threat implicit in involving many people in the decision-making process. It is a dual threat: ignorance and special interest. Uninformed and closed-minded persons only complicate the issues and, eventually, detract from the quality of the plan. Third, the discipline of the plan is very strict, forcing hard decisions that close doors and limit options in an attempt to concentrate all energies on a single purpose. Many chief executives still favor targets of opportunity.

One alternative, which many aggressive, operations-minded chief executives choose out of sheer practicality, is to make decisions on the spot by using whatever expertise is available (often from outside consultants) and trust that most of these decisions will be the best under the existing circumstances, and will eventually pay off. But that approach is also fraught with danger. First, it has all of the flaws of autocratic management. No one can know everything, and unilateral decisions generally do not elicit much support. Second, it presupposes, and therefore perpetuates, the assumption that no one else in the system has the knowledge or ability to be involved in decisions. Third, it actually prevents any original thinking and total system transformation. Decisions arise strictly out of existing circumstances.

The dilemma lies deep within the traditional organization. That construct often required people to perform but withheld the wherewithal for performance. It expected them to know but guarded information. It required them to grow but denied them the opportunity. It wanted them to be self-motivated but denied them incentives. So it should not be surprising that in such a system, the action followed the idea by a great distance. Inertia, gravity, and resistance precluded immediate action, or even the acceptance of the idea.

The answer is not simply to speed up the process and curtail the discipline—as in fire, ready, aim! That would only compound the error. The only way to resolve the dilemma, ironically, is by removing it altogether and creating a new organization by which the lag time can be eliminated, a system in which the idea and the action occur synchronistically. For most enterprises, since there is no such thing as a zero-start (these airplanes are always built in flight), that means pursuing strategic thinking, strategic planning, and strategic action to their ultimate. That is to say, a traditional corporation-model system cannot achieve the synchronicity of idea and action unless and until it meticulously and religiously goes through all of the generative processes described in the previous chapters. Once that has been experienced, a system of time-instant, continuously creative action will be a natural consequence. In fact, the enterprise can never go back to the confines of traditional corporation-model organization, nor to the science of management. All action in the new system is spontaneous, yet directed toward the same intent, in concerted harmony. To make that reality actual requires three things throughout the system: *simultaneous knowledge, the capacity and freedom to act, and dedication to mutual strategic intent.*

It has already been pointed out that the design of the new organization cannot be depicted as a chart or diagram, and that it could have an infinite variety of forms, even in time passing for a given enterprise. So attempting to prescribe a particular organization would be not only impossible but a contradiction. However, it may be helpful to consider an actual case in which a company, during the strategic action phase of strategics, actually allowed the action itself to create the form of organization.

The company was a well-established, very successful enterprise that had been in business for over a century. The recently appointed chief executive officer, who knows no fear, was earnestly seeking to lead the enterprise into new dimensions and new realities, both in its lines of business as well as in its organization. In fact, he knew that one was contingent on the other, and he was insistent that organization must follow, not dictate, the action.

After the company's strategic plan was approved by the board, the chief executive officer immediately introduced, throughout the system, mutual commitments and expectations. During the many discussions entailed in this process, new patterns of organization, impossible to predict in advance, emerged. The old positions gave way to relationships, and formal titles were given up. Clusters of action were identified, and interactions with other clusters were acknowledged and strengthened.

The overall design of organization that was perceived in the action had four distinct but interrelated features. These the company called *today's work, the creation of futures, the development of capacity,* and *presentation of identity*. No attempt was made to establish priority among them. On the contrary, each were held critical to the company's present and future.

An interesting designation was then applied, casually at first, but taken seriously after reflection. The four "core action areas," as they were called by the chief executive officer, corresponded closely to the four dimensions of organization. "Today's work" easily was seen as *action;* development of capacity, obviously as *capacity*. The two others were more of a stretch, but "futures" was related to *beliefs* (who they are) and "identity" was roughly paralleled to *purpose* (why they are). That being the case, at the risk of suggesting an overly complicated scheme, *commensuration* and *essentiality* became the dynamics pervading and harmonizing the action in each area. And action was understood by the company as being of three kinds: *poiesis* (implementation), *theoria* (invention), and *praxis* (discovery).

Just for the sake of the visual learners in the company, a tentative design was suggested. But that design was not held to be a formal structure. It was not printed as a replacement of the old pyramid structure. The old chart simply disappeared and the new design was translated into ongoing action (see Exhibit 39). That was the only place it could be seen.

Each of these common core actions can be easily understood, and there may be here a concept of organization that other enterprises could, or will, emulate. A brief consideration of each reveals the soundness of the design.

TODAY'S WORK

Sooner or later, someone has to do something. Work may be a dirty word, but that is the business of organization—whether physical labor, personal service, rationalistic exercise, or artistic creativity. There is only one thing more important than planning; that is, today's business. However, the corporation-model organization, by its basic assumption and disposition, was anti-work. It normed down productivity through standard efficiencies. It "promoted" people further and further from the actual business and rewarded them for their escape, while those performing the work often were disparaged and, as was the case, looked

Exhibit 39
A Holistic Concept of Organization

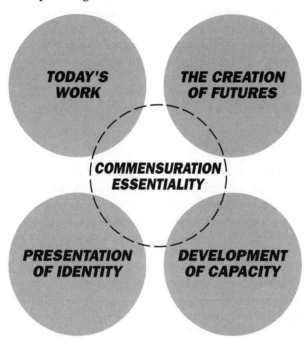

Source: Author.

down upon. It presumed to develop "human resources" in fits and starts, completely disassociated from action. And it diverted energy into auxiliary activity aimed at compensating for the inherent dysfunctions of the corporation model—teams, committees, councils, and endless meetings. In the final stages of the corporation-model, most work was replaced by voice mail. If work was lost in the typical corporation-model, it was actually opposed in the bureaucratic version. Most public sector systems were perpetuated by work-like activity.

Within the corporation-model organization, distraction was often prized. Time and presence were the measures of work. And, despite claims to the contrary by various consulting firms, there was seldom any real correlation between work and reward. That was always strictly determined by demand and supply—a function of the marketplace. Wage and salary were never based on the value of the work. The fact that no way was ever invented to reckon the value of work is striking testimony to the corporation's total disregard for the whole matter. It simply was not that important.

In the whole-context system, work is the quintessential reason for being—the highest calling, the noblest purpose; after all, it is the common good. Remuneration starts and ends here. It is to the benefit of all that work be done best, and that means an uncompromising commitment of energy to that work by the individuals who, at any particular time or in any particular circumstance, can best realize the strategic intent of the organization in practical, everyday action. Whether they are the most talented, most highly trained, or most specially equipped does not matter. The only requisite is that they are both committed and free to realize the fullness in immediate action—unrestricted, unperturbed.

CREATION OF FUTURES

The possibilities implicit in action, however profound or explosive, even when fully developed, even when consistent with the present strategic intent, do not constitute the future of the enterprise. One simple reason: strategic intent may change. The discoveries in action may have a defining influence on that change, and are, in fact, expected to do so, but there may be other reasons and purposes apart from any particular action.

The corporation-model organization very seldom appropriated the possibilities discovered in action, so the attempt to deal with the future was typically long-range or comprehensive planning—one reactive, the other inactive. Even the planning approach detailed in the previous section is only as good as the current intelligence. The future is nothing more or less than intelligence realized, so the creation of futures is the creation of intelligence.

The corporation-model, through management science, made several assumptions about this intelligence. Autocratic management assumed only a few had it; consultative, some had more than others; democratic, no one had it; laissez-faire, everyone had it—but it did not matter. Participatory management held that everyone had a part of it, and the world would be set right if the parts were "synergized" together. In their own strange way, all were true—within the context of the system.

The creation of futures in the whole-context system must be only the work of futurists—and their only work. Futurists are those persons in whom the enterprise has vested the responsibility of knowing possibilities beyond those derived from even the most revelatory action in the existing organization. It is a sacred trust, not a job. Most assuredly, this is *not* the business of those engaged in today's work; to involve them in futuring is to lose twice. The rule must be: let those engaged in today's business take care of the business today, and let the futurists create futures.

Of course, it is tempting to speculate on the kinds of persons who make the best futurists, and whether they can be developed. Are they intuitive? Rational? Lateral thinkers? All of those traits surely are desirable, perhaps even necessary, but the only requirement of a futurist is that he or she live somewhere else.

THE DEVELOPMENT OF CAPACITY

The question is simple. Is it actually possible for systems to transform themselves from within? That was the hope and promise of strategic planning. Some serious thinkers, such as Karl Marx, have argued that radical change could not, or would not, occur from within—only revolution could bring about new order, after the destruction of the old. As a historical fact, revolutionaries always seem to forget what the new order was supposed to be.

But the argument is certainly valid, especially in the case of unyielding, intractable systems—those resistant to change of any kind, those in which only inconsequential, incremental "improvement" is to be tolerated. And even in the most forward thinking and courageous corporation-model organization, strategic planning was inhibited by ties to the past and present. The system even created its own big lie; that is, the doctrine that people naturally oppose change. But nothing could be further from the truth. People love change. They seek it. The word that sells more stuff, universally, is "new." It is only systems that are adverse to change.

Whole-context organization is by nature evolving. Change is the essence of its being; and it is not change of schematic makeovers, rather it is morphological creation. Nor is it incremental, nor cyclical. So degree is never the issue and neither is time. The only thing that matters is the constancy of creation. Whether that becomes reality depends not on abilities, techniques, and methodologies applied to the task but on the system's insistence of translating today's work into the future—thoroughly and completely.

PRESENTATION OF IDENTITY

Distinctiveness exists only in the risk of being something other. It is at once both assertion and denial. In that sense, identity partakes of logical definition—classification and critical attributes, and that is a meaningful concept. But identity has no significance in the abstract. In ordinary enterprises, it is perception; in the extraordinary, perspective. The purpose of whole-context organization is to turn perception into perspective. That is, to change the way everyone thinks about the enterprise, and about themselves.

Typically, corporation-model organizations devoted immediate time and money to identity as perception—to no avail. For example, in the

1980's, during the savings-and-loan fiasco, many thrifts converted their charters into bank status. Legally, technically, they were banks. Their advertising campaigns declared them so—their signage, their logos, their organizational structure. But, alas, their identity remained a thrift. What happened? Or more to the point, what did *not* happen? Quite simply, everyone's perspective remained that of a thrift mentality.

In the actual example cited here, everything about the system was redefined by having each of the core action areas answer several questions pertaining to relationships inside of the action area as well as with the other areas. The questions were:

1. What is the core action area made of, and how does it operate?
2. Where does the core action area begin and end? What are its present boundaries? What are its gaps and overlaps? What are its critical tensions?
3. What commitments will this core action area make to other areas and to the whole system?
4. What commitments are needed from the other action areas?

The answers provided by one core action area exemplify both the depth of thought and the impact of the subsequent discussions of these items on the entire systems (see Exhibit 40).

The results of this bold experiment were obvious even during the first year. There was, quite expectedly, considerable shock among those in the company who suddenly realized that they were actually having to think and behave in a manner completely foreign to their experience. But soon a whole new culture began to emerge—a culture based on sincere common convictions, committed to mutual purpose. Clarity of purpose and concentration of effort brought a new enthusiasm to everyone in the company. Self-directed job performance took a sudden quantum leap forward. And the innovation that was discovered in action, individual and system, moved the company dramatically into the new dimensions and into the new realities to which the chief executive officer had aspired—and still does.

Exhibit 40
Core Action Area: The Development of Capacity

ANALYSIS

What is the Core Action Area made of and how does it operate?

***This core action area is made of interdepartmental, interdependent
components which work together to enable performance through
developing and <u>protecting</u> organizational capacity.***

SPHERES OF ORGANIZATIONAL CAPACITY:

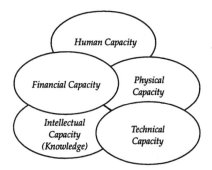

Activities Required to Develop Capacity in Each Sphere:

Human Capacity:
- Identify needs
- Recruit
- Articulate and nurture corporate culture
- Train
- Develop skill sets
- Establish compensation levels
- Ensure compliance
- Develop policies and procedures
- Benefits administration
- Employee relations
- Measure effectiveness

Technical Capacity:
- Enable technological advancement
- Provide concrete bodies of knowledge to support operations—architectural, accounting, sales, etc.
- Information infrastructure (IT)
- Administration of leases, other legal documents
- Tenant activities
- Budget success

Exhibit 40 (continued)

- Coordination of outside real estate/attorneys
- Detail plat/other land information

Financial Capacity:
- Goal setting
  —Budget
  —Proforma
  —Benchmarks
- Performance measurement
- Compliance
- Protection of assets
- Facilitator of profitability
  —Proforma
  —Financing

Physical Capacity:
- Program definition/clarification
- Planning
- Estimating/Proforma/Scheduling
- Team selection
- Project monitoring/control
- Follow-up/review

Intellectual Capacity/Knowledge Capital:
- Inventory of knowledge capital
- Capture and transfer new knowledge
- Package and sell knowledge

How the Support Core Action Area Operates:
- "Accountable" consultants
  —Plan/set goals/advise
  —Evaluate feasibility
  —Ensure compliance
  —Critical thinking/analysis
  —Saying yes/no
- Proactive mode: monitoring threats to capacity and seeking opportunities to enhance/increase capacity
- Information brokers
- Resource allocators
- Facilitators

Exhibit 40 (continued)

- Developers/Motivators/Cheerleaders
- Enforcer—Safety net
- Reality testing
- Network of bridges

DEFINITIONS

Where does it begin and end? What are the boundaries? What are the gaps and overlaps?

Boundaries:
- Questions about boundaries include:
    —Who is in control?
    —Who is ultimately responsible?
    —Who has the final say?
- The boundaries for support are determined by need for compliance/Support protects capacity by ensuring compliance:
    —Budgetary compliance
    —Legal compliance
    —Policy/procedure compliance
    —EEOC compliance
    —Strategic compliance

Gaps:
- Front-end consultation
    —Include in developing project scope
    —Involve IT/HR in proforma process
- Communication
    —Multiple vehicles
    —Different levels of use
- Management priorities
- Orientation to financial procedures
- Reactive manpower levels (we only support current operations rather than create capacity to move)
- Facilities gap—space and mobility

Overlaps:
- Synergistic overlap
    —Futures
    —Operations
    POS, Purchasing
    —Identify/Image

Exhibit 40 (continued)

Critical Tensions:

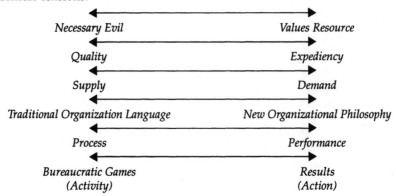

Necessary Evil	*Values Resource*
Quality	*Expediency*
Supply	*Demand*
Traditional Organization Language	*New Organizational Philosophy*
Process	*Performance*
Bureaucratic Games *(Activity)*	*Results* *(Action)*

COMMITMENTS

General Commitments to Others:

- Timely, accurate, accessible, and meaningful information and service to enhance profitability
- Reasonable and effective controls to protect assets and profitability

Commitments to Others Regarding Human Capacity:

- Get the best employees in the market
  —Compensation/benefits
  —Educate employees on the benefits of working at XYZ Company
- Provide information and learning opportunities to enable them to excel
- Provide developmental opportunities to enable management's capacity to maintain positive employee relations
- Performance consulting
- Identify, articulate, and nurture the corporate culture *(culture defined as an integrated pattern of human values, demonstrated in thought, word, deed, and artifact)*

Commitment to Others Regarding Financial Capacity:

- Provide a financial procedures manual and training program
- Provide a management reporting system

Commitments to Others Regarding Technical Capacity:

- Reliable communication infrastructure
- Ready access to IT resources
- Efficient expenditures of capital budget
- Meet operations expectations regarding quality and efficiency

Exhibit 40 (continued)

Commitments Needed from Others:

- Clear, time-sensitive expectations
- Clear procedures
- Strong communication
- Detailed information
- Increased commitment to the development of human capacity

Source: Author.

Conclusion

Sooner or later, all autonomous systems will be confronted with the imperative of strategics, and each will decide its own future. Some will refuse to engage in strategic thinking, planning, and action, and will by that one strategic decision set in motion their own decline. Others, however, will choose to create systems that are themselves characterized by constant creation—always vital, always new.

Historically, that has always been true: a few systems choose to thrive; many others do not. That is why the life of most systems has been cyclical. They rise to maturity and, unable to sustain homeostasis, they suffer obsolescence and quickly fall. Futuristically, the issue of strategy is of crisis proportions for every system in Western civilization. It is a matter of both timing and time.

The timing is critical. All systems exist at present in an epochal cusp between the traditional orders that have been built up over the past 400 years and the emerging new orders that are replacing them. Furthermore, each present system, within itself, is at some specific point in its own lifetime. This coincidence produces a compound crisis that is unprecedented in contemporary experience. Therefore, the strategic issues are also unprecedented. Strategy, as it is traditionally understood, must be reconceptualized in a way that more closely apprehends its original intent. That means embracing the totality of strategics.

Thinking is strategic only if it understands the full power of strategy, recognizes authentic leaders, distinguishes between condition and cause, appreciates all of the qualities of the life of systems, and is willing to abandon old schemes of organization for living forms. Planning is strategic only if it is the means by which communities of people continually create new systems to serve extraordinary purposes. Action is strategic only if it is creative, continuously prompting the discovery of new possibilities.

Ultimately, it is neither time nor timing that determines the future. That depends strictly on thinking, planning, and action—strategics.

Appendix

A Basic Guide for
Action Team Leaders

PREFACE

This Action Team Leader's Guide has evolved over several years as Cambridge facilitators worked with action team leaders in over 700 organizations. Written here in the second person, it is intended to offer practical, step-by-step assistance in dealing with the issues and concerns faced most often by team leaders. Admittedly, much of this information may be elementary, but usually it is the elemental things that determine the success or failure of any endeavor.

Since the development of action plans is the most important phase of planning, not even the smallest detail can be left to chance. And beyond that, the credibility of the entire plan depends on the action plans.

TOTAL-GAIN DECISION-MAKING

The decision-making method employed by the Action Teams is critical to the strategic planning activity for at least two reasons. First, the *credibility* of the entire planning process is at risk, so to speak. The slightest infraction of the principles of full participation and shared decision making, however understood by those involved, can not only destroy the effectiveness of an Action Team, but it can also seriously damage the organization's strategic planning effort. Therefore, extreme care must be taken to employ a decision-making process(es) beyond reproach. Second, the quality of the plans is at stake. Experience proves again and again that some popular management approaches to decisions (notably, any of the permutations of Machiavellian manipulation) are obviously counterproductive. Since they represent one, usually biased, point of view, the plans themselves are typically exercises in resistance to change. Furthermore, no plan, regardless of how good it is, which is developed in exclusion can expect to be inclusive in implementation.

But participation in decision making does not guarantee either credibility or quality. Even if the organization is sincerely committed to the full involvement of all concerned persons, sometimes it is difficult to escape the lingering influence of political and corporate systems that by their very nature are adverse to both participation and transformation. So most attempts of team or group decision-making do not live up to their promise because they are stymied by either "democratic" processes or something called "consensus." Both are fundamentally flawed and sure to end in disappointment.

THE DEMOCRATIC PROCESS

Democratic decision making is predicated on the twin axioms of political democracy: majority rule and voting. The first means that there will always be winners and losers; the second that nothing is ever finally resolved. Recently, the term "win-win" has captured the popular fancy as a happy way of overcoming the inevitable conflict in democratic processes. However, not only is this a logical impossibility, it also presupposes that decision making is a competitive exercise and that the group, team, and organization are permanently divided and contrary.

Ouchi's Theory Z Definition

"Consensus" decision making, as understood and practiced by most organizations today, derives from Ouchi's Theory Z definition: Consensus has been reached when participants can say:

- "I believe that you understand my point of view."
- "I believe that I understand your point of view."
- "Whether or not I prefer this idea or concept I will support it because it was reached openly and fairly."
- "I can live with this decision."

Since that decree over 30 years ago, all kinds of "consensus"-related terms and methodologies have been concocted and prescribed by a host of management gurus. But the consensus seems to be that "consensus" is both a rational *process* of negotiating a settlement and the resulting *decision*. That is to say, it is at once both a means and an end. It is "built" as well as "achieved." But no matter what definitions or techniques are used, in practice (and likely in philosophy, since both originate in the context of the corporation), "consensus" is nothing more than a nonvoting version of the democratic process in which the real losers are conned to peacefully acquiesce to the will of the majority. They do so because they have been peremptorily pledged to support an artificial process over their own convictions. So any "consensus" is, in fact, artificial and lacking the emotional support necessary for its complete realization. The vernacular of the day declares the truth: "majority consensus" (U.S. Congress); "significant consensus" (state education reform legislation); "quasi-consensus" (directive from state department of education). Whatever consensus might be, surely it has nothing to do with contemporary definitions.

WHAT IS TOTAL-GAIN DECISION-MAKING?

The only approach that guarantees both the credibility and quality of participative decision making has no popular cachet and, unfortunately, not much of a following. Even so, decision making is effective only to the degree that groups achieve, for lack of a better term, "total-gain agreement." That is to say, decision making in which 100 percent of the participants are satisfied that the decision reached represents a benefit or advantage to them that they could not have achieved without the involvement of the group. In other words, everyone experiences "gain" that would be impossible without the dynamics and contributions of the group.

"Total-gain" decision making requires a discipline beyond process or methodology. It requires constant adherence by all participants to certain principles. These commitments must be made before decision making begins and must be religiously honored:

- All decisions will be consistent with the organization's stated beliefs.
- All decisions will be made in the context of the organization's stated mission and strategic objectives.
- All decisions will be made in the best interest of the organization.
- All decisions will follow the golden rule.
- Participation will be commensurate with actual knowledge and/or experience.
- Each participant will always tell the truth.
- A final decision does not mean an end to conversation, review, and reconsideration.

Far more than cliché or methodology, this kind of decision making essentially reflects a mature organizational culture that, although rare, is certainly possible. However, it is achieved only when all participants are dedicated to a cause that transcends themselves.

ORGANIZING TEAM MEETINGS

When setting agendas, meeting dates and times, be aware that participatory techniques and decision-making require more time than do traditional information-sharing-and-voting processes. Be flexible, adjust when necessary and keep the team on task while providing adequate time for discussion.

Communication

Continuous, effective communication—both written and oral—is *critical* to keeping the initial spark of enthusiasm alive in the action planning process. Meeting agendas, minutes, schedule changes, and accomplishments must be communicated consistently to keep the team aligned with the strategy. Frequent communication, moreover, is essential to the retention of Action Team members, especially community volunteers.

Action Team Notification

First impressions are important. A letter of welcome and thanks signed by the organization's top leaders (chief executive officer, board president, or university president) and sent to each participant before the first meeting sets a positive tone. Equally important is the Action Team Leader's initial contact with individual team members. If possible, make personal contact through a short phone call, followed by an informative letter with the first meeting's agenda enclosed.

Post-meeting reports remind members of what occurred and what they are to do next. Absent members benefit from the reports and a call from the leader. They remain informed and are reminded that their absence was felt.

The Internal Facilitator

Keep this person informed about your Action Team's progress with meeting notifications, agendas, and meeting reports. Meet with the internal facilitator periodically to solicit feedback and coaching.

A PRE-MEETING CHECKLIST

Before the First Meeting:

- Establish the objectives for the meeting. For example, the first meeting's objectives might include providing a brief review of the organization's plan, explaining Action Team roles and responsibilities, and clarifying the assigned strategy.
- Select and reserve a meeting place. Meeting place criteria should include conve-

nience for most members, good lighting, comfortable seating or tables, if preferred, and easy access for handicapped individuals.

- Determine the activities needed to accomplish the meeting objectives.
- If possible, prepare and send the agenda with a cover letter and other pertinent information to each team member and to the internal facilitator.
- Send the agenda and cover letter to resource persons when appropriate.
- Gather or request any special equipment such as flip charts and large marking pens, pencils and pads, videocassette player, overhead projector, blank transparencies, and pens.
- Make name tags and table placards that are bold and easy to read from a distance for each participant.
- Plan for drinks and snacks such as fruit, cheese and crackers, nuts, water, coffee, tea, and juices.

After the Meeting:

- Call absent members, express necessary regrets, and provide information about the next meeting.
- Send meeting minutes and next meeting agenda to each member and to the internal facilitator.

CREATING A POSITIVE ENVIRONMENT: A REVIEW

- Call all Action Team members to welcome them to the team.
- Send out letter and agenda for the first meeting in advance.
- Start the meeting on time.
- Have members and newcomers introduce themselves. This may be done during a warm-up activity.
- Present a positive image of the organization's strategic planning process. Be supportive and enthusiastic of the process.
- Review the agenda and clearly state meeting objectives at the beginning of the meeting.
- Appoint a team member to keep accurate minutes.
- Be an active listener.
- Be aware of any tension or nonverbal hostile behavior and adjust your style if appropriate.
- Keep one eye on the clock and one eye on the agenda.
- Allow participants to leave the room briefly for smoking or other personal reasons, but do not plan a break if your meeting is less than 90 minutes.
- Provide stretch breaks (three to five minutes) every 90 minutes during long meetings or when the team is having a collective sinking spell.
- Share roles of responsibility; monitor assignments and give reinforcement as well as necessary corrective feedback to members.

- Give credit for ideas to team members when credit is due.
- Ensure that no one dominates the discussion and that all members have an equal opportunity to participate.
- Summarize all completed actions or assignments at the end of each meeting.
- Review the next meeting's date, time, place, and agenda at the end of each meeting. At the first or second Action Team meeting, set up a schedule of meetings based on the organization's strategic planning time frame and the schedules of team members. After work or early evenings are usually the most convenient times.
- Send a copy of each meeting report to team members and the internal facilitator.

Communicating the Results

Compose a summary report of the survey and its findings. Be sure to include:

- An executive summary—purpose, procedures, and results.
- Who conducted the survey.
- The characteristics and size of the target respondents.
- A sample survey form.
- The procedures used to conduct the survey.
- A complete report of the results.
- Conclusions and recommendations for follow-up.

SAMPLE SIZE TABLE

Population	Suggested Sample Size*
50	44
100	80
200	130
300	169
500	217
1,000	278
20,000	377
30,000	379
50,000	381
100,000	384

*Suggested minimum size

AN OVERVIEW OF ACTION PLANNING

The process of developing a strategic plan involves translating that which is strategic with the operational: the Strategic Planning Team describes the concept of what the organization will become; and the Action Teams describe how to make that concept a reality. For every strategy contained in the organization's Strategic Plan, an Action Team—composed typically of people who were not on the Strategic Planning Team—is formed to create operational plans to realize that strategy. These Action Teams work three or four months to create these detailed plans. At the end of that time the plans are presented by the Action Team Leader to the Strategic Planning Team.

The Strategic Planning Team will deal with each action plan in one of three ways: accept the plan as it is; return it for modification (along with a clear description of what kind of modification is necessary); or reject it (either because its costs outweigh its benefits or because its contribution to the strategy is inadequate or unnecessary). Additionally, the Strategic Planning Team will recommend when to schedule implementation of each action plan. Since the Strategic Plan encompasses five years, a sequence is developed in which roughly one-fifth of the accepted action plans are implemented each year.

The Action Teams are ad hoc and advisory—they have no formal power or authority. Essentially, they make recommendations to the Strategic Planning Team, which makes recommendations to the Chief Executive Officer and the Board. The Action Teams disband after developing action plans. They exist as design teams only and are not expected to implement their own plans.

Most Action Teams follow a logical sequence in their work which is paralleled by the organization of sections in this manual: Strategy Analysis, Information Gathering, Moving to Action, Action Plan Writing, and Cost-Benefit Analysis.

ROLE OF THE ACTION TEAM LEADER

It is assumed that you are a person of goodwill who has some knowledge of the organization and is willing to subordinate your own special interests to the good of the whole organization. You possess good interpersonal skills and are able to manage and facilitate groups of people. Typically you are not a member of the organization's Strategic Planning Team. You will probably devote upwards of 40 hours to this activity over the course of three to four months.

Your function is to guide your Action Team in developing a set of action plans that will ensure successful implementation of the strategy assigned to you. During the course of several months, you will find yourself in a variety of roles, including organizer, coordinator, facilitator, leader, liaison to the internal facilitator, and presenter to the Strategic Planning Team.

Coordinating Group Process

You will facilitate individual and group tasks—including the writing of action plans—using effective group interaction techniques. You will need to encourage participation of all team members and protect individuals and their ideas from premature judgment.

Organizing the Work

As an Action Team Leader, you are responsible for developing meeting agendas; arranging meeting dates, times, and locations; and chairing the meetings. You can expect substantial logistical support from the internal facilitator for arranging facilities, refreshments, and duplication and mailing of communication to Action Team members.

Leading Your Action Team

Ensure that the composition of the Action Team remains balanced. If attrition occurs, you may need to recruit new members to ensure that the team continues to reflect the diverse perspectives and points of view. This becomes increasingly difficult as the team's work progresses. Do it, if you must, very early in the process. Intervene assertively when necessary to keep the team focused and on task. You will be required to monitor the team's progress to ensure that time lines are met. Ultimately, you want to ensure that your team's action plans are aligned with the organization's mission, strategic objectives, and the assigned strategy.

Communicating with the Internal Facilitator

It is hard enough to ask for help when we really *need* it. Most of us shy away from seeking advice when we think we are doing just fine. Don't stick your head in the sand. The internal facilitator is there to provide support and to give you the kind of feedback and coaching from a perspective that only an outsider can have. Seek it frequently. Send meeting notices and minutes to the internal facilitator. Communicate problems, concerns, and progress.

Consider inviting the internal facilitator to observe some of your meetings and to offer suggestions on improving your team's process and interaction skills. The internal facilitator may periodically call a meeting of team leaders to share information on progress, obstacles to overcome (and techniques for overcoming them), and common problems.

Presenting Your Plans

Plan to write a cover letter to accompany your plans and to make a presentation to the Strategic Planning Team at the Second Planning Session. You will have 20 minutes to describe why your Action Team recommends its particular approach, and you will spend about 20 minutes answering questions. The internal facilitator may draw all the team leaders together for a practice presentation before the Second Planning Session occurs.

Considerations for Co-Leaders

Some organizations assign two Action Team co-leaders to each strategy. This concept can have symbolic as well as substantive benefits to the organization, but it also has some pitfalls which need to be avoided if the partnership is to be successful.

Co-leaders also may be able to divide a heavy workload. If the co-leaders have different strengths, then they can use their strengths to their advantage. Sometimes one co-leader does all of the meeting facilitation, and the other co-leader handles all other duties, such as logistics, distribution of minutes, and so forth. Sometimes one co-leader can be the "bad cop" and one can be the "good cop." One can be the hard-driving taskmaster, pressing the team to move forward to meet deadlines and follow the process. The other can move in afterward and heal the wounds and actually move the group forward after the other leader has "softened them up."

One potential pitfall of having co-leaders is the possibility that there could be no leaders. One co-leader could be assuming that the other would be taking care of a responsibility, while the other co-leader thinks the same way. The result could be that the responsibility is not carried out at all. Co-leaders, at the very least, need to reserve some time between meetings to plan the next meeting, which may add to the workload and require a common planning time between meetings.

Sometimes members can play one co-leader off against the other, as children do with their parents. If one co-leader develops the reputation of being "soft," team members may be more likely to ask that co-leader for special favors, which they know the other co-leader would not grant. Co-leaders need to be in sync on team issues so they can communicate those ideas to the team in unison.

ROLE OF THE ACTION TEAM

Your Action Team is an ad hoc group that translates the concept contained in the mission and strategic objectives into reality. The team is charged with creating not only the action plans describing how your strategy will be translated into daily operations, but also a cost-benefit analysis for each plan. Since the plans are developed by team members from a variety of roles inside and outside the organization, sufficient involvement is created to ensure support for implementing the action plans. The diversity of knowledge, experience, and perspective embodied by your team increases the likelihood that its plans will be creative, innovative, and outside the normal paradigm.

The team has no formal authority and is not expected to implement the action plans it writes. Action Teams must honor their strategy as it was written. They cannot change it.

Size of the Action Team

Action Teams vary in size from fewer than ten people to 50 or more. We recommend that teams have at least fifteen members in order to encompass a diversity of perspectives and to reduce the load on individual members. Teams of 30 and more, obviously, pose some organizational challenges. Most teams will achieve optimum size through self-selection. People tend to voluntarily drop off when they see that there are more than enough team members to do the job *and when they are comfortable that their particular perspective is already reflected by one or more other members.*

When necessary, team leaders may enlist additional members to ensure that the team reflects a cross-section of the organization. We recommend that you consult with the internal facilitator before actually adding additional team members. You also may enlist the help of experts as resource persons to the team when needed.

There will be times when you divide the Action Team into sub-teams for developing certain components of your plans. Sub-teams regularly report their work results to the whole team for input and agreement. In other words, sub-teams may draft the work, *but the entire team must agree to each sub-team's work before it can be recommended to the Strategic Planning Team.*

ROLE OF ACTION TEAM MEMBERS

There are certain qualifications for participating in this process. Action Team members must be people of goodwill who are willing and able to effectively express their views, make decisions by agreement, and subordinate their own private and special interests to the good of the whole organization.

Responsibilities of Action Team Members

Each member must accept the strategy as written and be committed to making it a reality. They must agree to participate actively without attempting to dominate or manipulate the group. All members work as peers and share in group decision making. The expectation is that people will deal frankly and candidly with the important issues, consistently attend the meetings, and remain active until the action plans are approved by the Strategic Planning Team.

Becoming a Team

A group of people pulled together to accomplish a task does not necessarily constitute a team. Becoming a team requires a process of sharing certain common experiences and conversations which bond the group in commitment and common purpose. We suggest that you design some of these experiences into your initial meetings to allow the group to become a team.

Effects of Action Planning

Let's face it. Action plans are where the rubber meets the road. The rest of the Strategic Plan is a fantasy if there are no detailed, implementable action plans to make it happen. Your skill as a facilitator and your team members' skills as innovators are crucial to the success of your organization's Strategic Plan.

Action Teams work long and hard and typically feel pride and satisfaction in having accomplished something important. Most who have done it describe it as a significant experience in professional growth and an education in the discipline of planning.

FIRST MEETING OF THE ACTION TEAMS

It is a good practice to have a common first meeting of the Action Teams. This first meeting ensures several things:

- It is an opportunity for the Chief Executive Officer to thank all Action Team members and leaders for serving in this important effort.
- It ensures that all Action Team members hear the charge and guidelines from the same person at the same time.
- It demonstrates a powerful symbol of the massive change effort under way in the organization as (often) more than 100 individuals are gathered in one place to work toward a common purpose and direction (as exemplified by the mission).

Agenda for the First Action Team Meeting

All Action Teams Together

1. Welcome and thanks
2. Set the context
   A. Overview of strategic planning process
   B. Review beliefs, mission, parameters, strategic objectives, and strategies
   C. Action plans as "linchpin" between strategic and operational planning
3. Review the charge
4. Review guidelines for operation
5. Introduce Action Team Leaders

Note: Items 1 through 5 should take no more than 30 minutes. The bulk of the meeting should be spent in the individual Action Teams. At this point the group should break into individual teams. All team members should be given copies of the draft plan, including beliefs, mission, parameters, strategic objectives, and strategies.

6. Introductions
7. Explain the nature of the task
8. Discuss the time line
9. Organize for work (meeting dates, time, location)
10. Clarify the intent of the strategy (see next section for details)

Note: Items 6 through 9 should take no more than 45 minutes. You want your team to be able to spend the bulk of the meeting discussing the strategy and getting into the meat of it. In this way the team members will feel that they have accomplished something of substance and that they will be better able to understand the strategy (they may find that they no longer wish to serve on this team once they truly understand what the strategy is about or what it is not about).

STRATEGY ANALYSIS

The Action Team is charged with creating a body of action plans which, taken together, are the most effective way to implement the strategy. To be successful in this endeavor, the members must have a clear, mutual understanding of the intent of the strategy. To ensure that you achieve this clarity, the team analyzes and discusses what the Strategic Planning Team intended the strategy to accomplish in the context of the Strategic Plan. Once there is clarity on this issue you are ready to move to the next stage in action plan development, but not a moment before. Consider these questions about the strategy: What does it mean? Why is it in the plan? What problems, circumstances, or aspirations prompted the Strategic Planning Team to develop it? (For this last question, refer to the internal and external analyses done by the Strategic Planning Team and especially to the Critical Issues.)

If you expect your Action Team to have difficulty grasping the intent of the strategy, invite the internal facilitator or even members of the Strategic Planning Team to assist you during the suggested group process outlined for this stage. You do not have the option of redefining or rephrasing the strategy.

At the end of this process of clarification, your Action Team will have developed shared operational definitions for key words and phrases, as well as a shared understanding of the intent of the strategy.

SUGGESTED GROUP PROCESS

1. Pass out a copy of the "Strategy Analysis" form to each team member.
2. Ask each team member to write silently and without discussion answers to questions 1 through 4.

3. Engage the whole group in a discussion of the first three questions. It is important for team members to see how their strategy fits into the overall context of the Strategic Plan. In discussing question 3, try to identify areas of your strategy that may overlap with other strategies.

4. Ask team members to suggest key words from the strategy. Write these on an overhead transparency or a flip chart.

5. Allow ten minutes for individuals to review synonyms and phrases for each key word.

Note: If you have a small group, you may be able to skip steps 6 through 9 and move to a full group discussion at this point. If you have a large group, do not skip these steps.

6. Break into groups and have each group identify no more than five synonyms or phrases for each key word. Allow no more than 20 minutes for group activity.

7. On a flip chart, list each word that was identified as a key word. Put one word on a page (you can do this while the groups are working so it is ready when they finish).

8. In a round-robin sequence, have each group give a synonym or phrase for the key word until all suggested definitions are exhausted. Repeat this procedure for all key words, one word at a time.

9. Only remove suggested synonyms or phrases if the whole group agrees.

10. Discuss each word and come to agreement on the operational definition of the key word. You may circle the words on the flip chart which the group feels are the closest synonyms.

11. The recorder should note the key words and their operational definitions for the minutes.

EXAMPLE

Suppose your team has a strategy dealing with technology. The term "technology" is a key word which may mean many different things to different team members. For some it means computers; for others it means much more (laser disks, overhead projection units, wide area networks, calculators, and so forth). The group needs to agree what will fall under the definition of technology for the purposes of this strategy (the dictionary definition is unimportant here).

The next step may be a homework assignment for the next meeting if time is running short.

12. Have all team members fill in this T-Bar, listing what they believe the strategy is about and not about. Ordinarily what the strategy is not about results from the discussion about the relationship with other strategies the organization is pursuing. It also can result from the discussion of the key words (for example, a technology strategy may be about computers and networks but not about overhead projectors and calculators).

STRATEGY ANALYSIS FORM

1. How does this strategy relate to the mission?
2. How does this strategy relate to the objectives?
3. How does this strategy relate to the other strategies?
4. Circle any key words in this strategy.
5. In the space below, write down what you believe this strategy is about and what it is not about.

This Strategy IS About	This Strategy IS NOT About

INFORMATION GATHERING

To paraphrase Albert Einstein, "The level of thinking that got us into these circumstances is inadequate to get us out." To develop innovative solutions you must look in innovative ways at your organization's circumstances. You must see through *new* eyes and search for solutions in new places. Information gathering involves immersing yourselves in the situation your strategy is designed to address and investigating as many conventional and unconventional approaches as possible to create the desired condition.

It is useful to start at the end and work your way back to the beginning. Identify the desired condition—how things would look if your solutions were truly innovative and effective—and research your way back toward what it would take to create this new reality.

Examine how similar situations are dealt with in other corporations, nonprofits, the military, universities, research organizations, and so on. Do thorough database searches on the Internet as well as business and scientific databases that might be relevant. You may need to bring in outside experts, visit other organizations, and purchase resource materials for your team. The important thing during this stage is to create the conditions that would allow your team to go outside the existing paradigms and assumptions and discover new possibilities.

SUGGESTED GROUP PROCESSES

1. "Seeing" the Strategy Completed

To give focus to your research, you want to open the mind to what exists and move it to new possibilities.

Creating Futures Meeting

The Product We Intend to Create

A chart of this group's hopes and dreams for the future as a result of implementing the strategy.

The Experience We Want to Have

Excitement about our common aspiration for the future.

Procedures (30 Minutes)

1. Clarify process. Give a picture of the whole process: how we got to this point; where we go from here (common aspiration, obstacles, action planning); and what we do in this session (create a common aspiration). In this process, we need the wisdom of everyone. There are no wrong answers; nothing is thrown away; group wisdom grows as others are heard.
2. Discuss the strategy.
3. Highlight a focus question. For example, "What do we want to see going on in our organization in five years as a result of the implementation of this strategy?" Write it at the center of the board or flip chart paper.

Brainstorm (30 Minutes)

1. Brainstorm individually. Ask the group to think about this question for a minute and write all answers they can think of on a piece of paper.
2. Ask each person to mark his/her two or three most important aspirations.
3. Brainstorm as a small group. Divide into small groups of three to four people. Have each small group choose the clearest ideas (total 20–40), honoring diversity but eliminating overlap.
4. Have each small group share its ideas on flip chart paper. Do not attempt to achieve agreement.
5. Have all ideas typed onto one sheet of 8 1/2 × 11 paper to be distributed at the next meeting.

2. Identifying Research Questions

Modified Nominal Group Process

1. Instruct all members of the team to silently record on a piece of paper all questions that they feel need to be investigated before action plans can

be written. Allow at least 15 minutes so that each team member can record all questions that come to mind.

2. In a round-robin fashion, have each team member read one question at a time. The team leader records the questions on easel paper, numbering each one and leaving space along the left margin, as follows:

1 _____
2 _____
3 _____
4 _____
5 _____
6 _____

If one question is clearly redundant with a question previously listed, do not repeat the question. If there is any doubt that a question is redundant with one previously listed, list the question. There is no discussion of the questions as they are being listed.

Continue to go around the group until all lists are completely exhausted. Typically, there will be 35–45 questions. Each piece of easel paper should be taped on the wall in clear view of the group. It is important to write large enough for all to see.

3. Begin with the first question listed, and ask the group the following two questions: (a) Does everyone understand this question? and (b) Is this redundant with any other question(s)?

This part of the process will generate considerable discussion. It may be necessary to rephrase a question(s) for purposes of clarity. If it is determined that a question is redundant with another (or perhaps two or more others), the group must decide which to keep. It is permissible to combine questions to attain agreement.

It is also important that if a question is eliminated because it is redundant, a line is drawn through it and reference is made to the question that was kept.

The team leader should continue in this manner until the entire list of questions has been covered. Typically, several questions will be rephrased for clarity or crossed out due to redundancy. This is an exhausting process. It is important that the team leader keep the group focused on the two questions, otherwise things can get out of hand.

4. Give each team member two 3 × 5 cards. Ask them to set them up as follows:

Points	Question number
5	_____
4	_____
3	_____

2   ——
1   ——

Next, ask them, without discussion, to place the number of the question that they feel is the most important to investigate opposite the number 5, the next most important question after the number 4, and so on, until each person has identified the top five questions.

Collect all the completed 3 × 5 cards. Have one team member read the number of points for each question, one card at a time. Have other team members assist in recording the points in the left margin and in totaling the points. After the points are totaled, have a team member read aloud the points each question received. Then repeat the ranking process.

The purpose of the second round of ranking is to more clearly identify the questions that the group feels must be investigated. There will likely be a clear break in terms of points between questions the group feels are important and those that are less important and do not need to be investigated. Of course, the number of questions that the team investigates will depend on the size of the team.

5. Make it clear to the group that once questions for investigation have been identified, they are not listed in terms of priority, regardless of the points a question received. List the questions in random order on easel paper as follows:

Question	Investigators	Sources
——	——	——
——	——	——
——	——	——
——	——	——
——	——	——

Have team members volunteer to investigate each question. Have the team brainstorm possible sources of information. Each sub-group of investigators (at least two people) is to focus the investigation and reporting around two questions:

a. What did we find out?

b. What implication(s) does this information have for writing action plans?

Finally, instruct the team that the next meeting will not be for two to three weeks to allow time for research and report writing. (This should have been made clear at the first meeting and appropriately scheduled.) For the next meeting, all sub-groups should have prepared a short written report addressing questions (a) and (b) above with sufficient copies for all team members and be prepared to give a fifteen-minute oral presentation.

Some Helpful Hints Regarding the Research Phase

1. Set a deadline for research to be completed and stick to it. Some groups will research for months in an eternal quest for the perfect solution to implement the strategy. Such a "holy grail" does not exist. Successful Action Teams usually implement their strategy by crafting a series of plans which, taken together, fully operationalize the strategy to the extent possible at that time. Rarely does a team discover one major initiative which, by itself, will solve the problem.

2. Teams should not conduct surveys. It is virtually impossible for an Action Team to produce statistically valid results. To create and implement an accurate survey, a team would need professional help and a considerable amount of time and money not available within the action planning framework. Furthermore, if many Action Teams were to conduct surveys, the organization would be inundated with them.

3. Distinguish for your team the difference between conducting research as opposed to finding and analyzing research. Your team will be engaged in the latter activity. Generally, teams do not have the skill, time or resources to actually conduct research studies. Rather, they will be reporting on research already conducted, successful practices elsewhere, recommendations of national organizations, and so forth. Your team is digesting existing research, not conducting original research.

4. Require that each team reduce its findings to writing of no more than two pages of text to be distributed at the next meeting (no attachments). Teams may have supporting data which may become useful later in the process (for example, to turn over to an implementation team), but it needs only to be summarized for the Action Team at this point in the process.

5. As the Action Team Leader, your role during this hiatus in meetings is to ensure that the research sub-groups are working properly. It is wise to identify a contact person in each team who agrees to keep you informed about the group's progress. You also are a resource person to the sub-groups in the event they need assistance in finding information on their question(s). Unless you have a very small team, the Action Team Leader should not be a member of a research team. Follow up with your research team at least once a week during this phase to ensure that time lines can be followed.

Note: The modified nominal group process may take up to three hours. Though some teams may prefer to break it up into two meetings, there is great advantage to keeping it to one meeting.

SHARING RESEARCH WITH THE ACTION TEAM

At the first meeting following the conclusion of the research, the sub-groups share the results of their research with the entire team. This sharing must be done in a collegial spirit in appreciation of the hard work each sub-group has completed over the past three weeks. It is not the time to pass judgment on some of the preliminary suggestions each sub-group may make regarding the implications of its research. There will be plenty of time later for judging the worth of various ideas.

To this end, it is incumbent upon you, as Action Team Leader, to set some ground rules for the conduct of the group during the oral reports of the sub-groups. Emphasize that the purpose of the meeting is to gather all relevant information for all members of the team and not to judge the merits of any idea. Team members should resist making negative comments (such as "That way is too expensive" or "Top management will never buy it") during the report, or engage in non-verbal offensive behavior (such as yawning, folding arms, and scowling). Behavior along these lines tends to stifle creativity.

Each group should bring enough copies of their written two-page summaries for each member of the Action Team and provide a fifteen-minute oral report, focusing both on the results of their research and, most important, on the implications for action within the organization. Assign a timekeeper and allow about ten minutes for clarifying questions and for discussion after each report. The written summary becomes part of the minutes for that meeting and is passed along to the internal facilitator. The number of sub-groups will determine the length of time necessary for this step in the process.

After all the reports have been given, the homework for the next meeting is to bring a list of activities that need to take place to operationalize the strategy to attain the mission and strategic objectives. These activities do not need to be phrased in any particular fashion. Team members must review the research presented to them and determine the most important actions the organization must take within the next five years. Suggest that each team member strive to bring in a list of five activities, but do not place a formal limit on the number.

MOVING TO ACTION

Once you have completed gathering relevant information, the next step is to distill an overwhelming amount of data and possible approaches to the strategy into an achievable number of specific results. You are methodically narrowing your focus to those results which must be realized for your strategy to become a reality.

Consider this analogy from landscaping: you have decided that your aspiration is to create a beautiful lawn. Identifying obstacles (weeds) and overcoming (pulling) them is essential but not sufficient to accomplish your aspiration. You also must plant something beautiful (specific results) in their place. In this stage of action planning, you determine which specific results are necessary to achieve your aspiration.

This is not a time to include every good idea that was ever mentioned, or to include all the "wouldn't it be nice" things everyone has always wanted.

This is where you boil things down to their essence—what *must* occur to implement your strategy. Nothing redundant is added, and no component essential to implementation is omitted. The group comes to agreement on the *entire* set of specific results before developing the steps to achieve them.

This cannot be overemphasized. If you skip this step (coming to agreement first on all the specific results), expect to encounter huge difficulties in developing agreement later on. When the specific results are expanded to include action steps and cost-benefit analyses, the stakes will be much higher for team members. At that point—since they will have expended considerable energy on each idea—you may find that the sub-teams become quite contentious when they are called upon to drop or significantly modify some aspect of their work.

SUGGESTED PROCESS

Begin this part of the process by giving your Action Team a "pep talk." It may be that some members have been feeling a bit overwhelmed by the amount of research they need to digest, the complexity of the strategy, and the fact that the team has not determined any solutions after more than a month of work. Tell your team that collectively they now know more about the strategy than any other group that has previously existed. It is critical that they "seize the moment."

1. Explain to the team that you need to identify the activities that are most important to achieve the mission and strategic objectives of the organization. Each team member has come to the meeting with a great number of ideas, and your team's job is to narrow that number to the most essential.

2. Pass out "Post-its" to each member. Have them individually write their ideas on the "Post-its," one idea per "Post-it." For members who did their homework, this is simply a matter of rewriting their ideas onto "Post-its." For those who did not or were absent from the previous meeting, they can write their ideas directly onto a "Post-it." It is best to use large "Post-its" for this activity.

3. Silently have team members place their "Post-its" on a wall. They need to group them according to common themes. Once all the "Post-its" are on the wall, team members may come up and sort the ideas into common themes, having no more than five team members sorting at one time. It is permissible to move anyone's "Post-its," but no discussion is to take place. The team will need 10–20 minutes to complete the sorting. Allow enough time for all team members who wish to sort to have an opportunity to do so.

4. Once sorting has been completed, the entire group should assign each category a name and go over all ideas on "Post-its" in this category to ensure that they are appropriately placed. Attach a label above each category. Some results may need to be moved or designated as belonging to more than one category.

Example

Suppose that your team is working on a technology strategy. Team members have various ideas needed to fully implement technology in your organization. Categories that typically might appear could be Hardware, Software, Training, and Technical Support. Under each category would be several ideas which may ultimately result in action plans.

5. At this point you explain to the group members that they need to turn their ideas into action plans. You will be doing some teaching about the first component of an action plan, the specific result statement.

Translating Your Ideas into Specific Results

At this point you should show the Action Team that a properly constructed action plan includes three parts: a specific result, implementation steps, and a cost-benefit analysis. Use an overhead transparency of a blank action plan form and some examples of properly written action plans. Explain that the first step in the process is for the team to agree on the specific result(s); writing the other two parts comes later.

Now it is time to check for the Action Team members' understanding of specific results. Although it may seem unnecessary, it is important that all team members understand how to write specific results. This is important for several reasons:

1. Specific results describe what actually will be accomplished in the implementation phase. While there is latitude in following the suggested action steps, implementers should be held tightly accountable for the end results. Therefore, there must be clarity about the expectation because it is non-negotiable.

2. Specific results are often the only part of the action plan which is printed and distributed for general information. The full text of the Strategic Plan, including all the action steps, is too bulky for mass distribution. It must be clearly written and free of jargon.

3. You must have agreement on all specific results before you move on to writing the other two parts of the action plans.

4. You may find that agreeing on the specific results is the most difficult part of the entire process, and with good reason. (That's why we call it "Creative Muddling.") Asking team members to write specific results according to the above criteria will help them clarify their thinking and, ultimately, will make it easier for your group to come to agreement. Force team members to think about the criteria before writing the result statements.

5. If your team does an intuitive "cost-benefit" analysis before approving a specific result, it may save itself a considerable amount of work later when the formal cost-benefit analysis is completed.

Sample Annotations for the Above:

1. This is a "plan to plan."
2. Good. The term "phase-in basis" solves the problem that this result is not fully accomplishable in a year.
3. Does not make a significant contribution to accomplishing the strategy. Probably would be better off as a step in another action plan.
4. Cannot stand by itself; probably need to read all the steps to fully understand it. Also, may not be measurable, demonstrable, or observable.
5. Good.
6. Probably fine, depending on how far away from the goal the organization is at present. Otherwise may not be accomplishable in a year.
7. Probably fine; may not be doable in a year.
8. Not doable in a year in most cases.

Once your team understands the concept of a specific result statement, then it is time to turn your attention to the ideas they generated and categorized earlier. Have team members volunteer into sub-groups for each of the identified categories. If there are five categories identified (as in the technology example above), then you will need five sub-groups. Give each sub-group the "Post-its" for its category.

Instruct each sub-group to write specific results for their category. They may be able to take one idea from a "Post-It" and easily write a specific result for it. They may modify an idea or combine some ideas into one specific result. The sub-group needs to discuss the merits of the ideas listed in their category and not automatically write a specific result for each idea. Remember that all ideas were listed, even those of little merit. Your sub-groups should refer to the criteria for specific result statements when working. During this phase a number of ideas with little or no merit will be cast aside by the sub-groups or will be subsumed by another, more beneficial idea. The number of results identified by sub-groups typically ranges from one to five, depending on the number of worthy ideas in each category. This exercise can be done at a meeting, if there is time, or it can be done for homework (or some combination).

Each sub-group should write its proposed specific results on an overhead transparency in preparation for presentation to the whole group.

AGREEMENT ON SPECIFIC RESULT STATEMENTS

Before attempting to gain agreement on specific results, review the criteria from the previous meeting. Have one group volunteer to display its recommended specific result to the entire Action Team for approval. Take one result at a time (cover up the others so they are not showing) on the transparency and ask the group if the specific result meets the criteria. If the whole group agrees to a specific result then the implementation steps and cost-benefit analysis will be completed for that result. If not, members may suggest changes to a specific result in order to gain agreement. If there is no agreement that a specific result should be included, then no implementation steps are written or cost-benefit analysis completed (and it does not go on to the Strategic Planning Team for consideration). Continue taking one specific result statement at a time from each of the sub-groups and discuss its merits. When all of the recommended specific result statements are reviewed, then you can summarize (by rereading aloud) all of the specific results your group has agreed to thus far.

There is no magic process to reaching agreement during this stage. Now is the opportunity for a full team discussion of the merits of the proposed results. This part of the process may go quickly or slowly depending on the number and complexity of the specific results. There are no shortcuts to take; however, if you have an unwieldy number of specific results recommended from your sub-groups, you can go through the following rank order process to narrow your discussion.

Optional Process to Narrow Specific Results (A Mini Cost-Benefit Analysis)

If you find that your sub-groups have come back with far too many specific results to be handled one at a time, then you may find the following process useful in narrowing the large number of specific results to a manageable number. It is similar to the rank ordering process used to narrow the list of questions that you may have used at the start of the research phase.

First, list all the specific results on an overhead transparency or flip chart. Number each result. Ask each team member, silently and without discussion, to rate the costs (in terms of resources, both human and financial) and benefits (in terms of helping operationalize the strategy) of each proposed specific result.

Rate the costs and benefits of each action plan on a scale from 1 to 5. For costs, 1 would be a high-cost result; 5 would be a low-cost result. For benefits, 1 would be a low-benefit result; 5 would be a high-benefit result. Explain that this is not a scientific or precise method for determining costs and benefits; that will come later, after the action plans are written. Team members should use their intuition to make a determination. Each member of the team would fill out a chart looking like this:

	Costs	Benefits	Total (Costs * Benefits)
Specific Result 1			
Specific Result 2			
Specific Result 2			
Etc.			

After each person has filled out the first two columns for each specific result, ask them to multiply the costs and benefits. The highest score possible is 25, representing a very high-benefit and very low-cost item. This result is something the group should certainly pursue. The lowest possible score is 1, representing a very high-cost item with very low benefits. This result is something the group should certainly discard.

Once each person has recorded the results individually, tabulate an average for the Action Team and record it on the transparency or flip chart where the results are listed. Look for a clean break in the rankings and concentrate the group's efforts only on those results which have the highest rankings. Start with the highest-ranked results and attempt to forge agreement on those, and then work your way down toward the lower-ranked results. Any result with a total of less than 9 in column 3 has costs which exceed benefits and probably should not merit further consideration.

FINAL TWO QUESTIONS BEFORE WRITING ACTION PLANS

Action Teams frequently ask, "How many action plans should we have?" The answer is heavily dependent on the complexity of the strategy. Some strategies may be able to be fully operational with five action plans; others may require two dozen or more. Before moving on to writing the steps, you should have your team ask these questions:

1. Is each specific result necessary to implement the strategy?
2. Is the set of specific results sufficient to ensure the strategy will be fully implemented as intended?

Question 1 is designed to weed out any superfluous or duplicative specific results. Sometimes Action Teams approve specific results early in their discussion, only to have those results superseded by other results later in the discussion. Or, some specific result which sounded very promising early in the discussion now appears unnecessary, given the rest of the results which have been approved.

Question 2 gives the team members a chance to review the entire set of results to see if, in fact, they do have enough of them to operationalize the strategy. If the answer to this question is "no," then the team needs to identify where the gaps exist and devise some additional specific results to fill in the gaps. It is useful to review the opening night's discussion of what the strategy is about and what it is not about.

If you can honestly answer "yes" to each of these questions, then your Action Team is ready to move on to the writing of the steps for each specific result, and you are well on your way to completing your task. If there is any doubt in the group, try to resolve it at this point, before sub-groups begin writing action steps. Once groups start writing steps it is much harder to backtrack and correct errors or omissions.

ACTION PLAN WRITING

This stage should be entered *only* after the Action Team has come to agreement on the total package of specific results which are necessary to realize your strategy. To do so before that invites fragmentation, duplication of effort, and frustration.

Once you have created the big picture—the set of specific results—it is relatively easy to fill in the action steps or activities necessary to accomplish them, which is precisely what is done during this stage. Typically the work is roughed out by sub-teams, each of which is assigned a fraction of the complete set of specific results. They generate the sequence of steps or activities necessary to accomplish each of the specific results assigned to them, and they bring their work to the whole team for feedback, suggestions and, ultimately, agreement.

The bottom line for action plans is that they enable a staff member to move ahead with action—without having to do additional planning—simply by following the suggested steps. The action steps or recommended activities represent the team's best thinking about how to attain the desired result, yet they leave room for the creative prerogative of the person implementing.

Action plans must be assignable to one person (who, of course, may work with a committee or delegate portions of the plan to subordinates), and they should be achievable in one year. In designing the action steps or activities, sub-teams may discover that a specific result actually requires more than one year to achieve. In that case, simply break it down into smaller tasks and write an action plan for each task.

The process of generation and critique, feedback and refinement goes back and forth—from sub-team to whole team and vice versa—until the Action Team is convinced that each specific result is accompanied by the most effective action to accomplish it. Once you reach agreement on that, the work is simply transferred onto action plan forms.

SUGGESTED PROCESS

We recommend that you complete one action plan as a whole-team activity to develop everyone's competence before assigning the remaining specific results to sub-teams to develop the action steps.

Process

1. Select one specific result at a time.
2. Brainstorm all the steps necessary to ensure realization of the specific result described. Write these on an overhead transparency or flip chart.
3. Arrange the steps in sequential order. Eliminate any steps so broadly stated that they do not provide adequate direction. For example, "Develop and pub-

lish an employee handbook." Replace them with explicit steps that provide clear direction on how to obtain the desired result.

If any steps not only require more explanation but also imply another program or project for which an action plan needs to be developed, pull the step out of the original plan and use steps 1–3 in this process to write another action plan.

Note: When there is a step so broad that it requires creation of a separate action plan, its removal may indicate that the original specific result was too broad itself. Thus the original specific result may need to be more narrowly focused and the action steps rewritten with greater precision.

4. Eliminate steps which are overly prescriptive or micro-manage. You need to give the implementator enough direction to accomplish the specific result but not be so specific as to remove all professional judgment from the task. Writing steps in action plans is an art.

5. Once the team as a whole has completed writing an entire action plan, divide the team into small groups. Assign the agreed-upon specific results to the subgroups and have them draft action steps for each one. If time permits, you can begin this process during the meeting so you can monitor the work. If the subgroups do not finish, then their homework assignment is to bring in a draft of steps written on a transparency for the whole team to review at the next meeting.

6. At the next meeting, each sub-group reviews its recommended steps for each specific result on the transparency. The whole group discusses the suggested steps until agreement is reached. The length of time this activity will take depends on the number of specific results, the quality of the work of the subgroups, and the size and nature of the Action Team.

COST-BENEFIT ANALYSIS

Save this stage for last. Do a formal cost-benefit analysis for each action plan *after* you have completed writing all of the plans. Do a thorough job. These analyses are the primary reference for the Strategic Planning Team in assessing each plan's *return on investment*. This is a comparison of the action plan's contribution toward achieving the mission and strategic objectives (in the context of the strategy) against the total cost of making that contribution.

Benefits are the desired consequences of investing in this particular action plan—the contribution it makes toward moving the organization closer to achieving its mission and strategic objectives. Those that can be quantified are called tangible benefits. Those that cannot are listed as intangible benefits.

Costs are the allocation or reallocation of the organization's resources necessary to implement a given action plan. Like benefits, costs can be categorized as either tangible or intangible. Tangible costs include outlays of money, time, facilities, and other quantifiable expenditures. Intangible costs include such things as stress, resistance to change, community pressures, fear, and frustration.

The cost-benefit analysis is the Action Team's projection of the positive and negative consequences of implementing a particular plan. This information is essential to the Strategic Planning Team in evaluating your plans and forms the basis for decisions about which action plans will be implemented and when. Consider this as the sales prospectus for the plan. If your cost-benefit analysis for an action plan is skimpy or incomplete, the Strategic Planning Team will simply return that plan to you. They cannot accurately assess a plan's return on investment without a thorough analysis from your team.

SUGGESTED PROCESSES

1. Where appropriate, secure necessary information such as employee compensation costs and price lists before initiating the cost-benefit analysis. The internal facilitator should be able to direct the Action Team Leader to organization resources and, perhaps, resources outside the organization.

2. Set up a flip chart, clean transparency, or chalkboard and draw a large replica of the cost-benefit analysis form.

3. Provide the following to each team member: a copy of one action plan, a completed cost-benefit analysis example, and a blank copy of the cost-benefit analysis form.

4. Define the terms: benefits, costs, tangible and intangible, qualitative, quantitative.

5. Assign the action plans to sub-teams to complete a cost-benefit analysis for each plan. The sub-teams may want to meet separately to complete their cost-benefit analysis.

6. Taking one action plan step at a time and using any cost information previously gathered, each sub-team determines the tangible and intangible costs and benefits. If costs or benefits are expected to accrue only after a significant time delay, indicate when they are expected to show up. Be as specific as possible. It is not the responsibility of your team to recommend whether costs should be covered by allocation or reallocation of existing resources.

7. Using the lists developed in step 6 (above), consolidate ideas when appropriate to show a total for a specific category.

8. Upon completion, *each sub-team shares its analysis with the whole team for review, critique, modifications, and agreement.*

Note: Once again, we suggest that you do at least one cost-benefit analysis with the whole team before assigning the remainder to sub-teams to complete. This will give everyone practice in the discipline of completing this stage.

EVALUATING ACTION PLANS

Action Team leaders often ask: "How will we know if our action plans are any good?" If you and your Action Team can answer all of the following questions affirmatively, you can rest assured that you have developed high-quality action plans.

For Each Individual Specific Result:

- Is the specific result of each action plan clearly and understandably written?
- Is the specific result written as an outcome or achievement, not as a process? (Is each action plan a plan to *do* rather than a plan to *plan?*)
- Is the specific result of each action plan measurable, observable, or demonstrable? (Is it clear how we will know when we have achieved it?)
- Is each action plan a *separate assignable body of work?* (Is it reasonable to expect that a staff member could marshal the resources necessary to accomplish this specific result within one year or less?)
- Is it *necessary* to achieve this specific result in order to make the strategy operational?

For the Action Steps:

- Do the steps or activities for each action plan ensure that the specific result will be achieved? (Have we included every step that will require a significant amount of time, money, effort, or thought?)
- If the plan were assigned to you, are the steps clear enough, complete enough, and correctly sequenced so that you could accomplish it?

For the Cost-Benefit Analysis:

- Have you projected the value to be added to the organization, both tangible and intangible, if the specific result were achieved?
- Have you projected the resources required to achieve the specific result? Quantify these costs wherever possible.
- Do the benefits clearly justify the costs? If not, change or delete the plan.

For the Set of Action Plans:

- Are all of the action plans *necessary* to implement the given strategy?
- Is the set of action plans *sufficient* to ensure the strategy will be fully implemented as intended?

If you can answer "yes" to all of the above questions, you have developed the best action plans possible at this time.

PRESENTING THE ACTION PLANS

Your presentation actually begins when you submit your action plans to the internal facilitator for distribution to the Strategic Planning Team. Include with your plans a concise cover letter and a contents page to introduce your team's work. Consider including a summary of your investigative work, basic assumptions made by your team, and the reasons the team took the approach it did. The internal facilitator will include these documents with your plans and send out the entire package of action plans to the Strategic Planning Team at least one week prior to the Second Planning Session.

At that session you will make a 20-minute presentation, followed by a question-and-answer session of the same length. The purpose is to ensure that the Strategic Planning Team understands the meaning and intent of your plans, as well as their strategic and operational implications.

The Strategic Planning Team will not be evaluating the quality or appropriateness of your team's work while you are there; that comes later. They simply want to understand the plans, their benefits, and their projected costs. Their questions will focus on achieving clarity and understanding.

Preparing the Presentation

You can prepare for the presentation by creating overhead transparencies or flip chart graphic illustrations of the major concepts you want to explain. You will not be expected to read the plans or otherwise describe what is already written. Rather, explain *why* your team recommends these actions. You will want to communicate a compelling rationale for implementing the strategy in this particular way.

Orient your presentation primarily to the organization's mission, strategic objectives, and strategies, emphasizing your own strategy. Also, discuss the sources of innovation you have uncovered while gathering information.

Presentation formats vary greatly. Some team leaders prefer simple visuals while others use multimedia demonstrations, skits, or videos. If a choice needs to be made, a team leader's time is better spent on developing quality action plans than on an elaborate presentation.

Be aware that the Strategic Planning Team will hear presentations that day from every other Action Team Leader as well. They may listen to eight or ten hours of presentations. You will want to design your presentation with that reality in mind.

Note: The internal facilitator may want to call all the team leaders together for a practice run of their presentations before the Second Planning Session. This allows for feedback and coaching from the internal facilitator and other team leaders. It also provides an opportunity to see the total package that will be presented to the Strategic Planning Team.

Over the course of that evening and the next day, the Strategic Planning Team will analyze and come to agreement on the disposition of all the individual action plans. The Chief Executive Officer or internal facilitator will typically call you within 48 hours of the completion of the session to fill you in on the disposition of your plans.

Communicating the Results

Compose a summary report of the survey and its findings. Be sure to include:

- An executive summary—purpose, procedures, and results.
- Who conducted the survey.
- The characteristics and size of the target respondents.
- A sample survey form.
- The procedures used to conduct the survey.
- A complete report of the results.
- Conclusions and recommendations for follow-up.

Notes

1. John A. Byrne, "Strategic Planning: The Rise and Fall and Rise of Strategy," *Business Week*, August 26, 1996, 48–49.

2. Herbert A. Simon, "The Proverbs of Administration," *Public Administration Review* 6 (Winter 1946): 53–67.

3. T. Irene Sanders, *Strategic Thinking and the New Science: Planning in the Mind of Chaos, Complexity, and Change* (New York: The Free Press, 1998), 146.

4. Marvin R. Weisbord and Sandra Janoff, *Future Search: An Action Guide to Finding Common Ground in Organizations and Communities* (San Francisco: Berrett-Koehler Publishers, 1995), 5.

5. *Destin Strategic Plan* (Destin, Fla.: Destin City Hall, 1998).

6. Internet Services Corporation, New York, 1998.

7. "ASCD Vision Statement," *Association for Supervision and Curriculum Development (ASCD) Strategic Plan*, June 1998 <http://www.ascd.org/today/strat-plan.html>.

8. Noel M. Tichy and Mary Anne Devanna, *The Transformational Leader* (New York: John Wiley and Sons, 1986), 146.

9. Crystal Ear®, advertisement, *Time* (September 1997): 25.

10. Samuel Taylor Coleridge, "Biographia Literaria, From Chapter XIII," in *The Norton Anthology of English Literature*, ed. Robert M. Adams (New York: W. W. Norton and Company, 1968), 272–273.

11. Fetzer Center, *Management Development Programs* (Kalamazoo, Mich.: Western Michigan University, 1998).

12. Glenn Rifkin, "Leadership: Can It Be Learned?" *Forbes ASAP*, April 8, 1996; 102.

13. Michael Barrier, "Leadership Employees Respect," *Nation's Business* (January 1999): 28–30.

14. J. Thomas Wren, ed., *The Leader's Companion: Insights on Leadership Through the Ages* (New York: The Free Press, 1995), ix–xiv.

15. Rifkin, "Leadership: Can It Be Learned?", 103.

16. William Rees Mogg, "World Leaders in Mediocrity," *London Times*, March 20, 1995, 16.

17. Stephen R. Covey, *Principle-Centered Leadership* (New York: Simon & Schuster, 1990), 45.

18. William F. Allman, "The Serotonin Candidate," *FYI*: A Supplement to *Forbes* Magazine, September 23, 1996, 136.

19. Ibid.

20. Robert Greenleaf, *Servant Leadership: A Journey into the Nature of Legitimate Power and Greatness* (New York: The Free Press, 1983), 102.

21. Laura Sessions Stepp, "New Test of Values at Alcoa: Company Stunned as President Quits," *Washington Post*, August 4, 1991, H1.

22. William Ernest Henley, "Invictus," in *The Literature of England*, ed. George K. Anderson and William E. Buckler (Glenview, Ill.: Scott, Foresman and Company, 1968), 1397.

23. James Watson and Francis Crick, "A Structure for Deoxyribose Nucleic Acid," *LionBook Site*, November 19, 1998 <http://biocrs.biomed.brown.edu/Books/Chapters/Ch%208/DH-Paper.html>.

Selected Bibliography

Andrews, Kenneth R. *The Concept of Corporate Strategy*. Homewood, Ill.: Richard D. Irwin, 1980.

Bean, J. P., and G. D. Kuh. "A Typology of Planning Problems." *Journal of Higher Education* 55, no. 1 (1984): 36–51.

Bennis, Warren. *On Becoming a Leader*. Reading, Mass.: Perseus Books, 1989.

Bennis, Warren. *Why Leaders Can't Lead*. San Francisco: Jossey-Bass, 1990.

Bennis, Warren, and Burt Nanus. *Leaders: Strategies for Taking Charge*. New York: HarperCollins, 1985.

Brandenburger, Adam M., and Barry J. Nalebuff. *Co-opetition*. New York: Doubleday, 1996.

Bridges, William. *Jobshift*. Reading, Mass.: Perseus Books, 1995.

Caldwell, P. "Some Better Ideas from Ford Motors C.E.O." *Planning Review* (September 1984): 8–9.

Carse, James. *Breakfast at the Victory: The Mysticism of Ordinary Experience*. San Francisco: Harper Books, 1994.

Cook, William J. *Strategic Planning for America's Schools*. Arlington, Va.: American Association of School Administrators, 1990.

Costa, Arthur L., and Rosemarie M. Liebmann (eds.). *The Process-Centered School*. Thousand Oaks, Calif.: Corwin Press, 1997.

Covey, Stephen R. *Principle-Centered Leadership*. New York: Simon & Schuster, 1990.

Cribben, James. *Effective Managerial Leadership*. New York: American Management Association, 1972.

Donnelly, J. H., J. L. Gibson, and J. M. Ivancevich. *Fundamentals of Management*. Plano, Tex.: Business Publications, 1984.

Drucker, Peter. *Concept of the Corporation*. New York: John Day Company, 1946.

Drucker, Peter F. *The Practice of Management*. New York: Harper & Row, 1954.

Duckworth, A., and R. Kranyik. "What Business Are We In?" *The School Administrator* (August 1984): 6–8.

Ellis, Darryl J., and Peter P. Pekar, Jr. *Planning for Nonplanners: Planning Basics for Managers.* New York: AMACOM, 1980.

Famularo, Joseph J. *Organization Planning Manual,* rev. ed. New York: AMACOM, 1979.

Frankl, Viktor. *Man's Search for Meaning.* Boston: Beacon Press, 1992.

Gardner, John W. "Leaders and Followers." *Liberal Education* (March–April 1987): 14.

Gates, Henry Louis. "The End of Loyalty." *The New Yorker* (March 9, 1998): 34.

Glavin, G. "The Management of Planning: A Third Dimension of Business Planning." *The Business Quarterly* (Autumn 1974): 43–51.

Gortner, Harold F., Julianne Mahler, and Jeanne Bell Nicholson. *Organization Theory.* Chicago: The Dorsey Press, 1987.

Grossman, Lee. *The Change Agent.* New York: AMACOM, 1974.

Hayman, J. "Relationship of Strategic Planning and Future Methodologies." Paper presented at the annual meeting of the American Educational Research Association, Los Angeles, California (April 1981).

Heider, John. *The Tao of Leadership.* New York: Bantam Books, 1985.

Houston, P. "Involve Your Community in Planning for It." *The School Administrator* (August 1984): 11–13.

Humboldt, Wilhelm. *The Sphere and Duties of Government.* Bristol, England: Thoemmes Press, 1996.

Kastens, Merritt L. *Long-Range Planning for Your Business.* New York: AMACOM, 1976.

Kaufman, Roger, and Jerry Herman. *Strategic Planning in Education.* Lancaster, Pa.: Technomic Publishing Co., 1991.

Kay, Emanuel. *The Crisis in Middle Management.* New York: AMACOM, 1974.

Korton, David C. *When Corporations Rule the World.* West Hartford, Conn.: Kumarian Press, 1995.

Land, George, and Beth Jarman. *Break-point and Beyond.* New York: HarperBusiness, 1992.

Lubove, Seth. "Get'em Before They Get You." *Forbes* (July 31, 1995): 8.

Mintzberg, Henry. *The Rise and Fall of Strategic Planning.* New York: The Free Press, 1993.

Mueller, Ronald E., and David H. Moore. "America's Blind Spot: Industrial Policy." *Challenge* (January–February 1982): 5–13.

Naor, Jacob. "Strategic Planning Under Resource Constraints." *Business* (September–October 1981): 15–19.

Naylor, Thomas H. *Strategic Planning Management.* Oxford, Ohio: Planning Executives Institute, 1980.

Neill, S. "Planning for the Future." *Planning for Tomorrow's Schools* (1983): 7–30.

Ouchi, William G. *Theory Z.* New York: Avon Books, 1981.

Reich, Robert. *The Work of Nations.* New York: Random House, 1992.

Samuelson, Robert J. "Crackpot Prophet." *Newsweek* (March 10, 1997): 50.

Shafritz, Jay M., and J. Steven Ott. *Classics of Organization Theory.* Belmont, Calif.: Wadsworth Publishing Company, 1996.

Shlain, Leonard. *The Alphabet Versus the Goddess*. New York: Penguin Group, 1998.

Simon, Herbert A. "The Proverbs of Administration." *Public Administration Review* (Winter 1946): 53–67.

Soros, George. "The Capitalistic Threat." *Atlantic Monthly* (February 1997): 47–48.

Steiner, G. *Strategic Planning*. New York: The Free Press, 1979.

Thurow, Lester. *The Future of Capitalism*. New York: William Morrow and Company, 1996.

Tichy, Noel M., and Mary Anne DeVanna. *The Transformational Leader*. New York: John Wiley and Sons, 1986.

Tita, M., and R. Allio. "3M's Strategy System—Planning in an Innovative Corporation." *Planning Review* (September 1984): 10–15.

Wood, K., and S. Wood. "Are Corporate Strategic Planning Techniques Useful in Public Higher Education?" Paper presented at the Joint Conference of the Southern Association for Institutional Research and the North Carolina Association for Institutional Research, Charlotte, North Carolina (October 1981).

Zukav, Gary. *The Dancing Wu Li Masters*. New York: Bantam Books, 1979.

Name Index

Subject Index

About the Author

WILLIAM J. COOK, JR. is founder and chief executive of the Colonial-Cambridge Company, a firm that for the past quarter-century has specialized in strategic planning for corporate and non-profit clients throughout the United States and abroad. His knowledge of strategics is derived from his own experience as a U.S. Army officer, a university vice-president, and a vice-president of a regional wholesale-retail company. He is the author of several books and articles, and his daily radio commentary was featured on over 75 stations in the Southeast for several years.